FEEDING INDIA

Centre de Sciences Humaines (Centre for Social Sciences and Humanities): Created in 1989 and based in New Delhi, the CSH is part of the network of research centres of the French Ministry of Foreign Affairs. The Centre's research work is primarily oriented towards the study of issues concerning the contemporary dynamics of development in India and South Asia. The activities of the Centre are focused on four main themes, namely: Economic growth and sustainable development, International and regional relations, Institutional structures and political constructions of identity and Urban dynamics.

Centre de Sciences Humains, 2, Aurangzeb Road, New Delhi 110011, India, Tel: (91) 11 3041 00 70, Fax: (91) 11 3041 00 79
E-mail: infos@csh-delhi.com
Website: http://www.csh-delhi.com

Institut Français de Pondichéry (French Institute of Pondicherry): Created in 1955, the IFP is a multidisciplinary research and advanced educational institute. Major research works are focusing on Sanskrit and Tamil languages and literatures—in close collaboration with the Ecole Française d'Extrême-Orient—ecosystems, biodiversity and sustainability, dynamics of population and socio-economic development.

Institut Français de Pondichéry, 11, Saint Louis Street, PB 33
Pondicherry 605001, Tel: (91) 413 2334 168
Fax: (91) 413 2339 534
E-mail: ifpdir@ifpindia.org

Feeding India

The Spatial Parameters of Food Grain Policy

FRÉDÉRIC LANDY

MANOHAR

CENTRE DE SCIENCES HUMAINES

2009

This book was published with the support of the Centre National du Livre, The Institut Universitaire de France and the University of Pasis X-Nanterre.

First published 2009

ISBN 978-81-7304-796-1

Published by
Ajay Kumar Jain *for*
Manohar Publishers & Distributors
4753/23 Ansari Road, Daryaganj
New Delhi 110 002

Typeset by
Ajay Arts
New Delhi 110 002

Printed at
Salasar Imaging Systems
Delhi 110 035

Contents

Figures

Maps

Acknowledgements

The list of people to whom I am indebted for this volume is long and I will limit my expression of gratitude to all the Indians who have borne with me for around twenty years now, in particular the hundreds of farmers and government officials who patiently furnished me with information and statistics.

Thanks also to Anne-Marie Barthélémy, the cartographer of all the maps provided in this book.

This book is the updated translation of *Un milliard à nourrir. Grain, territoire et politiques en Inde*, published in French by Belin in 2006. It is the result of research conducted over several years, funded by the Centre d'Etudes de l'Inde et de l'Asie du Sud (CNRS-EHESS), the Maison des Sciences de l'Homme in Paris, the Laboratory Géotropiques-Gecko of the University of Paris X-Nanterre, the Centre de Sciences Humaines (CSH) in New Delhi, the French Institute of Pondicherry and the Institut Universitaire de France (IUF).

This Indian publication was funded by the Scientific Council of the University of Paris X-Nanterre, IUF, CSH, and the Centre National des Lettres.

FRÉDÉRIC LANDY

Glossary and Acronyms

APL	: Above Poverty Line
Bajra	: Pearl millet (*Pennisetum typhoideum* L.)
Block	: Development administration unit corresponding more or less to the *taluk/tehsil.*
BPL	: Below Poverty Line
CACP	: Commission for Agricultural Costs and Prices
Chapati	: Whole wheat pancake bread
Chief Minister	: Prime Minister's equivalent at State (provincial) level
CIF	: Cost, Insurance and Freight
Desakota	: 'Village-city', an Indonesian neologism for describing the densely inhabited countryside of Java
Dharma	: Duty, a religious law
FCI	: Food Corporation of India
FOB	: Free on board
FPS	: Fair Price Shop (or ration shop): PDS reduced-price shop
HYV	: High Yield Variety
IFPRI	: Internal Food Policy Research Institute, Washington
Issue price	: Subsidized sale price in shops of the Public Distri-bution System
Jati	: Caste
Kharif	: Monsoon (rainy) season crop
Mandi	: (wholesale) Agricultural market
Millets	: Term used by Indians for coarse cereals (sorghum, pearl-millet, finger-millet, etc.)
MMTC	: Minerals and Metals Trading Corporation, a public-sector corporation
MSP	: Minimum Support Price

Net production	: Production less 12.5 per cent for seed, losses, and animal feed
Niger	: Oilseed (*Guizotia abyssinica Cass.*)
NSS	: National Sample Survey
NSSO	: National Sample Survey Organization
PACS	: Primary Agricultural Cooperative Society, a local input and credit cooperative (extensively funded by the Government)
Paddy	: Rice that has not yet been husked
Panchayat	: (Here) rural village council
Physiocrats	: Eighteenth-century French thinkers who favoured agriculture-based development and free trade
Procurement	: (Here) purchase of agricultural products by the state
Rabi	: Cold season crop
Rice mill	: Mill in which paddy is husked and bleached
RSS	: Rashtriya Swayamsevak Sangh (National Volunteers' Association), a Hindu extremist organization
SHG	: Self-Help Group that mostly organises micro-credit
Statutory rationing	: Food supply system solely through the monopoly of government circuits, as opposed to 'informal rationing' where the private market operates at the same time
STC	: State Trading Corporation, a government trading enterprise
Shakha	: Local branch of the RSS
Swadeshi	: 'Of one's own country'
Swaraj	: 'Self-government'—political autonomy or independence
Tahsildar	: Government official in charge of a *tehsil/taluk*
TPDS	: Targeted Public Distribution System, 'targeted' since 1997, with the selection of BPL households
Varna	: Set of *jatis* or castes
VHP	: Vishva Hindu Parishad (World Hindu Association), a Hindu extremist movement
WTO	: World Trade Organisation

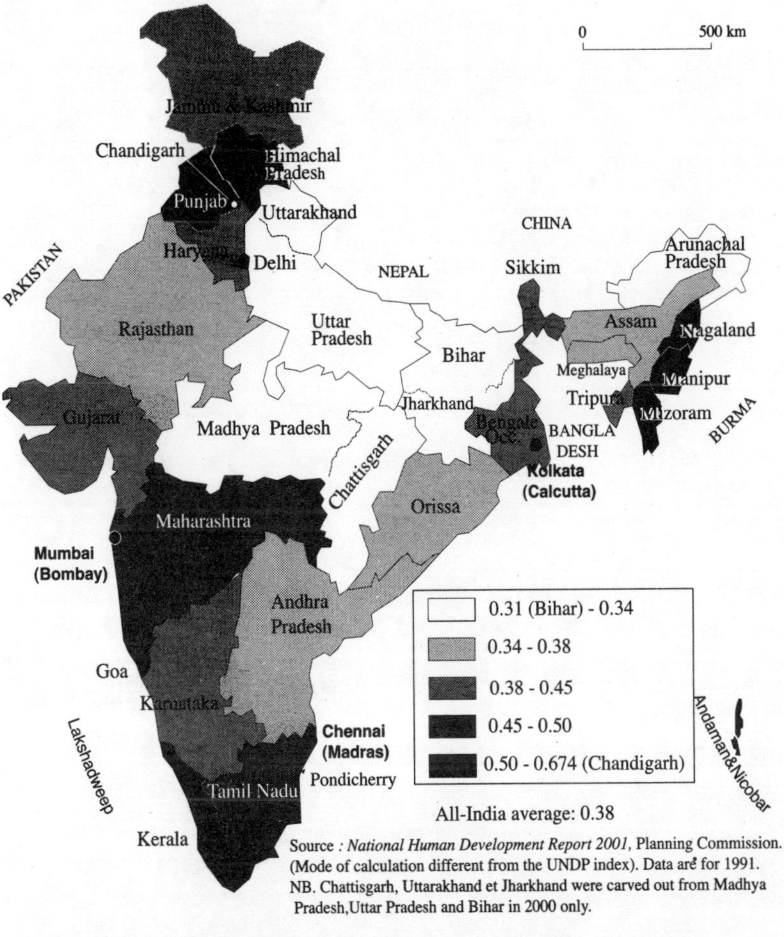

Map 1: Indian states and their Human Development Index

The new official toponymy has been used. Thus, Bombay is called Mumbai, Calcutta Kolkata, and Madras Chennai, except in case of anachronism.

One Indian Rupee is equal to 0.018 Euro in April 2007. Its local value in terms of purchasing power is, however, much higher. In the Telangana region (Andhra Pradesh), payment for a day's work at the rice harvesting is about Rs. 30, and the cost of 1 kg rice about Rs. 10.

Introduction

> Famine came, ghastly, staggering, horrible beyond words. In Malabar, in Bijapur, in Orissa, and, above all, in the rich and fertile province of Bengal, men and women and little children die in their thousands daily for lack of food. They dropped down dead before the palaces of Calcutta, their corpses lay in the mud-huts of Bengal's innumerable villages and covered the roads and fields of its rural areas.
>
> J. Nehru, *The Discovery of India*, p. 16

The subject of this book is India's public food distribution system — a complex organization that purchases up to one-fifth of the national output of wheat, rice and sugar from farmers, in order to guarantee market outlets and support prices. It redistributes these stocks to consumers—theoretically the poorest—at subsidized prices. It is a gigantic mechanism that covers almost the entire country and is an enormous economic, social and political issue in the public domain. Studying it means looking at much more than food security.

In 1943 the terrible Bengal famine left three million dead (Sen 1981). It is with this event that Nehru's famous book, *The Discovery of India*, opens, as it was a contemporaneous event. It was an India reeling under its wounds that was to gain Independence in 1947, and there is no doubt that a large part of the decisions then taken were marked by this disaster. This famine was depicted in Satyajit Ray's 1973 film, *Ashani Sanket* (Distant Thunder). The food situation remained precarious for a long time. In 1968, W. and P. Paddock, fearing the worst, asserted that with regard to international food aid, the sorting or selection principle should be adopted, as in the case of military hospitals: on the war front it is often the policy not to waste resources on soldiers with no chance of survival. In the neo-colonial framework of food aid, 'like doctors on the battlefield trying to make the best out of the limited resources, the affluent countries will have to decide which starving countries to save and which to sacrifice'.[1]

According to the Paddocks, India was one of the hopeless cases and would have to be forsaken.

Now however, till the recent change in 2006, during most years India's warehouses are overflowing and it is a net cereal exporter, despite its one billion inhabitants. We are far from the pessimism of yesteryears. But is this overproduction in the European sense? Are the stocks the result of astounding gains in productivity and full stomachs? Or is the reason the continuance of the very low purchasing power of a part of the population? Does the situation, rather than testifying to the country's success, point to a failure? After all, the famine-struck India of the nineteenth century was also a net cereal exporter!

BOUNDARIES OF THE PRESENT STUDY

For Westerners, travelling in India is sometimes akin to a journey in time. The rural roads still abound in Ambassador and Premier Padmini cars, built on European models of the 1950s; kerosene lamps, bullock carts and rural life as such may remind one of a not so ancient France. A similar association of ideas occurs in the case of India's food system too. The ration cards most families have, the closure of certain routes to the movement of cereals, the chequering of production zones by the administration during harvests, the monitoring of traders and transporters—all these are procedures similar to those in Europe during and after World War II. Most of them were instituted in India as of 1942. It is as if the country has not yet come out of the war and the famine.

This is not to overlook the fact that the distribution system has changed considerably in the intervening period: its techniques and modes of action have been modified and, above all, its reasoning and objectives have changed substantially. The concern is now about managing a relative abundance. It is precisely because the logic behind India's food policy has changed that criticism is now raining down on the continuance of one part of the system. It is alleged that distributing subsidized cereals is completely obsolete, that the pernicious effects of such a system outweigh the advantages. Deep-seated reforms have been demanded to do away with the former system to build a new, better-adapted mechanism.

Obviously, the approach that can be adopted to study this issue can only be a historical one. By following a chronological sequence this book will attempt to delineate the contours and developments of India's food policy. Recent history will not only define the way in which I unravel the story, it will also determine—at least partly—two points of departure: cereals on the one hand and the state on the other.

The limitation of the study of the food system to cereals may seem questionable, given the fact that India is facing a 'food transition', expressed in a declining consumption of cereals to the benefit of other products. The Public Distribution System or PDS also distributes, apart from wheat and rice, sugar, cooking oil, and kerosene. However, cereals constitute the cheapest source of calories, with the highest consumption, and are the central element defining India's former food system—at least, until the Green Revolution. The fight against hunger and famine was essentially a struggle to increase the availability of cereals. And it is by following developments in their production and marketing that the remarkable transformation independent India was to witness can best be perceived: the shift from a food policy based on the fight against hunger to a policy aimed at managing surpluses. The most remarkable aspect, perhaps, was that the same tools—though used a bit differently—that had been developed to fight famine in the past were to turn into factors for agricultural development.

A Green Revolution in cereal production was also happening in other countries, in Asia (Indonesia's BULOG system) and Europe (the Common Agricultural Policy). All were driven by the same compulsion: self-sufficiency, based on agricultural intensification that was enabled by state intervention. Subsidized food distribution systems were also set up in several other countries, from Egypt, Zambia, and Pakistan to the USA. What was original about India was that most of the food production and distribution mechanism established in the 1960s continues to operate while it was being dismantled in the rest of the world. In 2004 China wound up its system of state purchase and redistribution. Moreover, the redistribution there was essentially directed at city-dwellers only—i.e. a population that was half the size of the beneficiaries of India's PDS, though for an overall higher tonnage. And while the Chinese government purchased two-thirds of the production of cereals, soyabean and tubers, purchase prices were generally less advantageous than those Indian producers managed to get.

However, India eventually climbed on to the liberalization train.

Unlike China, it is a founder member of the WTO. Most Indian decision-makers believe that the prevailing systems are no longer relevant, as they lead to too much inefficiency and even corruption. Morever, structural change accompanying a certain withdrawal of the government went hand-in-hand with changes in production: more diversified products (poultry, horticulture) and higher added value. These were major changes for the domestic and international markets. To what extent shall they generate development? One is reminded of the factor of population pressure. It is not just by chance that China and India, the two most populated countries in the world, share certain elements in the policies they follow. Second, there is poverty and its various consequences. The victims of an agricultural exodus are unlikely to find a source of income in other sectors—India's rural areas have a far less diversified economic fabric than those of China. The domestic market cannot withstand high agricultural price rises. Budgetary constraints reduce the margin of manoeuvre of India's various state governments and its central government. Finally, apart from allying with other countries of the South, which it does, a developing country like India does not yet carry the same weight as the European Union or USA in international trade negotiations.

While it may seem strange that this study is limited to cereals, the emphasis on the state may also appear provocative. In these days of globalization, decentralization, and liberalization, post-modernism and de-constructionism, does it still serve any purpose to describe, justify, or criticise the state? It does, for at least three good reasons. The first is that even the most outrageous ideological liberalism has not yet managed to obviate the need for state action in a large number of fields, in all countries. The second is that the issue of food, which has to do with the very survival of all citizens, seems to be a subject that no state can afford to ignore, no matter how far from democracy it may be. The third reason is specific to India: despite liberalization since 1991, the state has retained a great deal of space there, both in the economy and in society. There is undoubtedly an urgent need to study the new actors in globalization, civil society, NGOs, and various other forms of participatory democracy. However, the pendulum should not swing too far—we should not forget about still-fertile existing scientific issues simply because we are examining new fields of inquiry.

Hence we need to speak of policies. The state is a fundamental component of what Sunil Khilnani (1999) calls 'the idea of India'—the at once vague and strong notion that has enabled a country born in pain in 1947 to remain united and democratic against all expectations. The Indian state—initially dominated by the Congress party that was at the forefront of the freedom movement—was endowed with a great legitimacy. To this was added its long history—the age of the state making the title of the collective work, *La greffe de l'État* or The Grafting of the State (Bayard 1996) rather unfortunate, particularly as more than a third of that book was devoted to India. A 'grafting of the state' may have taken place in several African countries, but in India's case, state institutions were too ancient for the state to be considered an import. In 1947, the state might in some ways appear abstract and impersonal to the people, but the food policy was a way of reducing its remoteness, as it had to do with the most widely spread occupation in India (agriculture) and a critical sector for all living beings—food. The risk was that the state could turn to populist policies in an effort to meet its citizens' aspirations, and in the course of reducing its anonymity it could loose its impartiality and concern for the long term, besides allowing the system to fall prey to corruption. The Indian government did not manage to avoid this pitfall.

In analysing these policies, we shall not underestimate the weight of the actors implementing them, subject to them, or hijacking them. The concept of 'public action' as defined by Drèze and Sen (1989: vii) emerges as a key notion: 'not merely the activities of the state, but also social actions taken by members of the public—both "collaborative" (through civic cooperation) and "adversarial" (through social criticism and political opposition)'. Another integrating concept, made popular by the World Bank, is that of 'governance', which includes the practices of non-state actors, in particular 'civil society' and the private sector. In this sense, a truly global study should not be limited to analysing the 'food policy', but rather, 'food governance'.

We shall try to analyse these policies in terms of both the discourse and the results. Announcements are obviously not always followed by the measures that are actually taken, even less by the desired results: an inclusive view is therefore desirable, combining the perspectives as seen in Delhi with those of the states of the Indian Union, without forgetting the results on the ground. Our analyses in terms of political science (both of the discourse and policy implementation), economics, sociology, and nutrition (for the outcome) are not fully detailed. If the food issue is considered a 'total social fact' (Mauss), the issues of cultivation, ecology, and politics are necessary, but you will not find them here. Indeed, just one approach has been highlighted here—the spatial approach. The originality of this text is that it proposes a geographic analysis of India's food system, mapping elements rarely explored until now. Indeed, the comments on maps are like the critique of a text that reveals meanings of which its author himself had been unaware. In the same way as Shakespeare's *Hamlet* can be analysed, we may research objectives, prejudices, and things left unsaid or of which its architects had not been aware—or at least, that had not been formulated as such in the available documents—behind the food policy. The maps make this possible; they are like footprints that lead a detective to the truth. That is probably one of geography's major contributions to the other social sciences.

It then appears that one of the food policy's objectives is *national integration* (making one nation out of the diversity of spaces and people) through dense and well-distributed circuits throughout the Indian territory. The various parts that make up the Indian Union should be linked to each other through a spider's web of diverse flows (particularly cereal flows) that together play a role in welding the national territory together through their circulation. This grid system, imperfectly built by both private and public actors, is not only the consequence of the country's general development. I shall argue that it is also the mark of a widely-shared conception—that of a territory to be integrated by cereal flows, politically, economically, and socially. The 'food system' therefore is not limited solely to nutritional, social, or productivist objectives—it also has an eminently geographic aim. We will see that the latter is based on two key spatial structures backing up the Indian imagination of the territory: on the one hand, the four cardinal points; on the other, dense flows linking these points and the areas beyond them. The predominant design therefore is not so much that of an egalitarian and homogeneous territory but rather of a territory to be 'irrigated' by cereal flows, this without necessarily leading to the disappearance of spatial inequalities. Turning this ideology of the national space into a reality was the task independent India decided to take up and its food policy played a role in this objective.

FOOD POLICY

'Food policy encompasses the collective efforts of governments to influence the decision-making environment of food producers, food consumers, and food marketing agents in order to further social objectives' (Timmer et al. 1986: 10). The last part of this definition is highly questionable, bearing in mind that there exist food policies that are totally against the interests of the food needs of the poorest, at the risk of triggering 'food riots'. Moreover, while this definition may be credited with the inclusion of the main food policy actors—governments, farmers, consumers, and traders—it remains thematically restricted. A population's nutritional condition depends on its conditions of health, education, and environment, almost as much as on its food bowl. Empowering women, ensuring literacy, caring, washing and cleaning are tasks that help in providing better nourishment. That is why more comprehensive studies are necessary, such as the one conducted by the M.S. Swaminathan Foundation (2001 and 2002) that took 17 indicators into account—from housing to the illiteracy rate—to prepare its *Food Insecurity Atlases.* It is also obvious that the general macro-economic policy and the vagaries of the world economic condition have a direct impact on India's food and agriculture. I ask the reader to excuse my granting these relatively little attention and focusing instead on cereal flows and the cereal circuit from state purchases to their redistribution—i.e. on the food policy in the strict sense, as described by Timmer and his team.

For the same reasons, I have underestimated the role of the swing of the pendulum with different political parties in power each time in centre and state. I believe that with regard to the food policy there have been very few sudden changes in direction with changes in government. What is striking is a certain continuity in policies and ideas, and the changes in direction that have taken place are more deviations than complete breaks with existing policies (Landy 2001).[2] Not even an event like the Emergency imposed by Indira Gandhi in 1975–7 could lead to an increase in the public distribution of cereals—although the contrary occurred on her return to power in 1980 (see Fig. 2.2). In the same way, the country's Independence in 1947 also barely stands out, since a food policy that merited the term was already in an embryonic stage in 1943 (even as early as in 1942 due to the attack by Japan) and no noticeable change occurred once the British left.[3] There are basically five pivotal dates to remember:

1942–3	Bengal famine and the initiation of the first food policy
1956	the beginning of major wheat imports from America, indicating the priority given to consumers, at the expense of producers
1964–5	the start of the Green Revolution and a return to self-sufficiency in food grains as the priority
1977	the beginning of cereal exports and the relaxation of coercive measures (the end of 'food zones')
1991	the initiation of a structural adjustment programme under the aegis of the IMF and the World Bank, which intensified the liberalization already begun.

However, an exceptional food situation can have a direct effect on political changes and people's mobilization. 'The 1970–3 drought in Maharashtra led to growing social awareness of the right to work, later enshrined in the state's pioneering "employment guarantee scheme". The 1987 drought in Rajasthan gave birth to a powerful movement for the "people's right to information". Even the Naxalite movement has important roots in the devastating droughts of the mid-1960s' (Drèze 2001: 4). This continued with the surprising defeat of the NDA alliance in 2004, which may have lost power at the centre partly because of three consecutive years of inadequate monsoon rains combined with increasing economic liberalization. Government passivity in the face of the food crises plaguing several regions led to popular support for opposition parties.

STATE, SPACE AND FOOD

Food is a 'nutritional commodity' that is, a commodity relevant to not just economics but also nutrition (Mooij 1999a). Thus it is necessary for us to discuss the nutritional context and we shall also follow as closely as possible, the path taken by bags of wheat or rice marketed by the public administration or private actors. The latter, will not be discussed at great length, however. Food is also a political commodity, and we will discover the stakes involved—stakes that go far beyond nutrition, as power in the matter of food may lie in the hands of junior officials and traders, and not only in those of the ministers in Delhi.

Yet at the same time food also takes on a geographic dimension. Very few studies on the Indian state reflect the spatial perspective, most studies being economic in nature. Extremely few go down to the 'field' level to examine what is happening beyond the plans drawn up in state capitals or in Delhi. There are two authors who must be set apart regarding this generalization. Barbara Harriss-White (1996, 2003) has conducted detailed political economy studies on markets and merchants in Tamil Nadu, and with regard to the role of the state in the food system, the cardinal study is by the sociologist Jos Mooij who analyses 'food policy as a tool in politics' (1999a: 39).

Mooij identified four streams of thought about the Indian state, which she used jointly in her study. The first stream was the least critical, as it attempted to analyse the long-term development policy, either in strictly economic (Chakravarty 1987) or more social terms (Amartya Sen 1981). The food policy is obviously a crucial subject in this perspective, given the problem of malnutrition. The state is then considered as a whole—at the risk of concealing the frauds and imperfections occurring in its daily functioning—in order to better study the development of the food policy in the light of changes in national development strategies or of international factors (relations with the USA, structural adjustment plan, etc.).

The second approach stems from predominantly neoclassical economics that places an emphasis on the 'rent-seeking state'. Wade (1982) is among the representatives of this approach, emphasizing corruption among government officials and the primacy of vested interests. The same perspective was taken up in a more Marxist-oriented approach by Harriss-White (2003). She laid the emphasis on a 'shadow state' that was often more real than the official state machinery and that was based on unofficial or even illegal practices. Studying the state therefore also made it necessary to take the social identities of individual officials into account. There was no opposition between the state and civil society—the state was present in the private homes of its officials, where some deals were settled, whereas the pseudo-civil society was present in a number of national ministerial wings or those of the local taluk offices. The interests of these officials and politicians lay in making the system inefficient, so that food insecurity could perpetuate the benefits they enjoyed in terms of their influence.

The third angle for Mooij was that of the political scientists who described the erosion of democracy by emphasizing the bankruptcy of parties and the collapse of civil society (Frankel (1978), Kothari (1988), etc.). Mooij then set out to present developments in the food issue and the stakes involved for political parties by calling to mind facts like the agricultural price rise of the 1960s, explaining that it stemmed from the coming to power of an agricultural bourgeoisie. However, this did not prevent pressure from being exerted for a reduction in food prices by an electorate that was increasingly aware of its prerogatives.

This brings us to Mooij's fourth line of approach, which was critical of the state and highlighted bureaucratic power. Bardhan (1984), for instance, condemned bureaucrats and technocrats for being a dominant class that confiscated power, as did the industrial capitalists and large farmers. Mooïj pointed out that if Bardhan's analysis were taken up, these three groups had different, but not contradictory, interests in the food policy: the industrialists wanted to bring consumer prices down, farmers wanted guaranteed farm prices, while bureaucrats placed an emphasis on the volume of food distributed, given that the power they enjoyed was proportional to it. However, Mooij moderated this perspective by stressing the fact that a large number of senior officials demonstrated a responsible approach, in terms of 'good governance' as well as generosity and honesty. She also pointed out that at least a fourth group needed to be brought out—that of politicians.

In my study I propose a fifth—spatial—perspective. This, in the footsteps of Raffestin (1980), will cast light on the 'geography of power', though in a rather restricted way, studying the spatial parameters of 'policies' rather than power as such. Providing a spatial perspective to all the power games existing in the food sphere was too difficult a task for a single book, not only because the topic is vast, but also because the theory of power space remains to be elaborated. True, following Edward Soja, some geographers have underscored the spatial aspects of Foucault's thought (Crampton and Elden 2007): approaching the Indian food policy in terms of state control and governmentality could probably have been possible. While 'space' is a neutral and abstract notion, territory is produced by a society, as Lefebvre argued, and more or less controlled by a state. It remains that Foucault was a philosopher, not a geographer, and even the reading of his works allegedly focused on spatial issues and territories is not very illuminating in this matter (Foucault

2004). According to Foucault himself, governments are concerned with the control of people rather than territories. Space and territory are at the forefront of neither state objectives, nor Foucauldian thought.

That we shall follow a more classical path in geography, highlighting the spatial aspects of the food policy, does not mean that we shall follow beaten tracks. There is little spatial research on development and economic policies in India, and most of it is conducted by economists rather than geographers. The fact that the food policy is rarely mentioned in Indian planning literature, in particular with regard to regional planning, should not prevent us from connecting the two issues and addressing the regional planning of the national space in the light of the food policy. Too often, the 'official claims of the state form the starting point of the analysis. The plans on paper define the research question: to what extent have the planning goals been achieved. In short, the perspective of the researcher is that of the state. What this implies for the conceptualization of the Indian state is that the self-image of the state, i.e. of the planners, is taken over by the researchers' (Mooij 1999a: 59). A more innovative perspective would be to suggest a number of new questions.

A convincing example is the discussion on the ideas advocated by the most famous theoretician of India's famine, Amartya Sen. For him, it was the democratic structure of the state—and the country in general—what enabled the prevention of famines. Pressure from voters, within the framework of universal suffrage, the threat of opposition parties, the dissemination of information, and media and opinion campaigns were effective tools that obliged a government to aggressively pursue preventive measures aimed not only at maintaining a certain stability in the supply of food products, but also at increasing the 'entitlements' of households and individuals. In May 1973 in Maharashtra, at a time when the government had organized massive infrastructure work sites to provide labour opportunities due to the recurring drought over three years, a strike by 1.5 million beneficiaries forced it to raise salaries (Drèze and Sen 1989: 133).

Yet counter-examples have also been offered opposing this theory —if only the fact that famines, although they may be restricted with regard to their geographic coverage, continue to prevail in the 'world's biggest democracy' (Etienne 2003). In the desire to find arguments on a national scale, we are likely to come up against quite different realities at the regional and local levels. The spatial perspective of Sen's analysis is limited. In fact, its main faults may lie solely therein. Thus, Banik (1998) underlines the extent to which the Indian democracy is incapable of preventing recurring famines of Orissa, in particular in the Kalahandi region;[4] close relations between politicians and mediapersons hinder any true freedom of the press; and drought relief is either badly targeted or diverted. Do these blunders, however, reinforce Sen's theory rather than gainsaying it? For there is no real democracy in Kalahandi district, and it is essentially due to the fact that civic rights and freedom are abused in this region that famines occur.[5] Sen and his adversaries may ultimately be right, but at different spatial levels, which should be differentiated. Since exceptions prove the rule, Sen's ideas, which stress the role of 'public action', could remain fully valid on the national scale ; if famines continue to occur on a local scale, it is only because of the almost complete absence of government action at this level—whence the advantage of a more geographic perspective underlining regional disparities.

The same perspective also enables us to study developments in food policy.

Over the relatively long period 1947–2007, it is difficult to identify clear trends in terms of policies. However, a certain swing between two trends can be seen, one succeeding the other, though often overlapping, and without necessarily corresponding to changes in political power. The two ends of the continuum are a policy of uniformity and equalization, and one of concentration and polarization. The first trend was essentially 'leftist', the second basically 'rightist', if these adjectives can really hold any meaning in this context. The first corresponded to what Drèze and Sen (1989: 183) call 'support-led security', whereas the second was part of 'growth-mediated security'. After Independence, land reforms and attempts at 'community development' marked the first phase aimed at introducing a certain uniformity in the name of social justice and the development of the whole of the young nation. With the start of the Green Revolution, the reverse took place when, faced with an emergency situation, there was a resolve that all efforts and investments had to be focused on certain regions, certain crops, and certain social groups. Whether consciously or not, the Green Revolution targeted mid-level farmers, the same group that

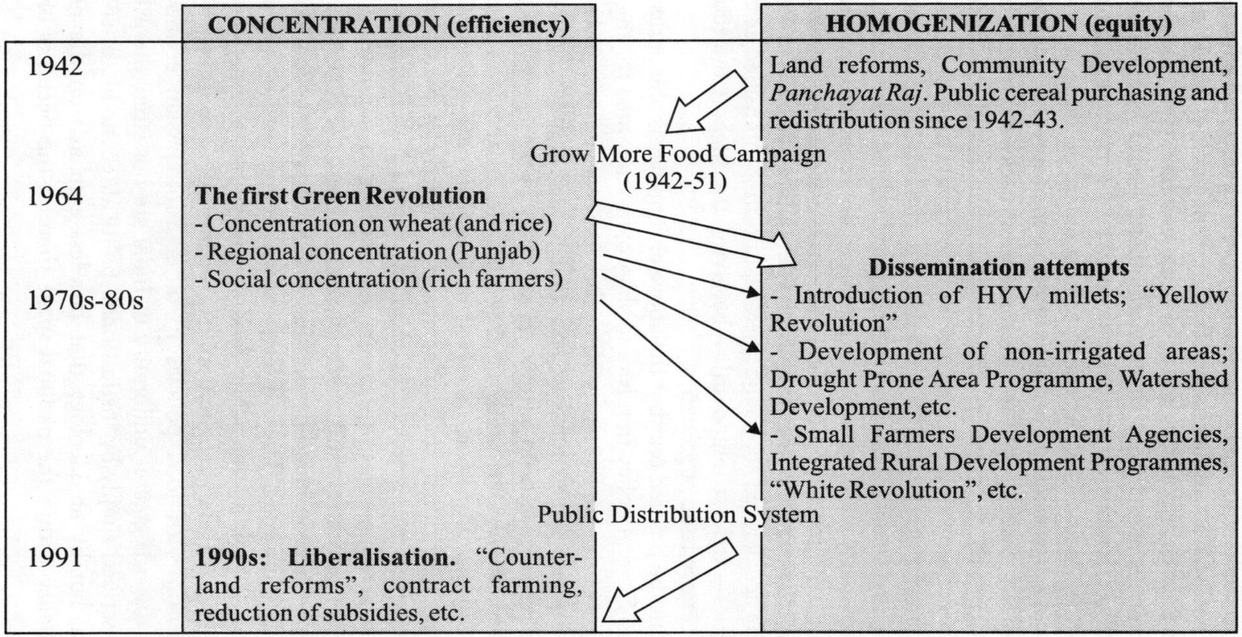

Figure 1: Concentration or homogenization – an impossible choice

constituted a solid support group for the Congress party that was in power in Delhi. The egalitarianism that governments had advocated until then was set aside—it was true that inequalities would arise, but the most urgent matter had to be dealt with first, given the threat of famine. It was hoped that development would 'trickle down' gradually. Trickling vertically would enable the poorest groups to have access to an improvement in their standard of living, after the rich would. It was also hoped that it would then spread like wildfire horizontally, thereby uplifting even the most backward regions and those deprived of irrigation. But since the benefits of the trickle-down effect were slow to emerge, a fresh policy was developed in the 1970s, attempting to restore the balance to the benefit of the crops, regions, and social groups that had been left behind. The defeat the Congress party suffered in 1977 prompted to accelerate the trend towards a policy that was more concerned about disadvantaged groups. However, the last swing in the pendulum occurred in 1991, with the accelerated economic liberalization that intensified certain disparities—at least temporarily—by giving the highest priority to the necessary issue of growth.

It must be pointed out that the above chronology is obviously not flawless. Several policy trends were able to, or attempted to, emerge simultaneously, sometimes within the same government, which obviously also led to tensions and ambiguities. However, the following pages have been written on the basis of the analytical grid described above. The study of developments in the food system is divided into three parts: a mixed review of success stories in the food and nutritional field, as against the tragedy of the colonial famines; the vagaries of policies based on a planned economy, swinging between support to producers and support to consumers, between concentration and dissemination; and last the new circumstances with economic liberalization and its attendant functioning and malfunctioning. These three parts will be followed by a fourth, which will look at the public food system within a larger framework—that of the imagination. As confirmed *a contrario* by a comparison with food policies in other South Asian countries, efforts towards greater uniformity in India are not strengthened or circumscribed simply by institutional, political, economic or social criteria, but by an ideology that lays less emphasis on the need for equality within the national space than on the necessity of its *integration.* That the Indian public food system has not yet been phased out in spite of the numerous criticisms from all political sides and the liberalization wave, can be explained by many factors, not to speak of vested interests. An important explanatory factor spelt out here is this imagined national territory, based on the four cardinal points that must ideally be interlinked by dense networks, be they flows of foodgrains or something else. Hence, the study of the public food system is a fecund entry point into the policies of planning and the idea of the national territory.

It is necessary to emphasize the fact that we shall highlight policies at the national level more than facts at the local level. The Indian reader knows well that the PDS does not succeed in integrating the nation—it contributes instead towards its disintegration. It enlarges gaps and inequities, fills the pockets of swindlers at various levels (from the small shopkeeper to the minister), and its persistence in the face of economic liberalization is less due to social priorities or spatial planning than to a nexus of interests at all scales (Harriss-White 2003). Other research is being conducted that takes the PDS as an entry into the study of urban governance and the compartmentalization of so-called 'civil society' (Landy 2007), but will be the matter of another book. There is no logical contradiction between these two perspectives, the national and the local, even though they provide somewhat opposite views.

NOTES

1. William and Paul Paddock, *Famine 1975!*, London, Weidenfeld and Nicholson, 1968 (quoted by Dantwala 1996 : 62).
2. It is remarkable that the abundant literature on the food *policy* fails to tackle its development in the context of India's political history—undoubtedly because it is, above all, the work of economists. Its institutional perspectives are limited, except for listing the various commissions set up.
3. In my view, it is therefore necessary to qualify the assertion made by Drèze (1995 : 154), that 1947 was a critical date for famine prevention, just as important as the initiation of the Famine Codes in 1880. His perspective is broadly set within the framework of the thesis Amartya Sen holds so dear, according to which there can be no food security without democracy. It is true that India's Independence would force the political and administrative authorities to *implement* measures with greater constancy than in the colonial era. However, these measures would long

remain the same as those applied in the British era, as described by Knight (1954) for the transition period of 1939–47.

4. Currie (2000) confirmed his survey and also criticised Sen.
5. Drèze and Sen (1989: 214) acknowledged that 'open journalism and adversarial politics provide much less protection against endemic undernutrition than they do against a dramatic famine'. Chronic poverty rarely makes headlines in the Indian media. As a result, over the last 40 years, there have been more deaths due to hunger in India than in China, despite the 15–30 million deaths that occurred during the Great Leap Forward in China. 'It is important to review how real is the idea that India has avoided famines since independence rather than not reported them' (Banik 1998 : 278).

CHAPTER 1

The Challenge of Food

> Unlike economists who are more concerned about the trade and distribution of food available within the framework of a nation-state or beyond, tropicalist geographers, even the ideologically neo-liberal ones, find the link between what can be produced locally and what will be consumed locally very important. So they cannot be expected to provide arguments about 'comparative advantages'—they would greet all calcu-lations to this effect very sceptically, using strong arguments. For instance, how can production costs in Asia and Africa be calculated and compared without referring to the structure of social reproduction? The idea of self-sufficiency seems less absurd to geographers rather than economists . . .. because unlike the latter, the former take the long term much more into account and put the nation's accounts into perspective by placing it in the position of Developing Countries!
>
> G. Courade 1992, p. 753

> Auto-nomy [*sic*] does not mean independence, but a negotiated dependence . . . in order to build an environment that one cannot build alone (due to limited means and rationality). Auto-nomy means being active in relation to dependence, be it natural or human.
>
> B. Dorin 1994, p. 218

SELF-SUFFICIENCY IN CEREALS, CONTINUING FOOD INSECURITY

India's development is marked by contrasts and fragility (Drèze and Sen 2002). The software and new technologies giant is also afflicted by persistent poverty—in 2006, India was ranked as low as 126 in the UNDP World Human Development Index classification. The issue of food is a good illustration of this situation. In contrast to the country's acquired self-sufficiency in cereals and milk, we find a continuingly deplorable nutritional record for the majority of the population: food security remains an objective and is not a reality.

Thus, agriculture is still a key sector, accounting for 58 per cent of the working population in 2003–4 and 22 per cent of the GDP. This means that its food function is augmented by its function in employment and income generation, which makes it a parking place' for all the working people unable to find a non-agricultural occupation. On a global level, however, during discussions in the WTO, the main functions of agriculture, identified as being non-commercial by international experts, were food safety, employment, rural development, cultural heritage, food safety, and environmental protection. Until now, the Indian agricultural sector only performs the first four functions, the latter two being looked upon more as playing a negative role given the far from 'ecological' nature of most cropping systems. However, this itself helps us understand the magnitude of the stakes involved in the 'multi-functionality' of agriculture, whose purpose, though incomplete, is to ensure that a billion people are able to live.

Achievement of National Self-Sufficiency in Cereals

Each of the words used above is important in its own way, as India has a very unfavourable trade balance in the case of certain agricultural products (oilseeds) and, above all, because national-level self-sufficiency in no way means that the needs of all its people are met—i.e. that there is any real food security.

In 1951, food grain[1] imports accounted for 9 per cent of net production,[2] with the percentage climbing to a 14 per cent high in 1966, hastening the advent of the Green Revolution. Since then, it has fallen continually and the trade balance has even been positive at times. India became the world's second largest rice exporter in 2002 (6.6 million tonnes) as well as in 2003, and the seventh largest wheat exporter (3.1 million tonnes) in 2002. In 2002, the government's food grain stocks rose to 65 million tonnes. That India had eventually to import 5.5 million tonnes of wheat in 2006 was the effect of a chosen liberalization of markets, not of a return to the pre-Green Revolution years.

In half a century, food grain production quadrupled, but the population tripled over the same period. Figure 1.1 can therefore be interpreted in two ways. One way would be optimistic, as the production curve follows and even overtakes the population curve. The other is more pessimistic, as the progress achieved in agriculture

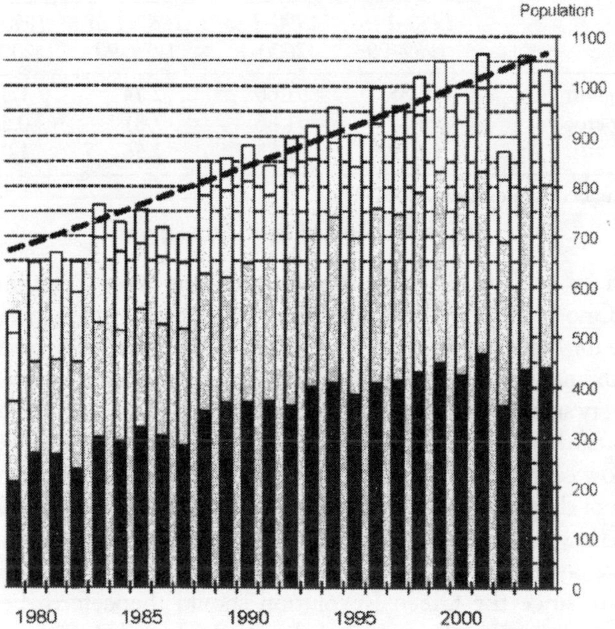

Source: Dorin and Landy, forthcoming.

Figure 1.1: Food grain production and area (1950–1/2004–5)

is largely wiped out by population growth. In fact, the growth in food grain production is no longer keeping pace with population growth (Figure 1.2): its rate of 1.66 per cent during the 1990s has been the lowest since the 1950s. The gains achieved by agricultural production came mainly from sectors, such as animal husbandry and those related to the food processing industry. Is a crop diversification taking place, which could threaten the wheat-rice duo that had become excessively dominant, as we shall see?

Other figures also indicate a similar ambiguity. One indicator is the food grain availability per capita—i.e. net production after deduction of net imports.[3] It showed a positive trend, rising from 395 grams of food grains per day per capita in 1951 to 438 g in 2003. However, the latter figure had already been reached several years earlier (469 g in 1961), and given the sawtooth curve that followed (510 g in 1991, 427 g in 2002–3), a number of observers laid

	Production		*Yield per hectare*	
	1980–1 to 1989–90	*1990–1 to 2000–1*	*1980–1 to 1989–90*	*1990–1 to 2000–1*
Food grain	2.85	1.66	2.74	1.34
Other crops	3.77	1.86	2.31	0.59
Total	3.19	1.73	2.56	1.02

Source: Economic Survey 2001-2.

Figure 1.2: Annual agricultural growth

emphasis on how disappointing the situation was (Chandrasekhar and Ghosh 2002). These quantities were three times lower than those for Europe, four times lower than in the USA and represented approximately 60 per cent of the total for China, particularly due to the very small share of grains that was used for animal feed. Excessive exports, the reduction in government investment in rural areas, and the low customs tariffs set by increasingly liberal governments were some of the factors responsible for this situation (Patnaik 2004).

However, there was something to be optimistic about with regard to the available production estimates—the better seed rate per hectare since the Green Revolution should thenceforth be taken into account, thereby reducing the share of seeds in any net production calculations.[4] Improved paddy milling too must be taken into account, thanks to its modernization, as it raises husked rice production figures.[5] In addition, animal feed was thenceforth partially provided by formula foods and cakes that had not been drawn from the harvest, which somewhat compensated for the fall in the availability of pulses (often fodder crops originally) which had halved since the beginning of the Green Revolution.

Food grain availability is just one indicator among many. Drèze and Sen (1989: 122) stressed the absence of any relationship between the end of India's famines and the growth in its agricultural production—famines began to become scarcer since the first half of the twentieth century, although per capita production was falling and population growth was accelerating. Whereas in the nineteenth-century, the growth in production (albeit low) in no way stopped famines from increasing in number. Thus, the Malthusian formula was not applicable, despite its popularity in public opinion today as with the nineteenth-century's colonial administrators. Currently, food grain production per capita is barely higher than at the end of the nineteenth century.[6] Apart from the African crisis period of 1971–3, the per capita production curve for India remained below the curve for the Sahel region during the 1960–80 period, at a time when the Green Revolution was in full swing (Drèze 1995). Thus, famines came to an end due to other factors: overall economic development, which enabled diversification and income stabilization to a certain extent; the end of the priority to cash crops over food crops; the reduction of fiscal levies on agriculture; the transition from irrigation based on mere diversion channels to a modern irrigation system based on storage dams (Durand-Dastès 1982), and so on. But they also ended due to the state food policy, which is the subject of this book.

The forecast is nevertheless far from reassuring. Given the continuance of a high population growth rate (1.7 per cent per annum) despite the fall in fertility, given the animal feed needs that compensate the fall in direct food grain consumption by humans, the estimates for cereal requirements in 2020 fluctuate between 224 million tonnes (194 million for human consumption and 30 million for animal feed) and 296 millions tonnes (246 and 50 million, respectively).[7] If we take a medium estimate (Bansil 2000), the same production growth rates that prevailed in the 1980s would have to be achieved again, at a time when Punjab's rice yields seem to have reached a plateau, when the environmental problems caused by the Green Revolution are increasingly evident and when a rise in non-food grain or fodder products is required in order to meet the diversification needs of India's food bowl. Currently, there is an estimated 8–10 per cent increase in the consumption of animal products (milk, meat, and eggs) due to the expansion of the class of wealthier citizens (Patnaik 1997). As 2 to 7 times more food grain calories are necessary to produce one animal calorie, we can understand why such a trend—which is normal given the rising living standards and cultural dynamics of one part of the population—may lead to increased tension over food grain, land, and water.

The overall review is, therefore, quite clear. Between the three-year averages of 1989–92 and 1999–2002, agricultural production rose by just 1.7 per cent per annum, i.e less than the population increase.[8] World commodity price trends are too uncertain for a country to be able to depend on cheap imports : global prices of wheat doubled between 2006 and 2007. Besides, India accounts for

22 per cent of world rice consumption and 12 per cent of world wheat consumption, so it should not hope to avail of low import prices, as its own purchases would themselves suffice to push the prices up (particularly in the case of rice, whose world prices are particularly tight). Some self-sufficiency and the maintenance of national buffer stocks are therefore necessary.

Absence of Food Security

The Famine Codes decreed by the colonial regime have turned into simple Relief Codes, but famine conditions continue to set in from time to time, and chronic undernourishment remains widespread.[9] The FAO came up with a figure of 221 million undernourished people in India in 2000–2, i.e. 21 per cent of the population.[10] Half the people living in hunger in the world live in India. According to the National Sample Survey Organisation (NSSO), 5.5 per cent of the rural population and 1.9 per cent of the urban population still cannot manage to earn enough for two meals a day. In addition, approaches based on chronic calorie deficiency (undernutrition) and the more qualitative nutritional defi-ciency (malnutrition) approaches have to be taken together. In fact, the latter take into account the share of the various nutrients in the diet and sometimes throw light on deficiencies that satisfactory calorie intakes may conceal.

(a) *Ambiguous Cereal and Calorie Intake Situations*

According to the NSSO, the average daily calorie intake is 2,150 kcal per head (1999–2000).[11] This is lower than the standard established by the Indian Council of Medical Research, which is 2,400 kcal for rural areas, but it may appear satisfactory since it corresponds to the FAO standard for South Asia (Varshney and Pandey 2003). That being said, as is the case with any average, these figures suggest truly tragic conditions in the poorest households. Households with monthly incomes of less than Rs. 525 (i.e. 67 per cent individuals) have an intake of less than 2,289 kcal, as against over 2,581 kcal for households with monthly incomes of over Rs. 615 (i.e. 23 per cent individuals). Two other factors make the situation even worse: the calorie intake is lower in rural areas as compared to urban areas, despite the higher physical effort demanded in the former, on an average. Besides, the calorie intake has shown a downward trend since the end of the 1970s in rural areas. It has only risen slightly (by 0.5 per cent per annum) in the poorest three deciles of the population, which get 1,696 kcal (in rural areas) and 1,715 kcal (in urban areas) (Radhakrishna et al. 2004).

The nutritional profile of the country is marked by the importance of pulses, given that *dal* inevitably accompanies *roti* in the north and often rice in south India. It is inevitably based on cereals, which constitute 65 per cent of the protein and calorie intake. The fact that cereals account for 33 per cent of the household food budget shows what an inexpensive nutritional source they represent. The poorest 40 per cent section in rural areas ingest 75 per cent of their calories from cereals, for which they spend one-third of their *total* budget.

However, according to NSSO surveys, per capita cereal consumption fell radically between 1972–3 and 1999–2000, going from 175 kg per capita per annum to 147 kg, above all due to the reduction in the consumption of coarse cereals (sorghum, *ragi* or finger millet, etc.). The quantity of cereals consumed also fell among the poorest sections, which meant that on the whole, the caloric intake of 30 per cent of the poorest section of the population showed a downward trend in the 1990s.[12]

There was a particularly marked fall in coarse cereal consumption. Rice and wheat consumption started falling only in the 1990s. Figure 1.3 attempts to distinguish the trends witnessed by these two cereals for different population groups. The poorer sections today consume a little more than in 1987–8, hence there has been a reduction in the social differences in consumption models. Spatial differences remain patently obvious: rural areas consume more cereals than do urban centres, but the greater fall in wheat and rice consumption among the rural rich (–14 per cent) as compared to the urban rich (–11 per cent) promises a reduction of social differences there as well.

How do we analyse the fall in cereal consumption? Inflation could easily be held accountable. Figure 1.4 shows a reduction in cereal prices due to gains in production since the Green Revolution and up to the 1980s. But wholesale cereal prices increased by 33 per cent in real value in the 1990s, probably—as we will see—due to State

1. Rural rice and wheat consumption

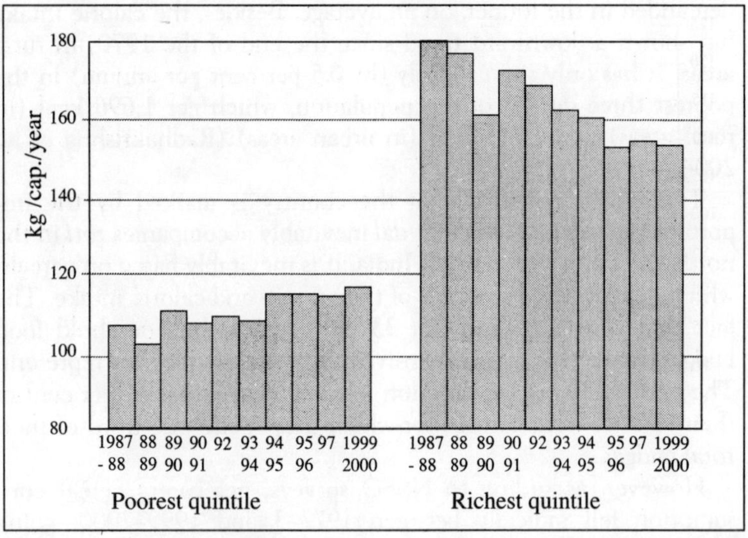

2 - Urban rice and wheat consumption

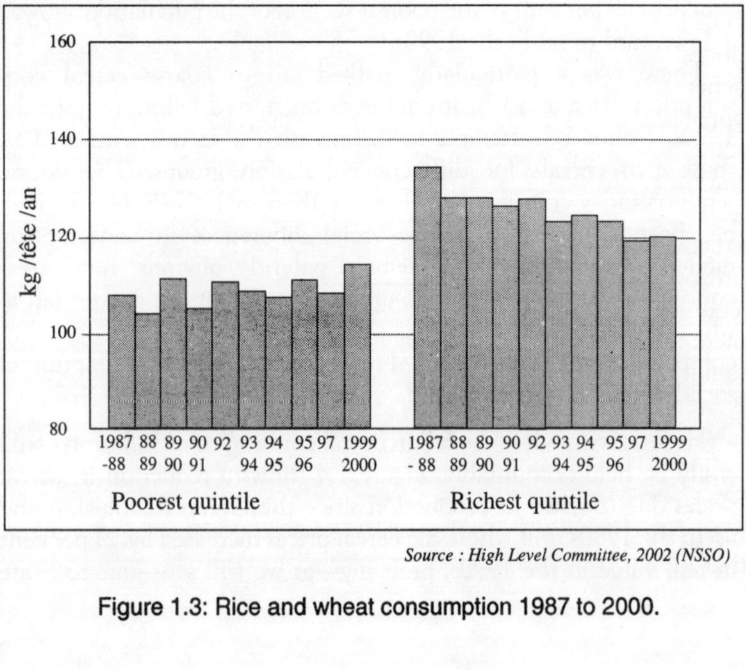

Source : High Level Committee, 2002 (NSSO)

Figure 1.3: Rice and wheat consumption 1987 to 2000.

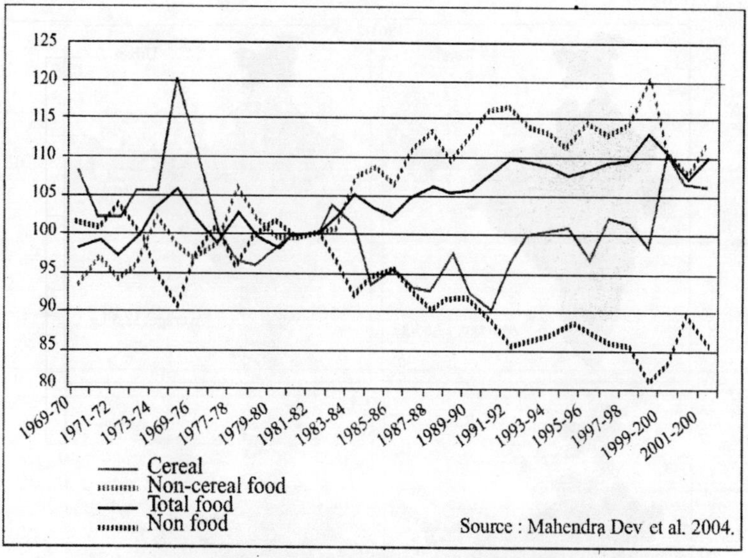

Figure 1.4: Wholesale price trends in proportion to the general price index (urban India)[13]

procurement (Landes and Gulati 2004; High Level Committee 2002). The price rise was probably even higher in the case of retail prices. Other causes included increasing urbanization and, more generally, changing lifestyles due to which both urban and mobile populations were obliged to have their meals away from home, sometimes on the run, often non-cereal dishes or snacks. An illustration may perhaps be seen in Map 1.1 on cereal consumption in 1999–2000, which is quite similar to the negative of India's urbanization map—it is as if the rural population of the most urbanized states (Tamil Nadu, Maharashtra, Gujarat) had been 'contaminated' by urban lifestyles.[14] More positively, an improvement in the standard of living of part of the population or the imitation of the food habits of the richest population groups by the poorest sections led to food with a much lower cereal content, and more meat, eggs, and vegetables.

The significance of the fall in the cereal content of India's food bowl, both in volume and percentage, is therefore rather ambiguous. For many, it is a sign of an improvement in living standards, given that a portion of the nutritive elements earlier provided by cereals

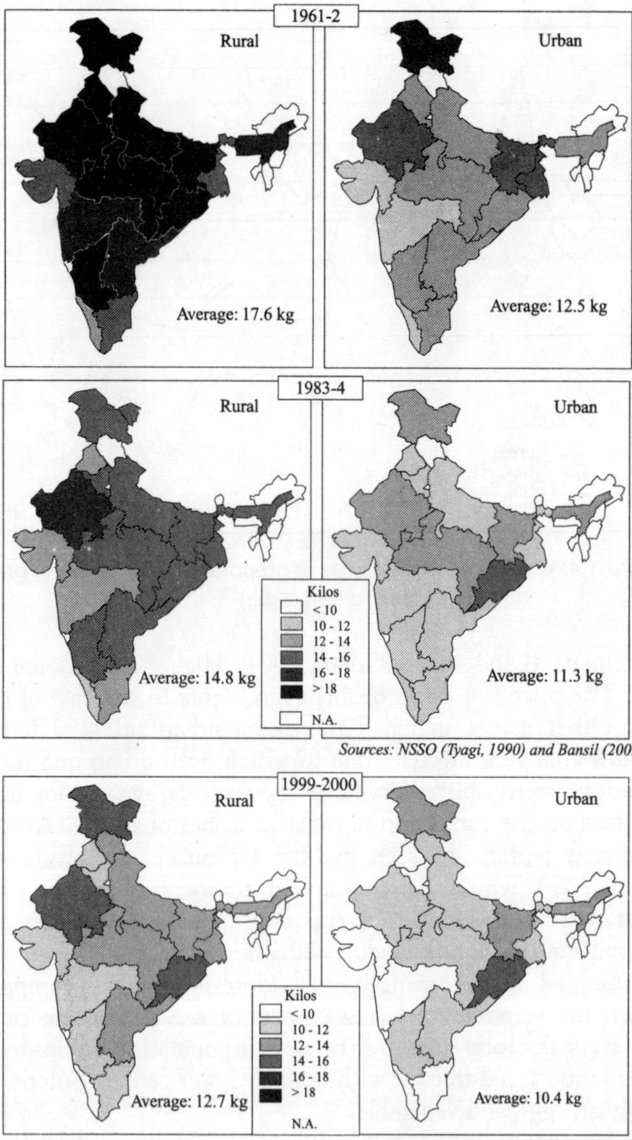

Sources: NSSO (Tyagi, 1990) and Bansil (2003)

Map 1.1: Per capita monthly cereal consumption (1961 to 2000)

now come from other, more costly, and better valued foods. The relative reduction of the weight of food expenditure in household budgets constitutes an illustration of Engel's law, which asserts that a rise in income is not followed by a similar rise in food expenditure. The reduction in the demand for cereals in rural areas was particularly marked in areas where infrastructural development (mainly roads) enabled the supply of more advantageous products (Rao 2000). In the same way, the diversification of the food bowl was, not surprisingly, said to correspond to Bennett's law, which asserts that a rise in income leads to the consumption of more costly food at the expense of cereals and tubers (Padilla 1996). The food budget falls in terms of total expenditure percentage, but rises in terms of absolute value.

However, food diversification is also a sign of crisis in a minority of households, those who have to reduce their cereal consumption. Their nutritional condition is in no way improved by doing so.

(b) *The Hindu Food Transition*

> Reports from the field point to chronic and severe undernutrition, even hunger deaths, from parts of the country as disparate as Andhra Pradesh and Rajasthan. In Maharashtra, the State government admitted to the High Court that 2,814 children, mainly from tribal areas, had died of starvation between January and July 2005. (*Frontline*, 27 January 2006, p. 110)

To go from a purely caloric analysis to a more qualitative one, it is necessary to refer to the nutritional situation in terms of proteins, carbohydrates, fats, and micronutrients (Dorin 1999). The nutritional condition of Indians has definitely improved. Kwashiorkor (severe form of malnutrition) is no longer endemic. The proportion of children suffering from acute malnutrition has fallen from 15 per cent in 1975–9 to 9 per cent in 1996–7 (Varshney and Pandey 2003). However, the situation remains far from satisfactory. Map 1.2 shows that 48 per cent of children under 3 years suffer from chronic or acute malnutrition (Radhakrishna and Ravi 2004). According to the FAO, 83 per cent of Indian women suffer from anaemia during pregnancy. In Mumbai, the country's richest city, over 750 children under 5 years die of malnutrition every year (Hatekar and Rode 2003).

The 'food transition', as it is called, is composed of two phases in the process of the change in food habits: an increase in the

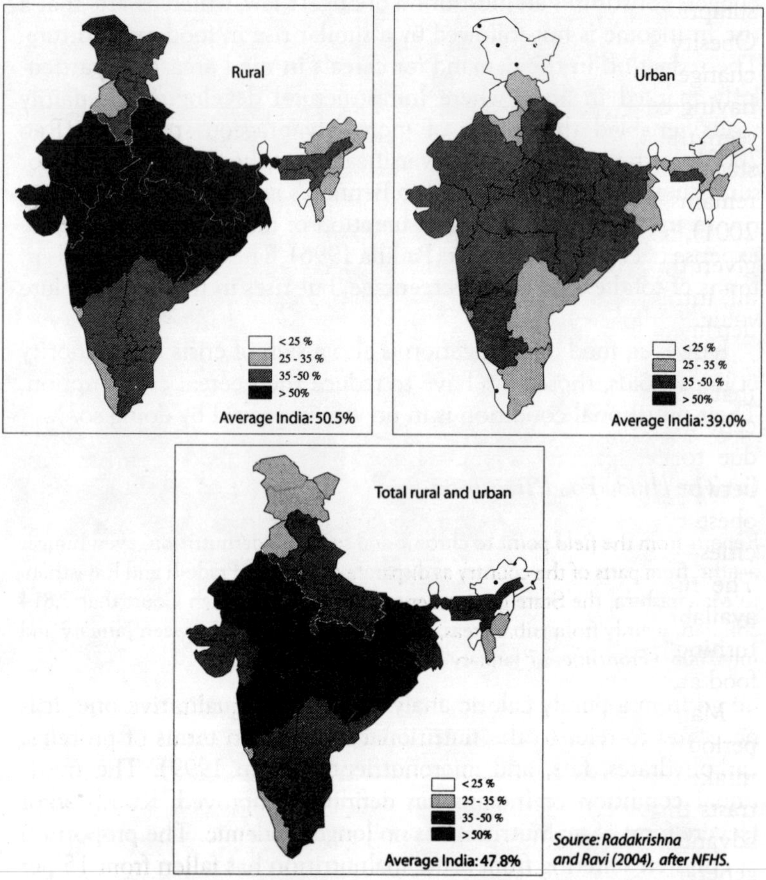

Source: Radakrishna and Ravi (2004), after NFHS.

Map 1.2: Undernourishment (severe and moderate) of children under 3 year of age (weight-age ratio) 1998–9

consumption of plant products when increased income makes it possible to ingest more calories; then a sharp increase in the consumption of animal fat, to the detriment of cereals, in particular. Obesity and cardiovascular diseases then ensue and reflect this change (Maire and Delpeuch 2004). India is obviously far from having completed such a transition. On the one hand, as we have seen, the poorer sections of the population have just reached the first stage of the food transition. On the other hand, urbanization, which remains limited in percentage terms (28 per cent city-dwellers in 2001), only marginally translates into more meat-based food habits, given the cultural importance of vegetarianism. It translates, above all, into the predominance of wheat and rice in food habits, to the detriment of other cereals.

The Body Mass Indexes published by the FAO in 1994 indicated that only 2 per cent of Indians were overweight (as against 48 per cent who were underweight). However, it is estimated that deaths due to cardiovascular diseases would rise by almost 50 per cent between 1990 and 2020 (IFPRI 2002). And the cohabitation of obese rich people and undernourished poor people—at least in the cities—is likely to place an additional burden on the health system. The rise in meat consumption will also weigh heavily on cereal availability for fodder. On the whole, the fact that malnutrition is turning into a dual phenomenon (deficiency plus excess) will make food an even thornier issue.

Map 1.3 shows the space-wise distribution of this data for the period between 1972–3 and 1999–2000. The change in calorie-intake conditions was characterized by a reduction in regional contrasts thanks to a slight rise in intake, but the south remained disadvantaged as compared to north India. This is contrary to the general opinion, according to which poverty is identified with calorie-intake deficiencies. Indeed, the tip of the peninsula is far from the country's poorest region. Given this fact, reference should be made to Engel's law instead, as relative development enables a part of the population to enjoy food that may not be particularly rich in calories but is more costly.

However, the protein consumption maps greatly resemble the calorie maps, with regard to both their aspect and their evolution over this period. This means that no deficiency in calorie intake is compensated by the intake of proteins. In particular, this means that a deficiency in the cereal ration is not compensated by qualitatively

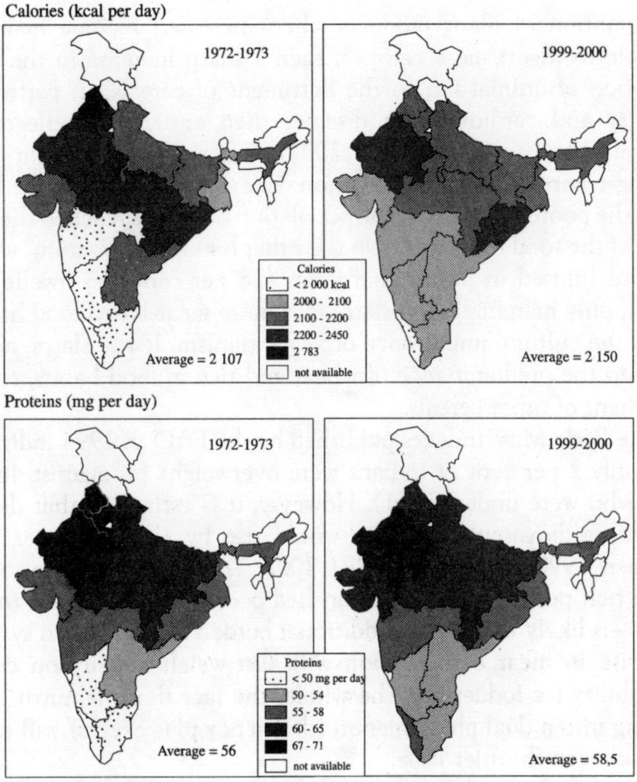

Source : NSSO

Map 1.3: Calorie, protein and fat intake (1972 to 2000)

richer food (eggs, meat). The hypothesis made by Engel's law is therefore far from verified.

The lipid or fat maps are the only ones to show a clear rise in intake over the period (+38 per cent in 27 years). The rural and urban population are both consuming more lipids than in the past.[15] However, regional contrasts remain marked, but this time the gap lies between eastern and western India. Could the differences in the overall development level constitute an explanatory factor? Perhaps not, since in any case, it cannot explain the good position currently occupied by Rajasthan: local consumption models would undoubtedly have to be used, along with the cultural importance of milk-based fats and oils in western India, the cradle of the 'white revolution' (Dorin 1994). It should also be borne in mind that cereals provide lipids in considerable quantities, which means that on the whole, essential fatty acid requirements are statistically covered (Dorin 1999). Therein lies what could be called the 'Hindu food transition'—the fall in cereal consumption is not compensated by a rise in meat consumption, which remains limited essentially for cultural reasons. MacDonald's in India offers a number of vegetarian burgers (and in any case, none contains beef). The transition is taking place more to the benefit of milk-based products and eggs—and to a lesser degree, chicken (Dorin 2005).

In fact, a difference should be made between growth rates and quantities in absolute value terms. Chicken consumption has witnessed the highest growth, rising by 10 per cent per annum since 1980; yet in 1999–2000, it only accounted for 60 g per capita per month (in urban areas)! Other meats have had much lower growth rates, with quantities being barely higher: 220 g per capita per month for fish, 100 g for goat meat, 80 g for beef, and 2 eggs.

The diversification of the diet cannot therefore be explained entirely by a rise in purchasing power. Food still accounted for 46 per cent of the household budget in 1999 (as against 14 per cent in 2001 in France). As can be seen in Map 1.3, the richer states generally have lower calorie intakes, but there is no real correlation. Above all, calories are not 'replaced' by proteins, i.e. the substitution of cereals by foods with a high protein-content that are far costlier is not the sole reason for the fall in cereal consumption.

The fact that even the poor are consuming smaller amounts of cereal even though grains are cheap sources of calories, means that they are facing an extremely serious food crisis—or at the least, additional expenses that they can scarcely afford. *A fruit of the Green Revolution, national self-sufficiency in food grains is also, therefore, partly due to the food transition and, to a lesser degree, to the persistence of malnutrition.* The richer the rich get, the less cereal they consume. The emptier the stomachs of the poor, the more the warehouses get filled. Government stocks, engendered by substantial supply, but also by the reduction in financially sound demand, therefore say a lot about India's poverty—at least as much as they do about its successes.

Furthermore, the increasing trend towards processing cereals into urban consumer products (corn flakes, pasta, etc.) risks limiting their availability for the rural masses. Probably paraphrasing the French Queen Marie-Antoinette, Patnaik (1997 : 1111) stressed that 'it is of no use to tell the rural labourer to eat noodles if he cannot afford wheat'. There is a purchasing power problem here, and one of physical access to food grains for landlocked regions, which hinders access to a satisfactory daily food ration, despite the statistical availability of cereals at national level. In particular, it should be noted that the states with the lowest calorie intake are also those with the lowest per capita cereal production. The transfer of food grains towards deficit areas through either private traders or the public distribution system, the subject of this book, still does not ensure economic access to cereals for the poorest households—although food grain circulation may have improved in the long term. The objective that became increasingly important after Independence, as we shall see—that of national integration through dense circuits well-distributed over the territory—is still far from being achieved.

So the question that arises is whether India really managed to eradicate famines. It is true that when Drèze and Sen (1989) distinguished countries suffering from chronic hunger from truly famine-struck countries, they placed India in the first group. In Bihar in 1967, Maharashtra in 1973, West Bengal in 1979 and Gujarat in 1987, famine was averted thanks to State intervention. Nonetheless, there were a large number of dramatic testimonies (Sainath 1996) pointing at the recurrent famines in Orissa (Currie 2000; Mishra 2005), Madhya Pradesh (CEHAT 2002) or elsewhere. The inadequate monsoons of the beginning of this century only highlighted a problem that was, in fact, chronic.

The fall in per capita cereal production is reminiscent of a similar reduction during the decades preceding the 1943 famine (Patnaik

1991). Unfortunately, India clearly illustrates the axiom according to which famines can occur even when a country has enough food statistically to feed its entire population. True food security implies that every individual has *access* to food—so the concept of 'entitlement' as defined by Amartya Sen comes in here. 'The "entitlement" of a person stands for the set of alternative commodity bundles that can be acquired through the use of the various legal channels of acquirement open to that person' (Drèze and Sen 1989: 23).[16] In other words, the loss of land, disease, or rise in prices may lead to a situation of hunger, as much as to the physical absence of available food grains. The fault lies in the agrarian structures of rural areas and all the social forms that remain fundamentally inequitable all over India.

Sen's theory only formalizes a view long recognized. Indeed, even Colonel Baird Smith, in charge of the 1860–1 famine survey (2 million deaths in northern India), wrote that the problem was one of 'hunger for work rather than food'; a purchasing power problem rather than that of a bad harvest. In the same way, after the Bengal famine, Nehru in his prison cell accused the British of having sown death—'the result of man's incompetence and callousness' rather than the vagaries of nature, in the 'rich and fertile province of Bengal' (Nehru 1985: 16). What Sen's theory does is to make it possible to arrive at a much better definition of the notion of 'food security', relinquishing the national scale and adopting a disintegrated vision at the levels of various social groups, households, and individuals. In fact, food security is something far removed from a mere production/population ratio (IFPRI 2002; Azoulay and Dillon 1993; Acharya 2002; Griffon 2006).

From Availability to Accessibility . . . and Beyond: The Five Conditions for Food Security

Guaranteeing 'access by all people at all times to enough food for an active and healthy life', that is the way the World Bank defined food security in 1986.[17] This would call for five conditions—and India is far from meeting all of them.

- *Availability of sufficient food products at national level*: This is the first condition and the only one that the country has been able to meet, since self-sufficiency in food grains has almost been achieved and imports of other agricultural commodities do not place excessive strain on the balance of payments. However, the situation remains fragile, given payment capacities and the instability of world commodity prices.

- *Physical availability of products:* Food products reach final consumption areas with great difficulty, given the serious logistical and marketing problems the country faces. Some landlocked or inaccessible regions are difficult to reach, making it even more difficult for the market or public distribution system to function properly. An extreme case is that of areas subject to ethnic (Manipur) or Maoist (Andhra Pradesh) guerillas, where insecurity has led to a total segmentation of networks.
- *Economic accessibility to products:* 50 per cent of urban households have monthly consumption budgets (for food and non-food items) of less than Rs. 775, i.e. 14 euros. The median budget for rural households may even be as low as Rs. 470, i.e. 8.50 euros. For many people access problems are structural rather than having to do with the situation of the day. Even better-off households may face serious problems, as considerable seasonal variations lie unseen behind their apparently adequate annual income.
- *Qualitatively adequate nourishment*: Meeting calorie needs does not necessarily mean meeting nutritional quality requirements. A satisfactory fat, protein, carbohydrate and micronutrient content depends on the material conditions mentioned above, but also implies a normal assimilation of these foods and, therefore, satisfactory health and environmental conditions.[18] However, only 63 per cent of households have potable water, and 15 per cent of the population still lives more than an hour away from a local health centre. Food quality is another criterion—there is no real food security without *food safety.* In India this is rarely mentioned, because—rightly or wrongly—having something to eat is still considered as being more urgent an issue than the quality of what people eat. If we only look at subsidized food grain distribution, which is the subject of this book, it must be said that quality is a major problem.
- *Cultural access:* Food is a field that is strongly influenced by existing value systems, religious, caste-based, regional, and civilizational. The majority of Hindus (81 per cent of the population) are not vegetarians, but there are few that eat pork or beef. The caste hierarchy goes hand in hand with a food hierarchy. To this are added a range of local proscriptions or taboos. There is an entire range of food habits—from the north in which wheat is the staple to the south and coasts where rice is the staple food, and the centre

and peninsula where millets are the staple diet. Moreover, the *tridosha* theory or that of the 'heat' of different foods is generally widely accepted, although there are many variants according to the places and the people.[19]

Thus, it is necessary to analyse the internal distribution of rations at the family level, in particular according to age and gender (the status of women varies according to the region, the education level, religion, etc.) (Harriss 1995). Most south Indians prefer to eat less rice if they cannot afford it, rather than having to buy wheat as well, as although the latter is cheaper, it is essentially a north-Indian food model. High yielding varieties, often not as rich as traditional varieties, may be looked down on. Above all, vegetable and meat consumption is still limited, partly due to taste (only small quantities of vegetables are eaten, piled on one side of the plate) and cultural value.

Hence, we can only agree with Maxwell (1996: 156) when he proposed a 'post-modern perspective' of food security, highlighting three 'paradigm shifts' in the history of the concept: '(a) from the global and the national to the household and the individual, (b) from a food perspective to a livelihood perspective, and (c) from objective factors to subjective perception'. It is also important not to ignore the micro-scale in order to assess to what extent nutritional needs are met, along with the role of individual actors (ration shop dealers, traders, officials, etc.) in the food policy. Having said that, going from the macro to the micro level and underlining the diversity of situations in space and within the sector does not mean denying the legitimacy of general policies, nor their analysis. It is simply a way of ensuring a greater efficiency of measures and greater rigour in analyses.

The food issue has also entered the globalization debate. India had wanted to tackle it with the help of the Green Revolution and by gaining self-sufficiency at as nation-wide a level as possible. But productivity gains made it necessary for India to look at export markets, while being unable to definitely exclude imports in the name of food security. But opening to the world did not make the need for introspection less urgent, as true food security could only be assessed at local and individual level. The new challenge before India is that it has to work at four levels at one and the same time: local, national, international—and at the level of its states (Landy 2004).

It remains to say that one cliché appears to be fairly unfounded—the one according to which it was agricultural growth and, in particular, the Green Revolution, which put an end to famines and led to India's self-sufficiency in food grains. In fact, one of the causative factors is surely the reduction in the individual cereal intake, which has fallen by one-third over the last half century. Secondly, as we have seen, self-sufficiency in food grains has gone hand-in-hand with a change in food habits and the persistence of malnutrition. However, another factor is the greater entitlements for the majority of the population, both physically (grains are available in local markets) and economically (grains are not too expensive *vis-à-vis* household purchasing power provided the inflation of the 1990s is not taken into account). The private sector and the PDS are both to be congratulated for the first, while a major factor in the second was the country's overall development, along with the PDS which provides subsidized food grains on sale.

The rise in wheat and rice production went, paradoxically, hand in hand with a fall in consumption. How can this contradiction be explained? Is it the growth in exports? Export growth was not as strong as all that. Is it the growth in animal-products consumption, then? Perhaps partly, but there is very little information available on this subject. Is the answer the private stockpiling by big dealers? They could not have done so for too many years together. Therefore, State action must also have played a part: the government stockpiles often substantial quantities of cereals—more than a quarter of the annual production—although it may redistribute it to the most needy who suffer from food shortages or famine. And yet, the PDS does not function well, as we shall see.

We must also try and see whether this system is not at least partly responsible for the fall in coarse cereals consumption to the benefit of wheat and rice, given that these are the only cereals supplied in the PDS. It could be argued that this plays an auxiliary role, with the change being due purely to the fall in market prices for these two cereals in the long term, because of production gains. In that case, what was the reason behind the rise in cereal prices in the 1990s (a true paradox, given the reduction in consumption and the rising production)? Perhaps state procurement, to bolster market prices and ensure supplies for the PDS, was also responsible. Instead of supporting consumption, the system was often a hindrance.

HERITAGE OF COLONIAL FAMINES

Laissez-Faire, Letting Them Die

In case of famine, the king shall help his subjects by providing them seeds and provisions. (. . .) He can help them by distributing from his own stocks or the income accumulated by the richest of his subjects; or ask other kings who are his friends for help. . . .

Once [the King's] stocks have been established, half shall be kept in reserve for any disasters that may be fall his people and only the other half shall be consumed. Older harvests shall be replaced by new ones. (Kautilya, *Arthashastra*, third century BC)

Indian scholars writing on the food policy tend to begin by recalling the wisdom of Kautilya. In the sixteenth century, Sher Shah had established reserves to which farmers had to contribute in kind (Acharya 1983). Akbar set up soup kitchens during the 1630–1 famines. Aurangzeb did the same, and also purchased cereals and sold them at reduced rates in famine-struck areas. However, we may well wonder whether these wonderful examples may not hide the actual reality, i.e. a tax policy that placed such a burden on farmers that they were unable to find much comfort in the emergency measures launched by the State, which gave with one hand after having taken so much with the other.[20]

Whatever be the case, the East India Company's growing hold on India would be marked by famines. There were apparently no more than fifteen or so famines between the eleventh and eighteenth centuries, whereas their frequency seems to have accelerated during the second half of the nineteenth century, when they brought cholera, smallpox, and other epidemics in their wake (Bhatia 1991).[21] Between 1770 (10 million deaths?) and 1900, twenty-two famines were officially recorded. Each was triggered by drought, but excessive grain exports by the British together with overtaxation of the rural producer were the structural causes of shortages. Hence, the famine map does not correspond exactly with the map of arid and semi-arid areas and less-irrigated regions (Durand-Dastès 1982; Currey and Hugo 1984). The excesses of the *zamindari* tax system—named after the absentee large landowners of the time, have often been held responsible. However, Map 1.4 scarcely shows any correlation between the recurrence of famines and zamindars. True,

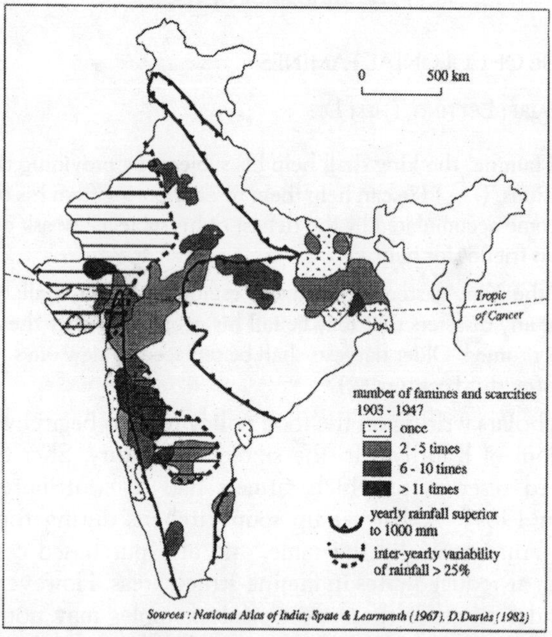

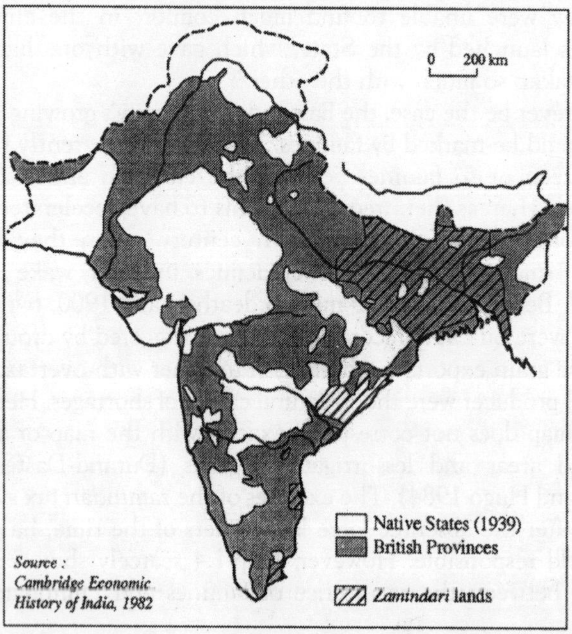

Map 1.4: Some factors behind colonial-period famines

information about the food crises shown in these maps is limited to the first half of the twentieth century. Above all, we now know that the situation in the *zamindari* system only rarely differed widely from the situation farmers faced in other regions (Markovits 1994). Indeed, the map suggests some other explanation—a more difficult situation in provinces directly governed by the British, as compared to a much less accentuated periodicity of famines in princely states under *indirect rule*.

Faced with these disasters, the measures taken by the British were marked by short-term concerns and the desire to avoid expenditure. Generally, they restricted themselves to purchasing food grains with public money—as in 1874 in Bihar—and distributing them, sometimes selling them to the most needy. After 1860 famines there were Famine Commissions, but their reports were often stamped with liberalism.

The 1880 Commission adopted a somewhat more systematic approach, prescribing a Draft Famine Code listing the measures to be taken in case of a food crisis. All provincial governments had to adapt these measures to local conditions, drafting a Famine Code (it may be noted that these codes survived even after Independence, under the name of Scarcity Manuals). Their establishment consisted of launching public works that were poorly paid for, in cash (it was then up to private business to bring food grain to the concerned areas, attracted by rising demand). Even if the grain was handed out, the ideal was for it to be distributed against work—only the infirm and aged were to receive gratuitous relief, as it was considered that too much charity lead to a 'demoralization of society and pauperization of the people' as the Viceroy Lytton asserted (see Acharya 1983: 37). Thus, in 1866 (when a famine struck, killing almost a million in Bihar–Orissa), the state purchased 40,000 tonnes of food grains, but only half this amount was finally distributed. The work was systematically offered far from the labourers' homes, in order to select only those individuals who were in extreme need.[22] In any case, political will was lacking—for instance, during the great Bengal famine in 1943, the Famine Code was never applied, for the good reason that the state of famine was never officially declared! It was only after Independence that the young Indian democracy, since it was a democracy, effectively implemented these measures.

The 1873–4 famine undoubtedly forced the British to somewhat systematize imports of rice in order to reduce shortages. Exports were prohibited—as they had been in 1867. Cotton, jute, oil seed, and opium exports are often denounced as the British encouraged these crops at the expense of food crops; in addition, cereal exports were notably high, at least in certain years. In 1910–11, for instance, cereal and oil seed exports accounted for 18 and 12 per cent respectively of India's total exports (Markovits 1994). An international price differential could easily trigger cereal exports to England, even if food were already scarce in India. Very little thought was given—and even fewer decisions were taken—concerning structural problems to be addressed in order to *prevent* famines. The first thing that came to mind was transportation: in 1865, the Orissa famine made Governor-General John Lawrence stress the urgent need to expand the rail network in order to transport food grain to the affected areas (unfortunately, trains would also be used for easier exports from famine-struck areas, whenever higher prices prevailed elsewhere). The telegraph would be used as another famine prevention tool. As regards irrigation, the canal network had not much expanded, except in the Himalayan foothills (Punjab), and the colonial government balked at building any infrastructure with funds from sources other than the normal tax receipts.[23] As far as targeted tax relief was concerned, it was not a famine prevention tool—it was only in 1902 that the Governor-General Curzon published an assurance that taxes should leave farmers with enough to 'meet the strain of exceptional misfortune' (see Acharya 1983: 118).

Finally, Lord Lytton put some of Lawrence's ideas into practice in 1878–9: a Famine Insurance Fund was set up, funded by an extraordinary tax until 1906, and transferred to the provinces in 1936. However, its budget was used only very diffidently, for fear of putting the state in debt. The relatively generous agricultural credit laws of 1883 and 1884, which followed the 1882 Commission, had barely any positive effect. Above all, the free-trade dogma, which was also brought up by the 1880, 1897, and 1900 Famine Commissions, remained sacred to the colonial rulers. It was only at the last that the administration had to intervene to purchase, transport, and distribute food grains, otherwise always giving free reign to private trade in the field as the only true remedy against food emergencies. Besides, the politically heterogeneous status of India did not facilitate an integrated view of possible solutions; the princely states—some of as small as a two to three villages—were only indirectly under British domination.

Another factor leading to the laissez-faire approach was that the 1880 Commission calculated that British India had a normal surplus of 5 million tonnes, and that there was therefore no need to maintain stocks, except in the event of enormous surpluses. Stocks were too expensive to manage, private business would be negatively impacted.

> The existence of a public granary in every village, ready to be thrown open whenever distress occurred, would be a standing encouragement to improvidence and recklessness. The plan would strike a death blow at that healthy development of the internal trade of the country, now in an early stage, but steadily striving under the encouragement given by the extension of railways and complete free trade, and it would raise a fatal barrier to the growth of those qualities of self-reliance in the community without which the country can never raise itself in the scale of civilization. (quoted by Acharya 1983: 44–5)

The 1943 Famine

We cannot thus speak of any real 'food policy' before Second World War, except by default. The reason why there were no more official famines between 1908 and 1943 was the railways and urban and industrial growth, which made it possible for the rural poor to migrate in case of disasters (Bhatia 1991). India stepped into the twentieth century seriously weakened on the food front. A study by G. Blyn, quoted by Dantwala (1996), though limited to British India, stressed the overall per capita reduction in agricultural production (–16 per cent from 1891 to 1946), all the more so in Bengal–Bihar–Orissa. On the whole, the colonial policies (Patnaik 1991), the marked population growth since 1921, and the consequences of the 1929 crisis were so many factors that foretold the tragic conditions that would be triggered by Second World War.

It has been said that independent India's entire food policy can be explained by the trauma of the Great Bengal Famine of 1943, which killed between 1.5 million people (directly) and 3–4 million (in the long term). This is not untrue, but it would be more accurate to say that the awareness of the need for a policy worth the name dated back to the start of the war itself, when food grain price inflation led to the levelling off of certain prices, even before Japan entered the war in 1941. At first, New Delhi seemed rather pleased with the rise in agricultural prices, which compensated farmers for the deflationary years. The government of the powerful Punjab province could not help but be pleased also. But it soon made them feel disturbed. Food grain was being distributed in Bombay and later in the larger cities, since 1939—that was undoubtedly the fruit of European experience in the field, going as far back as to First World War for England, with the imminence of Second World War inciting a renewal of the same policy (Mooij 1999a). The provinces were granted the right to prohibit grain flows and even to requisition food grain. In March 1942, the Central Provinces prohibited all exports, soon followed by Bihar, Orissa and then Bengal. 'The result was that soon every province, every district, every taluk in eastern India had become a food republic unto itself. The trade machinery for the distribution of food throughout this region was slowly strangled and, by the spring of 1943, it had died' (Chopra 1988: 28). In May 1942, a Food Grains Control Order was published against speculators. In July, a Civil Supplies Commissioner was appointed and, in December, a Food Department was set up.

In September 1942, the administration set up a purchasing programme in surplus regions with redistribution in deficit areas, particularly around Calcutta. The next year, this attempt was to turn into the All India Basic Plan, which was the embryo of the system prevailing today. However, the government had not yet thought of building stocks, given the emergency situation—food grains from domestic levies and imports were dispatched directly to needy provinces and states. Moreover, the plan did not envisage the national territory as an integrated whole, except in the case of wheat; for the other cereals, a more province-wise framework was planned.

In January 1943, the provinces had to impose a food grain export permit (for export outside their borders), and the department at the centre asked them to set up a public procurement system. But it proved difficult to get the surplus provinces to collaborate, as they balked at giving away their food grains. Soon, it was too late to avoid the Bengal tragedy, with the number of victims reminiscent of nineteenth-century famines, bringing back memories that people had believed they could forget.

The most famous analysis of the 1943 famine is by Amartya Sen (1981). He often told the story of how much his vocation owed to these terrible memories of his childhood—visions of dead bodies and gaunt, starving faces strewn across the streets of his native Calcutta. To feed the 13 per cent of the population who were urban in the early 1940s, the country depended on domestic production (30 per cent of which was marketed), but also on imported supplements, essentially around one million tonnes of rice from Burma every year. Most Indian regions that enjoyed a surplus grew wheat and coarse cereals, which did not suffice to feed the south, nor Bengal, both inhabited by rice-eaters (Map 1.5). Burma, though no longer a part of the Indian empire, sent supplies that remained crucial to India's economy. However, its occupation by the Japanese cut-off the supplies (Rangoon was abandoned in March 1942). The British took away rice and boats for fear of them falling into enemy hands. Then

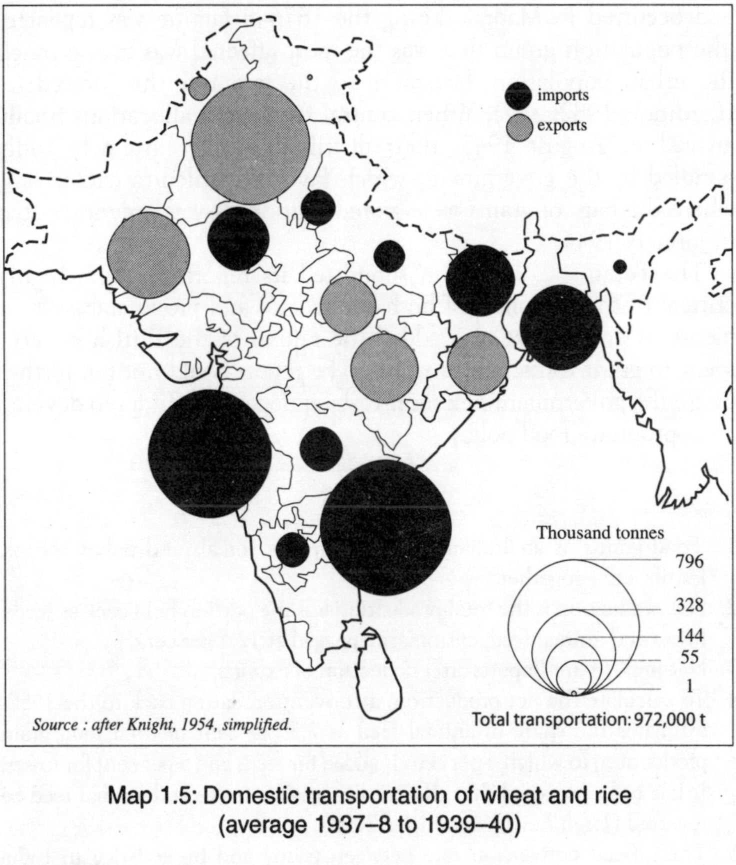

Source : after Knight, 1954, simplified.

Map 1.5: Domestic transportation of wheat and rice (average 1937–8 to 1939–40)

Bengal was hit by a cyclone in October.[24] The Basic Plan had provided for 350,000 tonnes of rice imports for the province from neighbouring regions, but barely any rice reached Bengal. In a desperate though inept effort to increase rice supplies, rice trade and prices were freed of restrictions in the entire eastern region, which only led to greater speculation.

However, this was a 'boom famine' (Drèze and Sen 1989: 5) : the war effort had increased the purchasing power of urban populations while abandoning the rural poor to their fate, in particular farm labourers and craftsmen, which led to a record grain price inflation. The authorities even went so far as to chase out the famine-struck who ventured onto the streets of Calcutta. The same situation that had occurred in Madras during the 1876–8 famine was repeated: 'the population group that was the most affected was not so much the urban population, but more so the migrants that flowed in' (Lardinois 1982: 387). When central food grain allocations finally arrived in August 1943, their distribution was extremely badly handled by the government, which favoured Calcutta exclusively, where the bags of grains were stored. Rationing was only instituted in January 1944.

The Famine Commission submitted its report in 1945, highly critical of the responses of both the federal and provincial governments. It could have also added the refusal of the British government to grant India import rights. The report could not but further incite the government of a soon-to-be independent India to develop an appropriate food policy.

NOTES

1. 'Food grains' is an Indian term that groups cereals and pulses (beans, lentils, etc.) together.
2. Net production is the total production less the portion held back as seeds, losses and animal feed, customarily pegged at 12.5 per cent.
3. Net imports are imports after deduction of exports.
4. To calculate the net production, a convention dating back to the 1950s estimates the share of animal feed as 2.5 per cent of total food grain production, to which 5 per cent is added for seeds and 5 per cent for losses. It has been proposed that the percentages for losses and animal feed be reversed (*High Level Committee* 2002).
5. The official conversion rate between paddy and husked rice in India remains at 66.6 per cent.

6. With an index of 100 for 1961 (i.e. 0.18 tonnes/inhabitant), the gross per capita food grain production stood at 146 in the 1893–4 to 1895–6 period. The index then fell to 99 in the 1936–7 to 1945–6 period, only rising beyond 110 once right up to 1985 (Drèze, 1995). It stood at 101 in 2001. This statement may be qualified by pointing out that the multi-year irregularity of the index has fallen, which limits famine risks. (One may also bear in mind the above criticism regarding the calculation of available production.)
7. Respectively, according to Dyson and Hanchate (2000) and according to Bhalla et al. (1999), though the latter seems the most questionable.
8. *High Level Committee* 2002. However, it must be pointed out that the official figure (*Index of Agricultural Production*) does not fully take fruit and vegetable production into account. The *National Accounts* give a figure of 3 per cent for agricultural growth, far higher than the population growth rate.
9. A large number of starvation deaths go unnoticed, either because they take place in inaccessible areas and are not declared, or because the administration refuses to record them as such. Given that the legal definition of 'starvation death' implies the total absence of food, those unfortunate enough to have been reduced to eat roots, mushrooms or mango kernels are often officially considered as having been 'poisoned'.
10. *2005 Report on food insecurity in the world* (www.fao.org/docrep/008/a0200e/a0200e00.htm).
11. NSS Report No. 471, *Nutritional Intake in India 1999–2000.* The FAO's figure for 1999–2001 was 2,490 kcal. For a critique of FAO's estimations, which are likely to lead to an overestimation of the under-nourishment rate in developing countries, see Svedberg, 2002.
12. It must be pointed out that there is some uncertainty about the statistics. Official figures on availability, based on production estimates (*National Accounts Statistics*), have very little to do with the consumption figures provided by household surveys (*National Sample Survey*). One may well believe that the latter are more convincing than the statistics on availability. But the trend is clear, whatever the sources: in 1961–2, according to the NSS, rural consumption was 17.6 kg of cereal per month while urban consumption stood at 12.5. In 2000–1, the figures were no more than 12.4 and 10.1 kg respectively, i.e. a fall of almost one-third over fifty years. Moreover, it must be pointed out that NSSO's results for 1999–2000 had been criticised for *overestimating* the consumption induced as compared to previous surveys, due to the interview methods developed in a shorter period of time. On the other hand, the NSSO's consumption surveys seem to under-estimate food quantities for several reasons (Cassen 2002), particularly because their

questionnaires call upon people's memories, but also because meals eaten outside the home are not taken into account, although these are all the more frequent with urbanization and socio-economic developments. Furthermore, it is also obvious that squatter settlements are 'left out' of surveys.

13. The graph for rural areas looks similar, with cereals being very slightly cheaper.
14. Among the few exceptions, that of Kerala can be explained by the well-known ambiguity of its forms of urbanization, but also by the continuing importance of tapioca (cassava/manioc) in the diet.
15. 37 and 50 mg per day, respectively, in 1999–2000.
16. Drèze and Sen include education and health, not just material items, in 'entitlements'.
17. *Poverty and Hunger: Issues and Options for Food Security in Developing Countries*, WB Policy Studies, Washington, 1986.
18. It appears that chronic malnutrition (*stunting*) which leads to delayed growth is far more prevalent in urban slums than acute malnutrition (*wasting*), which leads to inadequate weight gain according to the height. The reverse prevails in rural areas. Urban malnutrition could therefore be due less to the lack of food as such as to 'upstream' factors such as water quality, the lack of breast-feeding, or access to health care (Hatekar and Rode 2003).
19. According to Ayurvedic theory, foods are classified into three types ('hot', 'cold' and 'airy'), corresponding to the three elements (fire, water and air). Thus, white rice and coconuts are 'cold', while spices and meat are 'hot'—and can lead to 'dysentery'. Excess 'heat' or 'cold' can lead to illness.
20. In fact, the *Arthashastra*, so often quoted in the literature on the subject, devotes as many lines to the 'Controller of Prostitutes' as to the 'Controller of Agriculture'.
21. '[During the 1876–8 famine,] while high food price costs may have led to deaths, they were not solely responsible, as cholera played an equal role. What the livelihood crisis did lead to—by destabilizing epidemiological relations and economic and social structures—was the transition from an endemic to an epidemic situation' (Lardinois 1982: 379).
22. Just as cynical measures were taken, at some time, such as the distribution of cooked food alone (which was considered ritually polluted) in order to test the food taboos of the Hindus and to feed only those who were starving (Drèze 1995).
23. It was not so much the monsoon rains as such that were crucial, but the late-season rains between September and winter. The *kharif* or autumn

crops were often very coarse millets, which were not very demanding with regard to water, whereas *rabi* or spring crops were damned in the absence of showers. It was only in the case of rice—which had not yet spread so far and wide—that *kharif* crops were destroyed. However, on the whole, in case of weather hazards, it was not so much the reduction in food availability in itself that led to famine, but the disruptions in the rural economy as a whole, which led to a reduction in agricultural employment for the manual labourers who had already been weakened by the inflation in food prices (Drèze 1995).

24. Unlike Sen who underestimated the natural causes of the famine, Tauger (2003) reconsidered the importance of the cyclone and of a rice disease to explain the crisis. Also see Davis (2001).

CHAPTER 2

The Hazards of Spatial Equality

To describe the vagaries of the spatial food policy along a strictly chronological periodization is not easy. The PDS, which began to develop from the 1960s, had actually existed since 1942. Similarly, despite the fact that agricultural growth has recently spread to regions that had hitherto been ignored by the Green Revolution (e.g. Bengal), state procurement of grain continues to rely essentially on Punjab. In this chapter we shall follow a seemingly chronological plan, but one based on a structure that is actually thematic in nature. Highlighting certain processes or institutions that were at the forefront at a particular time should not lead the reader to forget other processes, which were admittedly secondary, but nonetheless effective for certain periods. Thus, the division of periods given below does not preclude some overlaps.

TIMES OF HESITATION (1943–1964)

> The government of independent India rapidly did away with the policy of strict non-interference with private trade of food, and its price stabilization measures in particular have often played an important role in averting famine threats. The punitive and avaricious nature of relief provisions has not altogether disappeared (far from it), but the value attached to human life has nevertheless appreciated compared to the colonial days. (Drèze 1995: 91)

> In times of scarcity, *fear*, by bringing convoys to a halt, makes scarcity a reality; by starting with the fear of a shortfall, you end by actually creating a shortfall. (Cobb 1965: 212, about urban supplies during the French Revolution)

In Figure 1, this period was placed under the rubric of homogenization rather than concentration.

These were the years of agrarian reforms, which began in 1947 and made it possible to do away with interlocking land tenures and

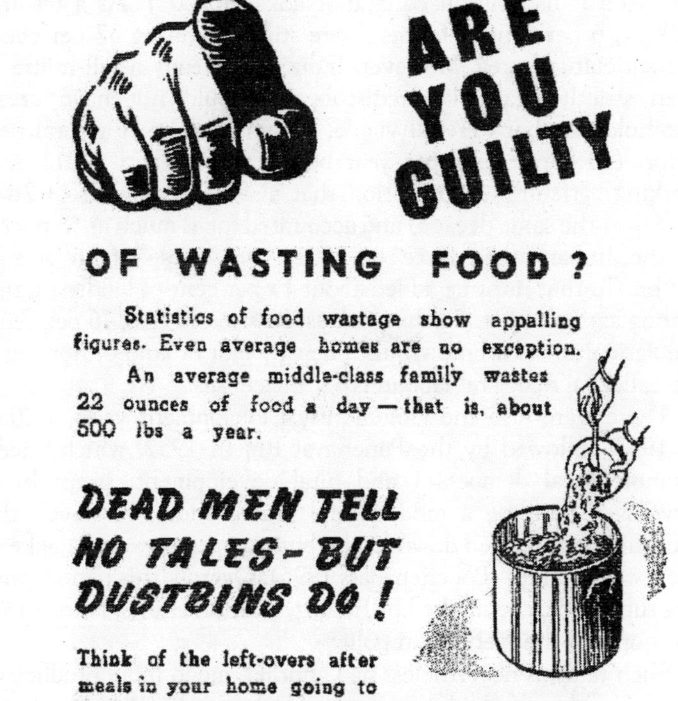
ARE YOU GUILTY
OF WASTING FOOD?
Statistics of food wastage show appalling figures. Even average homes are no exception.
An average middle-class family wastes 22 ounces of food a day — that is, about 500 lbs a year.
DEAD MEN TELL NO TALES—BUT DUSTBINS DO!
Think of the left-overs after meals in your home going to feed dustbins! Multiply it 5000 times. 5000 average homes in our cities guilty of throwing away good food — ENOUGH TO FEED 12,000 PERSONS!
REMEMBER YOUR WASTAGE IS THE NATION'S WASTAGE!
Leave a Clean Plate
Have a Clear Conscience
STOP WASTAGE
HELP BUILD
NATION'S FOOD
RESERVE

most semi-feudal systems of the *zamindari* type, but did not truly lead to a redistribution of land (Nadkarni 2002). As a result, in 2000–1, 6 per cent of farmers were still cultivating 37 per cent of the agricultural area. However, India was already a full-house and even strictly egalitarian redistribution could not have created farmholdings that were all viable. For an ever-growing rural population (+1.8 per cent per year between 1991 and 2001) and a working agricultural population that also kept growing (+ 26 per cent over the same decade) and accounted for as much as 58 per cent of the Indian work force in 2001, the average farm size was 1.3 ha. To that must be added about 15 per cent of landless farmers among agriculturists. Further, it must be stressed that 46 per cent of the agriculturists, who own just one tiny plot of land or none at all, are called 'agricultural labourers' by the census.

These were also the Community Development years, initiated in 1952, followed by the Panchayat Raj in 1957, which tried to promote local democracy and rural development, swept by the fervour of building a modern and united India. However, these initiatives got bogged down in the bureaucracy or were hijacked by the local notables (Pouchepadass 1996). Overall, this period, which was supposed to be marked by homogenization efforts, failed to fulfil the hopes of the Nehruvian policy.

Such reforms nevertheless had another, much more productivist, objective, that of combining 'equity and growth' (Bharadwaj 1998: 204). Smaller holdings allowed for more intensive farming; the fight against agrarian inequalities promoted investments in productivity, which would help India achieve food grain self-sufficiency. Thus, agrarian reforms replaced the other constituent, an increase in agricultural prices, that could have had the same effect. Nehru could never bring himself to raise food prices: ethically, politically, and economically, it was better to take on big landlords rather than poor consumers.

Smoothing Curves, Filling Bellies: Theoretical and Practical Tools

[In eighteenth-century France], there was a famine about every ten years, which automatically led to stockpiling by individuals, spiralling prices which then doubled and even tripled, market riots, blockage and looting along roads and rivers, the resulting interruption in food flows, the use of force against rioters and recalcitrant farmers, a rising fear of the future among the people, attempts to go back to the past (for instance, to the old prices of 1775 or September 1793), malnutrition, illnesses and epidemics, people's credulity, provocation and violence against women. Cobb (1975: 245–6)

These years were crucial for the choices made about major alternatives, some of which are still being questioned today.

Controls or Freedom?

Agricultural economics theory rarely legitimates total free trade (Timmer, 1986; Padilla 1996). Due to seasonal and annual variability in agricultural production added to limited demand elasticity in relation to prices, agricultural prices fluctuate extensively. Indeed, price variations are much greater than production variations (the King effect). Thus, agriculture is a very peculiar economic sector, where state intervention is especially justified in order to attempt to smooth out price variations (Boussard 2002).

Between 1943 and 1965–6, the Indian government was faced with alternatives. On the one hand, it was hesitating between a relatively liberal policy that granted market players a predominant role, or a more directive policy and a major role for the state in food grain marketing. In times of scarcity, it tended to incline towards the second solution, while in times of relative abundance, it was the first solution that prevailed. As for the second alternative, the government was undecided whether to go in for large-scale imports to guarantee people's food needs, or to purchase food grain from the domestic market.

In both cases, however, the government tended to look at farmers as those who fed the urban population. That was the major difference with the Green Revolution period that was to follow: many tools of the future food policy were already in place as far back as the 1940s, but what was missing then was a willingness to promote agricultural modernization through a pricing policy and guaranteed markets. Apart from cotton (since 1943) and sugar cane purchased by the refineries, the government imposed no prices in the agricultural sphere, except for certain (floor and ceiling) limitations that were defined occasionally for certain products. Food grain prices could be supported some of the years, and the states could announce maximum prices for these products. But until 1965, the policy in this sector remained for the most part ad hoc in nature.

In 1921 the state of Kashmir had already introduced a policy of forced paddy sales by farmers, along with a PDS for cities (Knight 1954). But the Bengal famine countermodel played a much greater role in the final choice of a highly interventionist policy. A Food Grains Policy Committee was set up in July 1943. While it essentially dealt with short-term perspectives limited to times of war, its conclusions underlined the inadequacies of free trade in times of scarcity, and its recommendations focused on the expansion of the state's role in food grain purchase and distribution. Finally, the colonial power realized that neither the railways nor the irrigation system were sufficiently developed to combat food risks. Indeed, to smooth out inter- (and intra-) annual variations, cereal stocks had to be accumulated, in order to be able to distribute them when required. The Famine Enquiry Commission set up in 1945 declared, 'It is abundantly clear that a policy of *laissez faire* in the matter of food supply and nutrition can lead nowhere and would probably end in catastrophe' (quoted by Acharya 1983: 60). The Bengal tragedy 'brought some realization of the terrible urgency of India's problems, of the overwhelming disaster that hung over the country' (Nehru 1985 [1946]: 500).

Thus, came the era of controls—wholesale and retail price controls, controls on food grain trade between districts, control over stocks held by traders as well as by consumers and producers, and so on. Food grain imports became a state monopoly in September 1943. Even the business tycoons were in favour of economic planning (see the 'Bombay Plan' in 1944). The commission presided over by the future American Nobel Prize winner, T.W. Schultz, affirmed in 1946: 'No country in the world, with perhaps the exception of Russia, has gone so far in controlling basic food distribution—not even Germany under the Hitler dictatorship' (quoted by Chopra 1988: 57). Indeed, a highly impressive mechanism was set up.

We can count at least five forms of public intervention in the food grain or sugar markets (or even other products, during some years). There was the state support price and procurement system; food stock management; subsidized food grain distribution (PDS); regulated markets, at which auctions are organized under the aegis of the state; and trade interventions: controls over speculative holdings, restrictions on domestic and foreign trade, on credit, etc.

While regulated markets emerged under the aegis of local, relatively participatory intervention, before finally falling under state control, government pricing and trade institutions set up at the federal level were gradually coupled with decentralized counterparts at the provincial level (Harriss 1984). The whole comprised the embryo of what would later be called the 'public food system': an enormous mechanism with all its parts connected to each other, (theoretically) functioning for the optimization of national consumption and (especially after 1965) agriculture production. It was left to the government to manoeuvre each of these elements in order to adjust the various pieces in a complex game aimed at feeding 400 million, then 600, now a billion people.

One of the major tools of the food policy was the 1955 Essential Commodities Act. Taking over from a legislation that emerged at an embryonic level during Second World War, this enabled the close monitoring of product flows by the administration. A whole range of products were covered—from cement to synthetic textiles, cotton to (soon) electric irons, food grains to plug sockets. The objective was 'maintaining or increasing supplies of any essential commodity or for securing their equitable distribution and availability at fair prices, or for securing any essential commodity for the defence of India.'[2] It is clear that production was not more urgent than 'equitable distribution', which placed this Act at the crossroads of the two types of policies described above—between concentration and homogenization.

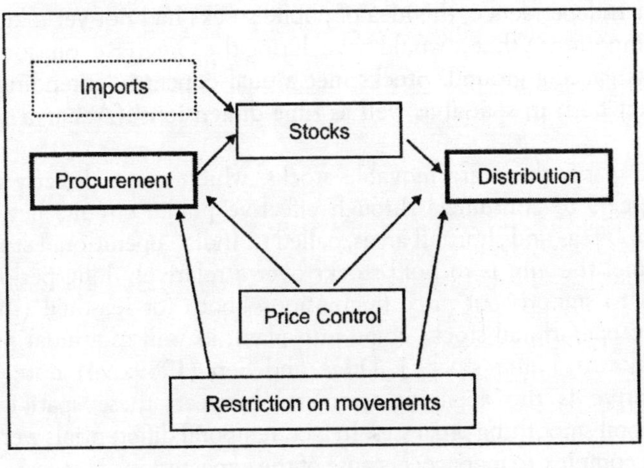

Figure 2.1: Indian public food system

There were two dimensions to the Act—one vertical, the other horizontal. The vertical dimension enabled the centre to exercise influence over the states with regard to food products. The Constitution had remained ambiguous on the issue, because according to the Seventh Schedule, agricultural and agrarian issues fall within the purview of the various states, but 'trade and production, supply and distribution of food grains' are shared by the states and the centre. The issue was legally clarified with the vote on the 1955 Act, which granted most of these powers to Delhi. It allowed the states to legislate, but their laws had to be first approved by the centre. However, the various High Courts retained the important role of validating or rejecting the decrees issued in this framework.

As for the horizontal dimension of the Act, it enabled control over the circulation of essential commodities for better management over the entire territory. Forced sales could be imposed, at prices fixed by the state and, theoretically, the cultivation of fallow could be imposed on farmers. By the time it was relaxed in the 1990s, the Act had been further reinforced by multiple amendments. In particular, the burden of proof lay with the accused, in this instance, the trader. And the number of commodities defined as essential rose from 10 in 1955 to more than 60 in 1992 (Mooij 1999a).

(b) *No Homogenization Without Stocks*

After Independence, the idea of public stocks had not yet taken on the importance that it would have during the Green Revolution, but it was gaining ground. Stocks met a dual concern, 'extending the market both in spatial as well as time dimensions' (Acharya 1983: 137).

In space, there are movable stocks, which move directly from producers to consumers through effective public circuits between surplus areas and shortfall areas, called in India, 'operational stocks'. In time, the aim is to hold stocks over a relatively long period in order to smooth out price fluctuations—both for seasonal (this is where operational stocks come into play), as well as annual prices (thanks to 'buffer stocks'). Drèze and Sen (1989: 94) note how deceptive is the apparent symmetry between these spatial and temporal smoothing processes. In fact, temporal differentials were far more complex to manage, because of the expectations, forecasts, and even speculation of the actors. Hence, there would be more place for public intervention in time, rather than in space; warehouses were better than trains. It was only when public stocks reached a certain level that price fluctuations could be virtually contained, both in space and time.

The aim was to counter the vagaries of the weather, which were responsible for agricultural scarcities: 'like the tower in a town's water supply, the buffer stock of grain acts as a "balancing tower" to be used and replenished in good time and not merely in the nick of time' (Chopra 1988: 263). It was also necessary to limit speculation, deemed responsible for many of the tragic consequences of uncertain weather patterns. While private traders build stocks in anticipation of profit during the end-of-season price hikes, public stocks constitute a reverse strategy, as the government tries to reduce the price increase that is the very basis of private storage (Sharma 1997).

It was feared that technical progress in storage mechanisms were facilitating speculative practices by unscrupulous private actors. In the eighteenth century, the French government too had similar fears when new steam treatment techniques had made it possible to improve wheat and flour conservation (Kaplan 1988). Above all, the memories of nineteenth-century famines were still alive in India, when cereals were shipped across to British markets for higher prices. It was rarely stressed that traders fortunately tend to support prices when they purchase post-harvest produce, while by reselling their stocks in times of relative scarcities, they tended to bring down consumer prices (Cummings 1969). Besides, the fiscal importance of the sales tax on traders was never noted, whereas it accounted for a third of the total revenue of Indian states. Until the 1990s, dealers and other traders were considered potential enemies of social and economic justice, whom the state had to thwart while encouraging practices that were more in line with public interest. Likewise, it was felt that farmers would be encouraged to sell to the government if they knew that prices could not rise very high because of public stocks.

At the end of war, the scarce stocks that remained were left in the hands of the states, but the central government took charge of transportation from one region to another. It was only in 1952 that the centre managed to accumulate a small reserve (420,000 tonnes). In 1954, it decided to build grain stocks up to an ideal level of 1.5 million tonnes—largely supplied by imports at the time. However, it was only in 1975 that a group of experts officially published the ideal tonnage for 'buffer stocks'. These stocks, indispensable for the long-term management of the food issue, later grew in size (15 million tonnes as of 1976), so much so that they largely exceeded the desirable quantities in some years.

(c) *Domestic Procurement or Imports?*

Supplies can be ensured in two ways: either by relying on food grain produced within the country, or by imports. In the first instance, the risk involves a rise in domestic prices, especially if the state becomes a major buyer for building public stocks. In the second case, the risk consists of exposing the nation's farmers to fierce competition because of grains purchased at lower prices in the world market, not to speak of problems of geopolitical dependence.[3] Until the Green Revolution and the achievement of cereal self-sufficiency, India continued to import large quantities of food grain. But it did not stop purchasing from the domestic market through procurement (Figure 2.2).

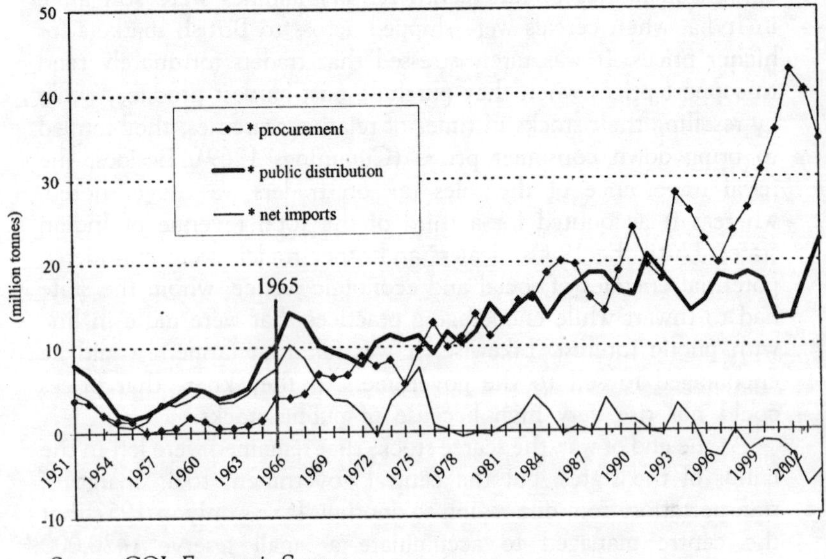

Source: GOI, *Economic Survey.*

Figure 2.2: Procurement, public distribution and net imports (1950–1 to 2002–3)

Contrary to what is often asserted by the literature in the field, a distinction must be made between the procurement *versus* import alternative and the alternative of a policy favouring farmers (by supporting prices) *versus* a policy favouring consumers (through cheap imports). The Indian case is not a good illustration of what is commonly called the 'food dilemma' (Padilla 1996), and even less an example of the opposition between cities and villages, which can be explained by two reasons at least. On the one hand, this is so because the majority of farmers are net buyers from the market, given the small size of their holdings. 'Many Western writers probably do not know that the majority of rural households are net purchasers of food, otherwise they would not have confused consumer bias with urban bias' (Dantwala 1996: 96). If you were to add the four-fifths of agricultural landowners with farmholdings too small for them not to supplement their cereal intake by purchases, landless agricultural labourers, and non-agricultural workers of rural areas (27 per cent in 2001), you would cover about two-thirds of the rural population, which would suffer from a hike in agricultural prices and from any 'improvement in the terms of trade' between agriculture and industry (Landy 1999; Varshney 1994).

The other reason for which procurement should not unduly be seen as opposed to the solution of imports stems from the fact that state purchases initially took the form of taxation, at prices that were often lower than market prices. Dandekar (1994) distinguished six modes of procurement that prevailed during the 1940–50 period, although the distinctions between them may not always have been very clear on the ground (Fig. 2.3).

(d) *Territorial Integration through Redistribution*

'The Basic Food Plan, owing to the selfishness of human nature and the constitutional handicap of the Government of India in dealing with self-governing provinces and states, met with many difficulties but undoubtedly saved India', says Knight (1954: 187).

State purchases took place at two levels—local and national. At the national level, from 1943 onwards, the Basic Plan attempted to allocate grains purchased from surplus areas (as well as imports) to deficit areas, thereby initiating a food integration policy. This actually covered the entire territory only several years later. The Food and Warehousing Corporation administered a Central Pool,

Name	*Mode of procurement*	*Areas most concerned*
Intensive procurement	The entire grain surplus purchased from producers at fixed prices. Free market theoretically abolished, universal rationing.	Madras, and with more flexibility in Travancore, Cochin and Mysore.
Monopoly purchase	No grain sale permitted outside the village, except to the government at a fixed price.	Punjab (and Bengal at the level of several villages). UP, Bihar & Orissa experienced flexible forms.
Levy-cum-monopoly	Only a significant percentage of the surplus purchased from farmers.	Bombay (and Hyderabad).
Levy system	Farmers had to deliver a fixed quantity to the state.	Saurashtra, Rajasthan, Hyderabad.
Trader levy	Fixed price purchase of a part of quantities marketed by a dealer.	Madhya Pradesh.
Open market purchases	Purchase by the state from the market.	Vindhya Pradesh, PEPSU.

Source: Dandekar 1994: 207.

Figure 2.3: The six modes of procurement from 1943 onwards

constituted by imports and compulsory sales in the few surplus states (above all, Punjab, which included Haryana at the time, and Sind), the beneficiaries being located above all in the south. We shall see that the geography of surpluses and deficits remain the same overall in this century. Map 2.1 shows inter-regional transportation following a bad agricultural year, hence higher tonnages than in preceding years: 3.2 million tonnes of wheat, rice, maize, and coarse cereals—78 per cent of which came from imports. It illustrates that already at that time, grain circuits, although corresponding to very crude estimations and planning (Knight, 1954) – could concern princely micro-states, hence a very local level. Besides, the maps present a highly simplified version of the available data.

At the local level, states and provinces had to try to define their purchases depending on their own needs, apart from those of the Basic Plan—something that already foreshadowed what the government was to rediscover at the end of 1990s with 'decentralized procurement' (see Chapter 3). Thus, a practice that failed to

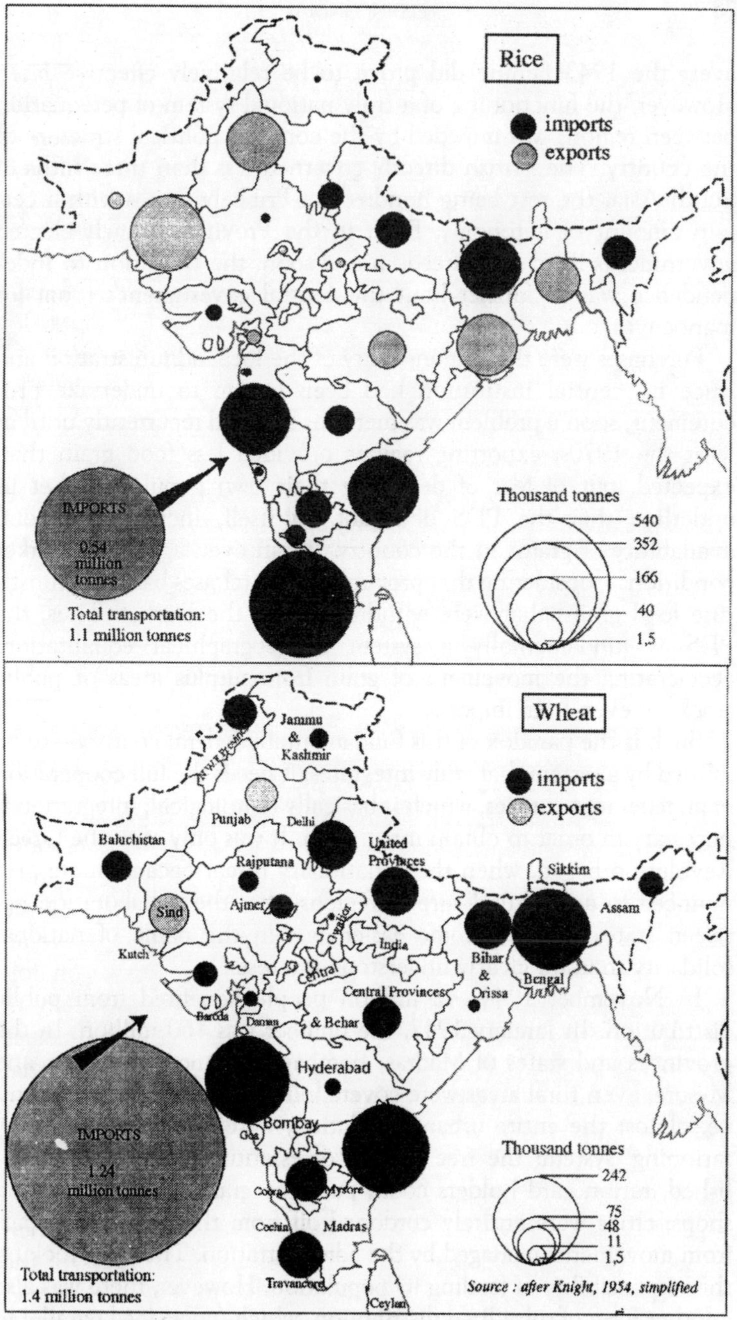

Map 2.1: Net balance of transportation undertaken by the Basic Plan in 1946–7

avert the 1943 famine did prove to be relatively effective later. However, the functioning of a truly national system of perequation between regions was impeded by the complex political structure of the country. The British directly governed less than three-fifths of South Asia, the rest being hundreds of Princely States with a certain amount of autonomy. Even in the Provinces, newly-elected governments liked their freedom and soon, the transition to Independence was to further limit the central government's room for manoeuvre.

Purchases were the responsibility of the local administration and since no central institution had been set up to undertake procurement, soon a problem was met that surfaced recurrently until at least the 1970s: exporting regions provided less food grain than expected, out of fear of depriving their own population. Let us underline that the PDS does not, in itself, increase the total availability of grains in the country. It can even aggravate market conditions, considering that procurement purchases basically constitute food grains that were withdrawn from the market. Thus, the PDS is fundamentally a system of geographical equalization, accelerating the movement of grain from surplus areas or public stocks or even from imports.

Such is the paradox of this fundamentally federal country—to be unified by a system that truly integrates, it needs the full cooperation of all federated entities, which is basically tautological; integration is necessary in order to obtain integration. It was only after the Green Revolution began, when the deflationary threat became more pronounced in agricultural surplus regions, that the collaboration between states would become easier, less in the name of national solidarity than for clearly understood interests.

In November 1944, 42 million people benefited from public distribution. In January 1947, the number was 160 million. In the provinces and states of Madras, Bombay, Travancore, Cochin and Mysore, even rural areas were covered. In 1947, 54 million citizens, i.e. almost the entire urban population, were under the 'statutory rationing' system: the free market of essential products was abolished, ration card holders could purchase grains only from ration shops; cities were entirely cordoned off from the hinterland apart from movements managed by the administration. The state took on the responsibility of feeding its population. However, there was also another form of subsidized distribution, which functioned parallel to the free market: 'non-statutory rationing' (Knight 1954).[4] The food distributed only benefited from a subsidy when the government imperatively desired a fall in market prices. Rations had originally been fixed at half a kilo of cereals per adult per day (giving due consideration to local food habits wherever possible) corresponding to day-to-day needs; but since 1946, these had to be reduced due to availability constraints.

Officially, statutory rationing was supposed to prevent excessive consumption in cities, which would have otherwise 'siphoned' off stocks from rural areas, as was the case during the 1943 famine, because of higher purchasing power. However, one could say that this was actually done to ensure minimum and cheap consumption for city-dwellers, thereby ensuring social peace and urban economic growth. The choice of a development that was increasingly focused on industry was to reinforce the need for less expensive food in cities so as to cut salaries and encourage industrial growth. Thus, in 1951, the First Five Year Plan officially provided for statutory rationing in big cities or in highly deficient areas such as Travancore–Cochin (the future Kerala).

(e) *Spatial Segmentation: The Mosaic Effect*

> The introduction of the May ceiling [for grain prices in France in 1793] made recourse to force necessary (. . .). From the moment that the maximum was applied with exactitude in one district and nonchalantly in a neighbouring district, a bonus was actually being offered for clandestine circulation and hoarding. Further, the maximum rates were too close from one district to another for encouraging grain movements over long distances, since carriers did not find it worthwhile. (Cobb 1965: 214)

A new segmentation began in the name of national integration. A partition of the domestic market was created, or at least, reinforced (Lele 1971). Since 1948 'food zones' were defined at the level of one or several states, with impenetrable borders during shortage years, both for wheat and rice. In the absence of specific permission from the centre, grain produced within a zone was to be sold within the same zone. This kind of segmentation of the domestic market was based on the following logic: 'Since the purchasing power of the different regions does not necessarily match their needs, there is the possibility that the surpluses of the producing regions may be moved out to areas of high purchasing power and a regime of high prices may prevail throughout the country, resulting in distress to the vulnerable sections and necessitating a large volume of supplies to be channelled through the public distribution system' (Tyagi 1990: 31). This kind of logic led to the monopoly over urban public supplies within the framework of statutory rationing, finally leading to a similar spatial segmentation. It was compounded by the concern for avoiding grain transportation over excessively long distances.

In the 1948–53 period, thus most of the time each food zone consisted of just one state, with inter-state grain trade closely monitored by the authorities. As supplies were becoming adequate, these zones then tended to increase in size, so that private trade could play the role of internal re-distributor: in 1957 (Map 2.2), there were three wheat zones in north, while the entire south formed a single rice zone. But the food situation became strained again, and strong tensions dismembered the zones formed by several states. The surplus states imposed 'executive restrictions on the movement of grain within the zone, by erecting some sort of road barriers asking the collectors to keep a watch on the situation under the ostensible garb of ensuring the discharge of levy obligations by the producers, traders and millers, etc.' (Chopra 1988: 249). Hence, the bigger zones were once again broken up officially (Map 2.3).

The spatial segmentation brought about by the food zones defined by the centre could be worsened due to restrictions on circulation imposed by the states. Their constitutional power in terms of the agricultural goods' trade made them 'natural food management units' (Dandekar 1994: 245) *sui generis*. Thus, it could happen that a state would close its borders, although the zone to which it belonged included neighbouring states. In general, there could be a contradiction between the restrictions imposed by the states and the federal integration system.

In any case, the system had a number of harmful effects, some of which were the reverse of the effects desired: the barriers raised discouraged production in surplus zones, inter-regional price differences increased,[5] corruption and contraband between zones worsened the situation, private trade could not function and centre-state relations were put to a severe test. The system had been conjured up in order to avoid trade from deficit zones, which happened only rarely (Drèze 1995). On the whole, the discourse of eighteenth-century French physiocrats—Turgot and Quesnay, for

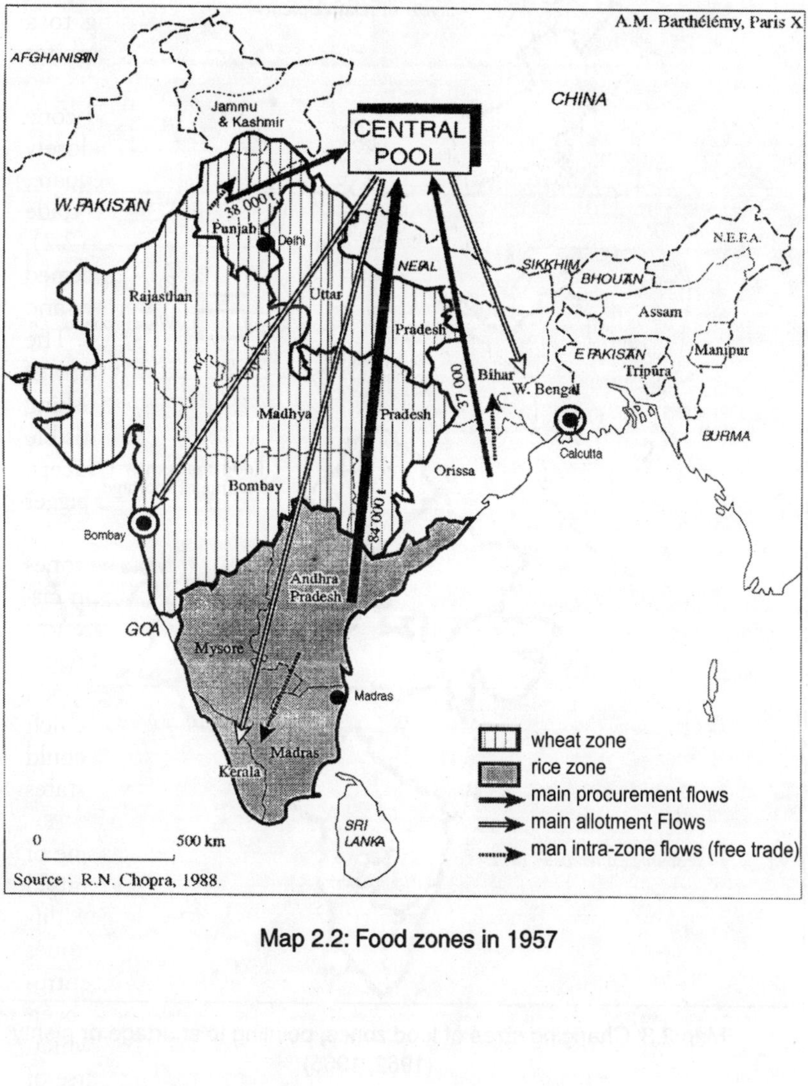

Map 2.2: Food zones in 1957

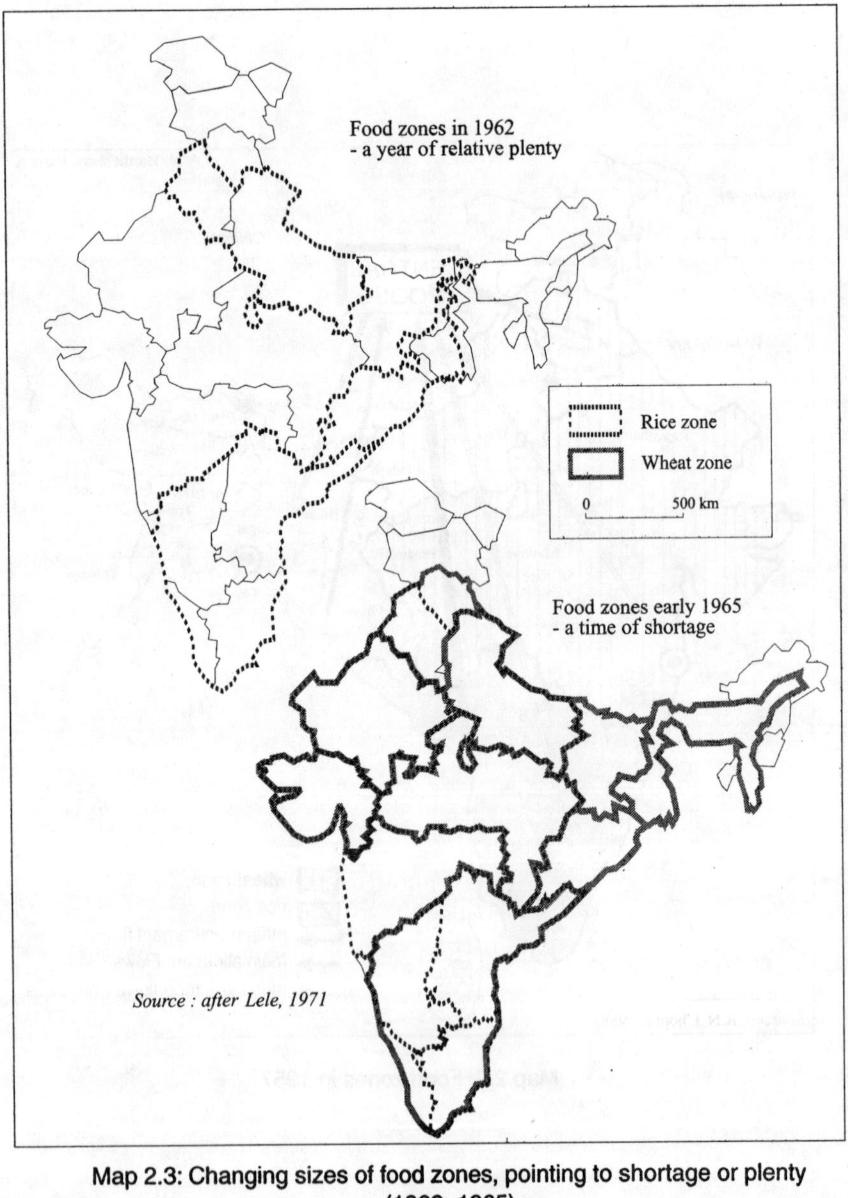

Map 2.3: Changing sizes of food zones, pointing to shortage or plenty (1962, 1965)

instance, who condemned trade barriers in France—could also have been used in India in the twentieth century. Grain redistribution by the centre to the benefit of deficit regions failed to make up for the creation of a spatial mosaic.[6] The food zones managed to reduce inequalities in grain availability *within* states, but not *between* states (Ray 1970). Finally, these were abolished for good in 1977.

The Procrastinations of the Food Policy

(a) *Controls and Decontrols (1947–1956)*

At the end of 1947, controls were relaxed under pressure from M.K. Gandhi, who was very liberal with regard to food, and on the advice of a new Foodgrain Policy Commission. This meant the removal of restrictions to movements within states, a reduction in price controls and distribution, and a greater emphasis on procurement rather than imports. Perhaps the latter point bore the stamp of the beginning of political independence. Although 1947 was hardly a landmark date in the history of India's food policy, it is hard to believe that the departure of the British did not have any repercussions on the government and public perceptions of food dependency.

The states and provinces were supposed to procure their supplies internally, rather than through the centre. The latter promised them 1.34 rupee per quintal of food grain procured internally, and the same amount per quintal 'exported' to deficit states. Although the restrictions on trade between states were not actually lifted, it was hoped that the relative liberalization would act as an incentive to production, which in turn would keep a check on rising prices. However, the procurement process failed to take off, and inflation shot up. New ration shops had to be opened and the government resigned itself to increased imports.

Hence controls were re-introduced in September 1948. Gandhi, assassinated in January, was no longer there to protest. The states could now set a price at which they had the right to purchase or requisition food grains. (The Rs. 1.34 system was retained.) Rice polishing was banned, to enhance its nutritional value. Food grains purchased within India were not subsidized by the centre, unlike imports, but provinces had to pay one-third of these subsidies while the former princely states had to pay half. However, these measures did not have much of an effect. Imports rose from 1.6 million tonnes in 1944 to 4.9 in 1951. Paid for in foreign exchange and at rates higher than domestic prices, what was henceforth to be called the 'food subsidy' was turning into a problem. In 1950, the start of the Korean war and bad weather worsened the situation: procurement was increased drastically, at the risk of accelerating inflation, which was already quite high,[7] and the government had to ask the US for a loan of 2 million tonnes of wheat. The 1947–52 period witnessed the distribution of 7.1 million tonnes of food grain on an average each year. Similar tonnages would reappear only during the mid-1960s crisis. In 1951, 122 million inhabitants benefited from 'rationing', of whom 47 million were covered by statutory rationing. Since procurement remained stagnant at around 4 million tonnes, imports could only go up.

In 1952, the financial weight of imports was such that the government had to do away with subsidies. PDS prices had to be raised in all the states. But the end of the Korean war and good harvests helped improve the inflationary situation. It was in 1952 that for the first time the centre managed to build food grain reserves for the following year (420,000 tonnes). Liberalization was thus decided upon, under the aegis of R.A. Kidwai, Food Minister between 1952 and 1954 and a staunch liberal. Procurement was gradually reduced and even done away with in certain states, while statutory rationing completely disappeared in 1954. Customs barriers around major cities too followed suit. Trade between states was restored, within the limits of the 'food zones', which too were abolished in 1956. Imports declined: while they accounted for 10 per cent of the total food grain production in 1951, they fell to 1 per cent in 1955. Indeed, food grains were exported for the first time since the war in order to keep prices from falling too low, which was becoming a matter of concern. Support prices had to be announced as of 1954 for sorghum, pearl millet and maize, followed by wheat and rice the following year (not that a lot of food grains were actually purchased by the state).

1955 was the harbinger of another change. The coarse cereal harvest was poor and, well aware that public stocks were at their lowest, traders raised prices further. The Suez crisis did not improve matters. Food grain exports were stopped in 1956 and the Reserve Bank ordered banks to adopt drastic measures *vis-à-vis* traders (increase in rates, reduction in advances). An agreement was signed with Burma for rice imports over three years; another, more important one, was concluded with the US, for the import of 3.4 million tonnes of cereals over three years, with a 30-year credit, in accordance with Public Law 480.

(b) *Imports—A Short-term Option (1956–1965)*

This PL 480, which was voted in 1954 and still exists, enables the export of US wheat to 'friendly' countries against credit in local currency, which can only be spent in the buyer country, thereby contributing towards its development. In return, the US is happy to offload its surplus wheat, demand that half the food grains be transported under the American flag, oblige imports of a minimum quantity each year, and restrict any possible re-export of food grain by the client country (Acharya 1983). India was a major beneficiary under this law which guaranteed a steady supply of relatively cheap food grain. There was also the possibility of ensuring continuity in the PDS, at least in urban areas, although the PDS had already been scrapped twice. But the agreement also marked India's acceptance of a threefold defeat. Defeat in the battle for self-sufficiency, an objective announced in 1943 to be fulfilled by 1952. A defeat of nationalism for this young nation, officially at the head of 'non-aligned countries', now drawn under the American food umbrella. And finally, a defeat for Indian farmers—at least those who were surplus food grain producers, for they had to face competition from foreign wheat. The shock was even harsher given that 1956 was also the year when the Second Five Year Plan had to be launched, which was to mark India's initiation into a process of development based on industrialization (heavy industries to begin with), at the expense of capital allocations to agriculture. This was no simple coincidence—imports would push prices down, thereby enabling sufficiently reduced salaries to accelerate industrialization. The country was ready to pass seven years living 'from ship to mouth'.[8]

The agreement was accused of leading to the maintenance of inflation (which was nonetheless restricted to 2.5 per cent per year) and, in particular, of generating fairly high interests for the country to pay—although most of the money was eventually adjusted in the form of a donation to the Indian government in 1974. However, in the agricultural sphere, the consequences in terms of competition for national production need to be measured.

Between 1957 and 1964, imports accounted for 5-7 per cent of the total food grain production: the PL 480 accounted for 80 per cent of imports of wheat, 40 per cent of rice and 100 per cent of maize between 1956 and 1971, the last year of imports under this law (Chopra 1988). They peaked at 8 million tonnes in 1966. However, affirms Dantwala (1996), they represented hardly any competition for national production: while wheat prices were relatively low during the period, it was simply because of higher production levels. Dantwala recalls that there were years of low prices even before the PL 480 (1954–6), just as there were years of inflationary wheat prices afterwards (1963–5). Moreover, imports under the PL 480 were far from cheap in view of the high cost of transportation by American ships. On the other hand, there were considerable incentives for national production, as wheat procurement prices remained higher than the CIF prices of imports till 1972, as was also the case with the least appreciated rice varieties.[9] But a major objection has to be raised: the area under wheat stopped increasing in 1956, stagnating at around 13 million hectares, while it had risen by 43 per cent in the five preceding years. Beside the vagaries of the weather, which were responsible for variations in production, this should be considered sufficient proof of the competition offered by imports. And finally, import prices were not by themselves as important—the presence of imports itself discouraged the sowing of wheat in new areas.

The 1957 Enquiry Commission did not care—quite the contrary: 'Imports under such concessional terms not only relieve us of our immediate foreign exchange commitments but also help us to build a rupee fund which can be utilized for development purposes. . . . That assured supply of food grains from abroad would enable the formulation of a stable and long term food policy needs no emphasis' (quoted by Dandekar 1994: 219). If the notion of food security had already been in fashion in 1957, there is no doubt that the Commission would have brought it up, as it was happy to find a middle path between a policy based on controls, public monopolies and restrictions, and a policy giving full reign to market forces and, therefore, speculation. It must be stressed that PL 480 imports were expensive, but on credit. What is more, long-term supplies were ensured. In retrospect, we can add with Acharya (1983), that imports brought in their wake both American technical assistance for agricultural development and Ford Foundation aid in formulating an improved seed distribution programme. While from the economic viewpoint, the Green Revolution was to run counter to PL 480 imports, in political terms, it constituted an extension of it.

On the domestic front, the government officially opted for nationalizing the wholesale trade in foodgrain. At least that was the objective announced in 1958 for the long term. For the time being, the government was content to impose a minimum price that buyers had to pay to farmers, and a maximum price that wholesalers had to comply with. Located between the two, the state paid a procurement price if it wished to buy the whole or part of the wholesalers' stock. The food economy seemed to be under permanent control.

However, it was clear that domestic procurement was no longer the priority, as indicated by Fig. 2.2 above. Wheat procurement was halted in 1960 and rice procurement carried on only in Madhya Pradesh and Punjab. Map 2.5 below shows India's dependence on wheat imports, with redistribution from major ports. Private food grain marketing intensified further, since credit conditions were relaxed in favour of traders. The objective of nationalizing wholesale food grain trading was abandoned shortly thereafter. In fact, as elaborated below, it was achieved only once in 1973.

Then came the crisis. Food grain production fell in between 1962 and 1964. The quantities distributed by the PDS doubled in two years. Statutory rationing was re-established in 1965 in the four major cities, and was then extended to others. The whole of Kerala was placed under informal rationing in 1964. The same year, food zones were defined for wheat. In the case of rice, zones constituted by single states further restricted food grain trading (Map 2.3). States had the power to ban trade in coarse cereals. The usual private trade restrictions re-surfaced. Procurement resumed on a somewhat larger scale, using all formerly tested methods—from free sales to compulsory levy. It was in these already difficult circumstances that the two 1965 and 1966 droughts occurred. With just 72 million tonnes, food grain production was down by 19 per cent in 1965–6 as compared to the previous year and only rose by 4 per cent in 1966–7. Thus, India faced two successive bad years, affecting practically the whole of the country—a situation eminently favourable to a serious food crisis, one that had not reached proportions such as these since the 1899–1900 famine (Drèze 1995). With inflation of food prices, procurement and public stocks at their lowest, cereal imports peaking at 10.3 million tonnes in 1965–6 (i.e. 17 per cent of production) to enable the subsidized distribution system to function,[10] the crisis renewed the spectre of the terrible famines of the past (2,353 'supposedly dead from starvation' according to official statistics for 1966–7). Bombay's restaurants remained closed on Mondays to save food. The ambition was to provide food supplies through the PDS to all cities of over 100,000 inhabitants (but it could not be fully realized), by setting up a food cordon to cut them off from their hinterland, and by doing away with public distribution in certain rural areas due to the food grain shortage! In January 1967, 30 million people were covered by statutory rationing and 201 million by informal rationing, i.e. almost half of the Indian population, was covered.

Such a crisis was to accelerate a growing awareness in many minds: the policies adopted since 1956 had led to a deadlock. The way had been paved now for the Green Revolution and the quest for true food grain self-sufficiency.

It must, however, be noted that the agricultural crisis alone did not lead to the initiation of the Green Revolution. The unfavourable conjuncture of circumstances was not at the root of such a structural change, given that new improved wheat seeds were already available in the Indian market during the 1965 drought. In fact, as we shall see, new options had already been taken up two or three years earlier. The crisis only confirmed these choices of prime importance.

The general political context also explained this change in direction. The 1960s were years of immense upheaval (Varshney 1994). Nehru died in 1964, and his successor, Shastri, who was more liberal, very soon after. Industrialization-based planning was reappraised, all the more since the Third Plan (1961–6) renewed strong support to agriculture. In 1964, the energetic C. Subramaniam became Minister of Food and Agriculture, and launched reforms in the agricultural research institutions and administrations. The USA delayed the departure of their cereal freighters to India in retaliation for the latter's criticism of the Vietnam War. The conflicts with China in 1962 and with Pakistan in 1965, which led to the suspension of American aid, also revealed the fragility of India's situation, as it was excessively dependent on imports and international aid. The devaluation of the rupee in 1966 and the restrictive clauses that were added to PL 480 in 1967 (payment in dollars, ban on trade with Cuba and North Vietnam), not to speak of the US rapprochement with the Chinese enemy from 1971 onwards, were the last straw that accelerated the quest for self-sufficiency. The term had not yet been used, but 'food sovereignty' became a priority.

Besides, imports were not the only issue. The expansion of the cropped area and irrigation as well as institutional reforms (co-operatives, land distribution) had shown their limitations. With demographic growth playing its part, grain surpluses on the market were decreasing. It was therefore necessary to implement technological changes that allowed for an agricultural take-off. But technology on its own was nothing without acceptance from the main actors, the farmers. We shall see that the technological miracle was actually based on institutional reforms, which essentially concerned marketing structures allowing incentives to be provided to farmers.

CONCENTRATION NOT WELL ACCEPTED (1964–1991)

There are two parts to the Green Revolution: the beginning, when the new technological package was prescribed (concerning the most urgent matters and promoting concentration processes), and the subsequent years, when the concern for homogenization once again came to the forefront. Most development structures had already been set up at the start of the Green Revolution, if not before (pricing, research, credit policies). Development schemes implemented later, such as the Integrated Rural Development Programme or the progressive use of high-yield seeds for coarse grain, were slow to show results, probably because motivation was basically lacking. Thus, the concern for equalization was not a change in direction as such, but rather a 'revving up' of the engines that were in place since the end of the 1960s. The fact remains however, as the following pages will show, that 1976-7 was a turning point. While earlier, the emphasis was on managing scarcity and emergency situations, later, with food grain self-sufficiency, development programmes could be further developed or reinforced, whether on the basis of cereal stocks (Food for Work) or not (Integrated Rural Development). Before 1977, the food crisis compelled the concentration of effort and investment in the most favoured regions and social groups. Thereafter, a more egalitarian policy could be developed, though with mixed results (Venugopal 1992).

Hunger Justifies the Means: The Green Revolution

If, as a result, disparities are widened, it will at least be as a consequence of a forward thrust; *and* those who will be pushed ahead will not necessarily be a privileged few: there would be millions of big as well as medium and small farmers and even tenants who, but for HYV, would have remained poor for a long time. If this is to be viewed as dualism, it is at least partially benevolent and must be preferred to a more egalitarian stagnation. Dantwala (1996 [1970] : 78–9)

A regionally more balanced growth of foodgrains is certainly desirable but the pursuit of this objective should not be at the cost of pushing up the marginal cost of production of foodgrains. It would be economically more sensible to assist each region to make the optimum use of its development potential, instead of seeking product uniformity in the growth process. Ibid. [1986] : 118

Precursors to the Green Revolution

The Green Revolution was more an *evolution*, at least if you consider food grain growth rates, except for wheat. The production and productivity gains of the years following Independence were anything but negligible. Between 1949–50 and 1964–5, annual agricultural production growth stood at 3.2 per cent and 3.0 per cent for food grains. It was almost 30 times the growth rate obtained in the first half of the century under colonial rule, when per capita food availability fell by 25 per cent between 1900 and 1947. The crop area had increased by 15 per cent, with irrigation of the Thar region by the Rajasthan canal and the development of the sub-Himalayan Terai. But the largest proportion of growth in production had already come from an increase in per hectare yields, thanks to more use of chemical fertilizers and irrigation. Thus, food grain yields rose by 45 per cent between 1950–1 and 1964–5. Overall, the production of major crops—except wheat—increased as much in the 1950–65 period (in fifteen years) as it did between 1965 and 1990 (in twenty-five years).

Admittedly, the annual demographic growth rate was 2.2 per cent over those first fifteen years, and India did not escape from maverick weather conditions, as for instance in 1965 and 1966. A part of the crop area expansion concerned less fertile or fragile land, or the conversion of rather useful pastureland misnamed 'waste lands'. The fact remains that British colonialism had created an entire agronomic research infrastructure, its more remarkable elements being the Council of Agricultural Research and the Agricultural Research Institute, set up as far back as in 1928. Irrigation had been first developed on the upstream plains of the Ganga, which was definitely inadequate, but provided some foundation and experience. Last but not least, if the age-old 'tradition' of intensive agriculture in many of these regions was also taken into account, it could be said that the Green Revolution did not begin from scratch.

The Grow More Food campaign launched in 1942 lasted till 1951. When Japan entered the war in December 1941, the colonial government realized (rather late) that rice imports from Burma were under extreme threat. In April 1942, a conference that brought together representatives from the provinces and princely states had recommended the adoption of the first agricultural policy covering the entire country (Chopra, 1988). The objective was food (actually cereal) self-sufficiency by 1952. Thenceforth, subsistence crops found favour over commercial crops such as cotton. In particular, the Grow More Food campaign had emphasized irrigation and chemical fertilisers to increase agricultural production, exactly as the Green Revolution was to do much later (Knight 1954). However, there are two differences between them. The first left a lot of room for the clearing of waste land and range land, thereby combining agricultural intensification, with agricultural expansion, the latter with the increasing use of tractors. The Green Revolution, on the other hand, looked only to intensification (to increased yields); it would only try to increase the cropped area by systematizing the annual two-crop strategy with the help of irrigation. The second characteristic of the Grow More Food campaign was that it lacked a pricing policy, which we shall describe later for the Green Revolution, as well as a sizeable technological component: the very effective improved varieties of the 1960s.

From 1951 onwards, the campaign became more geographically selective and appeared as such in the First Five Year Plan: concentration of programmes promoting the widespread use of seeds and fertilizers in irrigated or sufficiently rainy zones, development of tubewells, etc. Indeed, these were just precursors to the Green Revolution. On the whole, only 2 to 4 per cent of the sown area was actually covered by the campaign. Most certainly, if we were to revert to Figure 1, which provides a synthesis of agricultural history on the basis of the equalization/concentration diptych, this campaign mainly fell under the latter, as did all policies based on productivity gains until the 1970s.

Besides, the low coverage area was less and less considered a shortcoming. In 1959, while wheat imports under PL 480 were in full swing, a group of experts funded by the Ford Foundation emphasized the fact that neither imports nor rationing could provide a permanent solution to the crisis. The group suggested an aggressive but selective agricultural policy, which would concentrate inputs that were available in limited quantities in the most favoured regions, for a rapid increase in production: the 'selection of certain crops and certain areas for more intensive efforts' (Dandekar 1994: 148). It also advised the implementation of a guaranteed price system through a dense market network. The idea of concentrating efforts in certain regions was later incorporated in the Third Five Year Plan (1961–6). The new Intensive Agricultural Development Programme first concentrated on seven districts in 1961, and on eight districts later, in 1962. The seeds of the Green Revolution had already been sown.

Three Fundamentals of the Green Revolution

Dantwala (1996) refers to three groups of factors that explained agricultural growth after 1965: Institutional factors (land structures, credit, marketing, agricultural extension, education); economic factors (incentives/restraints, prices, taxes, subsidies, etc.); and technological factors (seeds, fertilizers, and irrigation).

According to him, some of these had a limited influence: thus, institutional changes, such as the abolition of semi-feudal tenures and the *zamindari* system, did not seem to have any effect on the Gangetic plains in terms of agricultural production. The same was true of the Community Development programme. The issue of farm prices is particularly complex to analyse, given the low response of farmers because of the difficult socio-economic context, but also since these prices fluctuated greatly at different times and for different products. According to Dantwala, the factor that truly triggered the Green Revolution was high-yield varieties: 'the technological barrier had for long rendered the much-needed institutional changes practically sterile and ineffective' (ibid.: 79).

Without taking sides in the hierarchy of trigger-factors, three fundamentals can be distinguished for the Green Revolution: a technological triptych (improved varieties, fertilizer, irrigation), a production-incentive price policy, and a distribution policy for inputs and services such as credit. Let us address them successively.

In 1963, the Ministry of Agriculture invited to India Norman Borlaug, the inventor of dwarf and semi-dwarf wheat varieties produced in what was later to become the International Maize and Wheat Improvement Centre (CYMMIT), in Mexico. Borlaug sent back 100 kg of seeds to India upon his return. But despite all efforts, it was not clear how the seeds could be acclimatized and propagated in a short span of time. Hence, 250 tonnes of wheat seeds were imported from Mexico in 1965 and, in particular, 18,000 tonnes the following year, funded by the Rockefeller Foundation. The largest tonnage of seeds ever to have been sold in the world thus ensured the national distribution of these varieties (Dandekar 1994). In 1965, the Intensive Agricultural Areas Programme had already covered 114 districts (out of 325).

The International Rice Research Institute (IRRI), set up in 1960 in the Philippines, was going to popularize semi-dwarf rice varieties, of which the first (Taichung Native-1) had been created in Taiwan in 1956. Others were to follow—less sensitive to wind because of their small size, non-photoperiodic in nature, and requiring just about fifty days of maturation as against the 5 to 6 months taken by traditional Indian varieties, while producing twice, if not three times the yield. IR-8 reached India in 1966, followed thereafter by many others, with added resistance to insects and diseases. As India perhaps had the largest rice germplasm resources in the world, it was relatively easy for its researchers to cross IRRI varieties with local varieties to ensure better adaptation to the conditions prevailing in the country.

In 1967–8, while HYV-sown areas already amounted to 6 million hectares (6 per cent of area cultivated by cereals), wheat production came close to 17 million tonnes for the first time and rice production broke records the following year with almost 40 million tonnes. 'Even Mexico . . . had needed fifteen years to do what the Punjab did in five years' (Chopra 1988: 158). Here we understand the term 'Green Revolution', used for the first time by an American in 1968 though not specifically in relation to India. Let us also point out that these varieties were not hybrids. Some hybrids were developed for maize, pearl millet, and sorghum, but they were found to be susceptible to diseases. On the other hand, since hybrid seeds are almost sterile, they cannot be re-used for the following crop, while the Green Revolution took place without making farmers dependent on the seed industry—a point of great relevance today, in view of the GMO controversy. Even today, India sows very few hybrid cereals.[11]

To enhance the use of fertilizers, credit and agricultural extension were required. Subsidies had not been mentioned, although nitrogen fertilizer prices were controlled even before Independence. Sale prices were fixed higher than production costs so as to encourage the private industrial sector to develop. The objective was to avoid fluctuations in global market prices, level out import prices and domestic prices, remove differences in production costs between different factories, and standardize sale prices throughout the country (Desai 1993). Thus, price fixing did not address the concern of making fertilizers economically accessible to farmers, but rather that of making them physically available. Thus, spatial equality did not yet go hand in hand with social equity favouring poor farmers—the fertilizer budget proved excessive, until the early 1970s. The Green Revolution was born with non-subsidized fertilizers—except in mountainous regions and occasional seasonal discounts, in particular for popularizing new fertilizers. The view was that the best dissemination tools were not prices as such, but an increase in industrial production or even imports, along with an increased use of HYVs or irrigation.

The system exploded during the 1973 oil crisis: the rise in prices of imported raw materials made Indian production costs higher than sales prices. Now more than before, the watchword was self-reliance and the development of national production. It became necessary to find the means to draw more private capital to the fertilizer sector—thus the 'Retention Price Scheme', implemented in 1977 for nitrogen fertilizers and in 1979 for phosphate and potassium fertilizers. This was a challenging dual-purpose system as it concerned both supply and demand. From the perspective of supply, the needs of industrialists had to be met if the aim was self-reliance in fertilizer. But from the demand point of view, sales prices had to be contained so that farmers could use fertilizer more and ensure food self-reliance for India. There was only one solution: cut all links between production costs and the selling price for farmers. The difference would be paid by the state, which undertook to subsidize users and some of producers. We shall see that such a system took up from what had just been implemented for foodgrains: purchases from farmers at high prices and redistribution to consumers at subsidized prices.

It was thus that a 'retention price' was fixed for each factory and product, so as to ensure industrialists a net income of 12 per cent per year, irrespective of production costs. So the state fixed a different raw material price for each factory, again due to its concern for perequation (Gulati and Narayanan 2003). The choice of manufacturing processes and production capacities for all producers, private or public, had to be approved by the administration, which in turn enjoyed monopoly over imports, thereby protecting the national industry. Imported fertilizer prices were brought to the same level as domestic fertilizers. The retention price system enabled industrial India to reach near self-reliance in terms of chemical fertilizer production. On the other end of the chain, the subsidies offered to farmers for these fertilizers facilitated self-reliance in food grains.

In 1951–2, less than 18 per cent of the area under cultivation in India was irrigated. In 1964–5, the percentage was still just 19 per cent. Ten years later, it was 24 per cent. In 1999–2000, it had reached 41 per cent (and 51 per cent for food grains). Today, 86 per cent of wheat is under irrigation, which is logical since it is cultivated in dry season. But rice, although originally a monsoon crop, is also now irrigated up to 52 per cent, which demonstrates the importance of the second crop of the year.

Progress was particularly spectacular in another field : the Green Revolution was actually a well-digging revolution: not shallow open wells, but deep tube wells or bore wells, equipped with diesel or electric pumps. Today, 60 per cent of irrigation water comes from underground water. (And many areas irrigated by wells have not been listed officially.) In 1970, wells accounted for more than 20 per cent of irrigated areas only in the Gangetic plains, Tamil Nadu and along the Delhi-Gujarat diagonal. As of 1990, the diagonal extended towards the east, covering a large part of Madhya Pradesh, and Andhra Pradesh has almost caught up with Orissa.[12]

There is undoubtedly a regional equalization factor at play here, given that this spread covered regions that had not been affected by the large dam constructions that began in the mineteenth century.

Several development programmes promoted the sinking of wells and offered credit at preferential rates. However, many wells are located in areas that were already experiencing the early benefits of the diversion dams built by the British in the Himalayas. Thus, the Green Revolution consolidated the progress which had already been achieved in the Punjab–Haryana region, although the intensively cultivated areas did expand.

As agricultural electricity is subsidized more than 80 per cent on an average (about 294 Billion rupees in 2001–2) (Gulati and Narayanan 2003), irrigation is a heavy financial burden. Ecologically, the trend is extremely worrying, given that the water table is threatened in sedimentary areas as well as in Punjab and even more so in the Deccan crystalline basement. Between 1980 and 1998, the water table fell in almost a third of districts by more than 4 m (Dorin and Landy forthcoming). Cheap electricity in contrast to diesel costs and free water hardly offer any incentive for preservation. And socially, these wells pushed their owners to abandon ancient collective irrigation modes (channels, village ponds, etc.), which rapidly became quite disorganized. Hence farmers who did not have any wells faced a very difficult situation. Many got into debt trying to sink wells.

Under the inputs and services distribution policy, extension services are provided by the Development Block administration, and Village Level Workers work under it. Inputs are managed by the administration (surface water irrigation, electricity) or distributed by 'cooperatives' (fertilizers, credit), competing with the private sector. The origin of Primary Agricultural Cooperative Societies goes back to the pre-Independence period, but in 1947, they only accounted for 7 per cent of total credit to agriculture (Dandekar 1994). The entire planning effort consisted of developing these cooperatives, which function on the basis of a pyramidal structure (village–district–state). Their members' share represents a small portion of their capital, which make them para-public agencies. While their number had been reduced at one point during the early days of the Green Revolution in order to improve their functioning, there are more than 90 million members of various cooperatives today. By providing reimbursable crop credit at preferential rates, cooperatives played a major role in intensifying cropping systems (about half the loans are in kind, mostly fertilizers).

A little later, the nationalization of commercial banks in 1969 enabled credit management as per the planners' wishes. Thus, agriculture was defined as a priority sector, with banks granting a minimum credit quota (18 per cent even today officially), though this was never actually achieved. At the same time, the Food Corporation of India no longer depended on credit from the State Bank of India for its functioning, but could henceforth also take the help of commercial banks, which until then were not really interested in funding the heavy food mechanism. In 2003–4, 5 per cent of gross bank credit issued by these banks was used for 'food credit', and up to 21 per cent in 2001–2 and 2002–3 because of the grain surplus to be stored.

However, according to the National Sample Survey, only 58 per cent of the credit provided to farmers came from official institutions in 2003, as against 26 per cent from agriculturist and professional moneylenders (often with a license), 5 per cent from traders, and 9 per cent from friends and relatives. Usury exploitation does not come just from the interest rate but also from cheating with regard to the weight and quality of crops that debtors have to sell to their creditors (Alary and Hache 2001). And yet, the informal sector proves to be more flexible and offers greater ease of access than official credit. That is why it is indispensable, although it may encourage over-borrowing for farmers to be able to survive.

Seeds, fertilizers, water—the three fundamentals of the Green Revolution—were like the three musketeers, as there were actually four. Technological and pricing policies had to proceed *in tandem* in order to obtain results.

Apart from the Green Revolution in tropical Asia, the 1960s also saw the European Common Agricultural Policy (CAP) emerge. The CAP used tools that were common to the Green Revolution: protectionism in the face of imports, the role of irrigation and new seeds (particularly for the spread of maize), the development of chemical fertilizers, and enhanced specialization of farms and regions. Another common point was the pricing policy, which made it possible to offer producers incentives. The risk involved was that enhanced production could lead to a fall in prices, which would not be compensated by increased productivity per hectare. The main difference was the mode of subsidy used: in Europe, consumers could afford higher food prices, and farm subsidies were originally based on taxing consumers. In India, the average purchasing power made such a policy untenable, hence consumer prices could not be as high as in Europe. It was necessary to keep them down by subsidizing inputs in order to bring down production costs and, consequently, selling prices. That was why, contrary to the mode followed in the CAP, fertilizers were subsidized, not just irrigation water, electricity, or credit as was the case in Europe. Finally, when Indian agricultural prices lost their relative value after the oil crisis and obtaining self-reliance, the situation that emerged was common to other sectors beside the farm sector: a general 'low cost economy' in which the low prices of farm products were compensated year after year by low prices of manufactured products and services.

All this coincided with the political strategy adopted by Indira Gandhi, who came to power in 1966. The elections the following year, marked by setbacks for her Congress party, revealed the emergence of new rural classes that had benefited from the Green Revolution and land reforms—the 'bullock capitalists' (Rudolph 1987) who set up their own unions and soon, their own political parties. They could not yet lay claim to power, though they did succeed in doing so ten years down the line, but they could easily make the Congress lose. Already influential in their states, farmers entered the national Parliament in large numbers.[13] Indira Gandhi saw this as a motivation to develop an input subsidy policy and as a reason to maintain tax exemptions for farm income (Varshney 1994).

The concern for self-reliance was necessarily combined with protectionism. Cereal imports were drastically reduced, not just to save foreign exchange, but also to protect national production. Most imports were then used to build buffer stocks rather than to compete directly with Indian farmers. At the same time, an increasing share of the national produce was purchased by the state at relatively high prices (above support prices). This was partly the reason for the wheat productivity gains recorded in the mid-1960s. In 1968–9, for instance, the government purchased almost the entire food grain sold in Punjab. When prices declined relatively after 1974, wheat productivity continued its upward trend thanks to the introduction of more productive new high-yield varieties. Rice productivity gains emerged relatively later, because of the late dissemination (in the early 1970s) of varieties such as IR-8 on a large scale, but also because it was only at that time that the procurement price for rice began to match wheat price.

It is understandable that price management is a valuable economic policy tool. Free market trends were closely monitored by statistical institutes, just as the Indian Meteorological Department monitors the advent of the monsoon. In the event of difficulties, price management is coupled with credit management, so as to make use of private trade strategies. It must be recalled that the central government has the right to control food grain purchase or selling prices, but also to prevent hoarding, thereby checking speculation. In case of a shortage, the government can enhance the subsidized quantities offered by the PDS. Generally speaking, it may be said in fact that the efficacy of public action was due less to the fixing of prices than the mere presence of the state on the market, i.e. the volume of food grain it controlled through its purchase and redistribution (Dandekar 1994), not to speak of the psychological effects of discussion and reform.

Spectacular Results

Till [the 1960s] the maximum production of wheat in India was 12.3 million tonnes, achieved in 1964–65, when productivity was at the highest level of 913 kgs per hectare. Until 1964–65 the maximum area under wheat had been 13.6 million hectares. By 1970–71, within four to five years of the introduction of high-yielding varieties, the area under wheat increased to 18.2 million hectares, production jumped to 23.08 million tonnes and the average yield reached 1,307 kg. This dramatic increase in production and productivity could be achieved through the expansion of area under high-yielding varieties. The area under HYV increased from 2.9 million hectares in 1967–68 to 6.5 million hectares by 1970–71 and further to 19.4 million hectares by 1983–84. As a proportion, the area under HYV to the total area under wheat increased from 19.6 per cent in 1967–68 to 36 per cent in 1970–71 and further to 78.6 per cent by 1983–84 [and 86 per cent in 1998–99]. Apart from this, the proportion of irrigated wheat area also increased phenomenally from 43 per cent in 1967–68 to 54 per cent by 1970–71 and 72 per cent by 1983–84 [87 per cent in 2001–02]. In this increase of area under irrigated wheat, expansion of irrigation by tubewells played a major role. The proportion of area irrigated by tubewells to the total area irrigated in the country increased from 0.6 per cent in 1960–61 to 14.3 by 1970–71 and further to 27 per cent by 1984–85 [and 41 per cent in 2001–02]. (Tyagi 1990 : 59 and indiaagristat. com)

Such an accumulation of figures in the text quoted above reflects the besetting sin of many Indian researchers and administrators. Yet it reveals the systemic nature of factors of production that contributed to agricultural growth, interlinked through feedback loops. The fairly widely used term of 'technological package' does not really fully convey the idea of a *system*, because it gives the impression of an accumulation of new factors, each of which seem to have had individual positive effects. On the contrary, their interdependence needs to be underlined. Without HYVs, productivity gains would have probably not have exceeded those of the Grow More Food campaign. But without irrigation, there would have been no High Yield Varieties grown. Without the technical progress in tubewells, enabled by more accessible institutional credit, irrigation except for large dams, would not have developed.

Strangely, the term *self-sufficiency* was barely used in official documents on the beginnings of the Green Revolution. However, the seeds of the concept did lie in them. In fact, between 1951 and 1969, imports accounted for on an average 5.8 per cent of the net food grain availability. The percentage later became negligible, if not negative, although the situation with pulses (and oilseed crops) was much less satisfactory. In fact, in 1970–1, for the first time since Independence, procurement exceeded public distribution needs. PL 480 imports stopped in 1972, the year when some stocks were resold in the open market, and would resume only in 1975 and 1976. Imports stopped in 1977–8 and India even managed to export some wheat and rice to friendly countries. In March 1977, 'with a stock of over 18 million tonnes and a country-wide network of over 240, 000 ration/fair price shops, the country had now secured the two most important elements of the national food security system' (Chopra 1988: 200). The 1978–9 *Economic Survey* already referred to the need to encourage exports and the 1979 drought emerged almost as a godsend for the disposal of surplus stocks.

In 1975 it was possible to decide to build buffer stocks entirely in kind (without saving foreign exchange for imports), with quantities varying between 4.4 and 8.8 million tonnes according to the seasons, and an ideal rice/wheat ratio of 40/60. Their volume was finally fixed in 1978 at 12 million tonnes (reduced to 10 million in 1981), with operational stocks being added depending on the season.[14]

There were very few quarters with tonnages below the minimum levels, and most stock-related problems were due more to excess food grain than any lack of them. The buffer effect made it possible to

(Million tonnes)	1st April	1st July	1st October	1st January
Wheat	4.0	14.3	11.6	8.4
Rice	11.8	10.0	6.5	8.4

Source: High Level Committee, 2002, §3.8.

Figure 2.4: Minimum wheat and rice stocks per quarter (2002)

prevent food grain prices from falling below the support prices, as much as to prevent food shortages and famines. However, their efficacy was limited. The numerous food grain distribution restrictions till the 1980s often made it difficult to lower prices in certain regions that were not integrated in market terms. On the other hand, the substitution effect between different cereals, extremely variable according to the regions and their food habits, made it difficult to calculate standards for each type of grain, given that in certain regions the public sale of wheat would hardly be able to check an increase in rice and sorghum prices (Krishna and Jha, 1969). Finally, in budget terms too there were limitations. In the past, foreign exchange was necessary to purchase food grains and replenish stocks in the event of an agricultural crisis. Now, stock management costs had to be financed in the event of procurement that would be much higher than the amount needed for distribution.

The Two Balances

In an ideal food policy, a government has to balance two perspectives. 'Let us recall that the food dilemma is presented in terms of a conflict between consumers and producers. . . . The issue at stake is whether budgetary allocations should be used in order to support consumption or to support production. While the former means a short-term equity policy, the latter can lead to an efficiency policy in the long-term' (Padilla 1996: 168). This is the first equilibrium, one that is more economic in nature (Landy 1999). The second balance is geographic in nature, and concerns the equilibrium to be managed between food surplus areas and food deficit areas. The two balances have sometimes been identified in terms of an opposition between cities and villages, cities constituting food deficit areas but populated with consumers, while producers were found in rural areas (Lipton 1976). We have already seen the limitations of such a perspective.

'The benefits of input and food subsidies have been shared by all the sections of the society, i.e. surplus producing farmers, other farmers who are net purchasers of food grains, landless labourers, urban consumers and the industry' says Acharya (1997: 16). The objective was to satisfy consumers with fairly low prices, without however discouraging farmers, who had to be suitably remunerated in order to incite them to invest. We have seen that this kind of equilibrium often corresponds to the self-sufficiency/import alternative, insofar as international prices are sometimes much lower than domestic prices because of the inadequate competitiveness of Indian agriculture (due to low productivity or subsidies granted by exporting countries). In this regard, India's food grain history can be illustrated by Figure 2.5.

There are three ways of ensuring low consumer prices. First, they can be subsidized through what may be called a downstream policy (a policy India was to adopt, both for food grains and agricultural inputs). Secondly, by adopting a supply-side policy and paying the price of substantial imports, with the expectation of having adequate supplies to keep retail prices down (a policy India had opted for till the 1960s). And third, by encouraging national production. In India, the latter, upstream policy took the form of a high degree of state intervention, often with strict protectionism. All in all, it must be noted that these methods are far from being exclusive, as India continues to use the first and third together, which shows the seriousness of the challenges faced in the food sector (Fig. 2.6).

The Second Five Year Plan in 1956 cut down the share of agriculture and community development from 15 per cent of the credit allocated in the First Plan to 12 per cent. But Dantwala

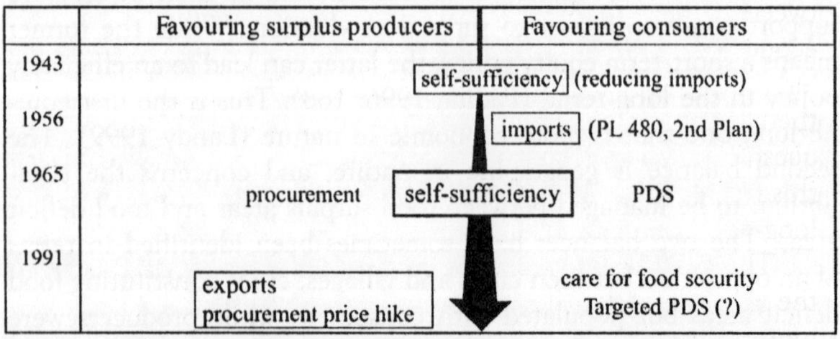

Figure 2.5: Food dilemma from the Indian perspective

Factors involved in rising food prices	Factors involved in falling food prices
Structural	
Public and private investment, general development of the country pushing up demand.	
Inflationary funding by budget deficits and credit growth.	Increase in the purchasing power of certain sections can compensate such price hikes in real terms.
Population increase.	Increase in production and market surpluses.
Greater flexibility of demand in relation to income elasticity for poor households.	For food grains, relative decrease in their share in daily rations (rising living standards, urbanisation, etc.).
Temporary	
Increase in procurement prices.	PDS distribution.
Decrease of imports, increase of exports.	FCI sales in open market.
Storage and speculation.	Higher procurement prices, other FCI measures.

Figure 2.6: Factors in food price trends

(1996) rightly observed that it was not advisable to unduly pit agriculture against industry since the construction of fertilizer or tractor factories directly concerned agriculture. A lot of ink has been spilled over the issue of agricultural prices and terms of trade between agriculture and industry in India. While a majority of economists—particularly those who believe in the existence of an 'urban bias'—consider it as being unfavourable to agriculture and therefore the intensification of production (Dandekar 1994), others question the figures and at least partly justify the policies adopted in this field (Dantwala 1996; Sarkar 1995), while also laying stress on long-term development (Varshney 1994).

The fact remains that in the first three five year plans, to 1966, the government had favoured consumers (and industrial capital interests) by refusing to encourage a rise in agricultural prices. The PDS, intended to meet urban needs and prevent any agitation there, was a political tool at least as much as a food security tool. The Green Revolution saw the birth of new capitalists, this time in the farm sector. Frankel (1978) showed how the new concern in the 1960s to ensure decent prices for farmers corresponded to the political rise of an agrarian bourgeoisie. In the states and the Union, political change has almost become the rule. Thus, it became a matter of urgency for the party in power to reinforce its legitimacy by developing initiatives favouring the maximum of voters.

A difficult corner was then successfully negotiated (Varshney 1994). It was not that the consumers were at less of an advantage this time as compared to producers, but the authorities refused to opt for one over the other. Instead, they chose the path of dual support—to both agriculturists and consumers, which the 1966 Food grains Policy Committee called an 'integrated food policy'. Chopra (1988: 153) and Dandekar (1994) both affirmed (with the same words!) that the new policy was, 'more or less, the same policy which was in operation during 1943–7 and, with some brief experiment with decontrol during 1948, up to 1952'. Indeed, it laid the foundation for the preparation of the National Food Budget, dreamt up by the 1966 Commission in order to move food grains from surplus areas to deficit areas, depending on their capacities and needs. However, I argue that this policy is quite different from the earlier one, in that food grains would henceforth be purchased from farmers at incentive prices, without national production having to face fierce competition from imports. From an era of coercion and forced sales, there was a gradual shift (except for certain bad years) towards an era of incentives. Admittedly, the state accepted the rules of the market, but intervened with all its force through purchase and sale. From the farmers' perspective, it was more a carrot rather than a stick.

However, there was a stage between that and what Bharadwaj asserted (1998: 205)—that an attempt was being made 'to solve separately the problem of "production" (or "growth") and that of "distribution" and welfare'. On the contrary, the two remained linked, because it was an increase in production that would benefit consumers in the long run. No doubt that this required a radical change in perspective, which also reminds us of Foucault (2004) who recalled the physiocrats' victory over the old mercantilist trends in France. The price controls implemented in France in the seventeenth century, as they were in India in the 1950s, were perceived as useless, even harmful, by many. In order to offer low consumer prices in cities, the best approach was still that of paying farmers a correct price. Like the architects of the Green Revolution, when France's physiocrats were heard by the royal government in 1764, 'with the promulgation of freedom for cereal trade, they re-introduced agriculture, farming profit and peasant welfare in the objectives of policy intervention. The countryside was thus at least as important as the cities, if not more so, as a privileged subject of governmental intervention' (ibid.: 350). The concern for making distribute replaced the concern for making produce.

'The kaleidoscopic problems of food administration at the national level' (Acharya 1983: xii) stem in particular from the existence of two kinds of regional imbalance, depending on whether consumption and production are considered separately or together. In the production sector alone, Indian regions are characterized by major deviations in productivity (Map 2.4). Likewise, in the consumption sector, the needs of less densely populated areas are smaller than those of highly populated areas, particularly major cities, where agriculture is practically non-existent.[15] Thus, estimations that are used in order to assess the production balance minus consumption and to be able to define surplus and deficit regions, are extremely complex. However, this is what has been done in India since the beginning, essentially due to its concern for regional parity.[16]

Spatial inequalities are in fact the *raison d'être* of the Indian food network. 'The affirmation of discontinuity and heterogeneity at the root of the notion of network must be acknowledged. (. . .) It is this heterogeneity that is the basis for the need for the links and relationships provided by the network. If all the nodes were strictly identical, they would not have anything to exchange among themselves and linking them would not make sense' (Dupuy 1994: 145). Gradually, a full 'territorial system' was set up for food (Raffestin 1980), consisting of:

- *Areas* covered by an increasingly dense network over the years. These are the regions covered by the PDS, which theoretically has to supply the whole country. (On the contrary, as we shall see, procurement areas tended to become scarcer with the concentration of public purchases in high productivity zones.)
- *Nodes*: These nodes correspond to railway stations, truck depots

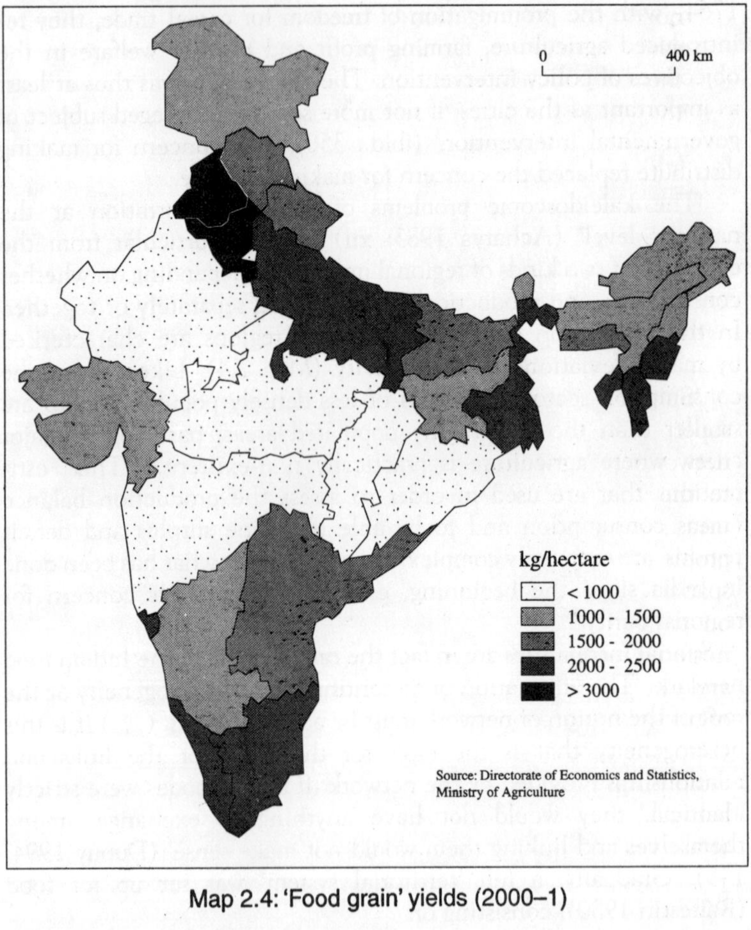

Map 2.4: 'Food grain' yields (2000–1)

and all storage areas. Their sizes vary in a reverse U-shaped hierarchy: state-procured food grains originally come from a small purchasing centre, rice mill, or even the farmer's own granary, and they are initially transported in trucks. Then, the node grows in size until it corresponds to bigger marshalling yards and major national warehouses. Further downstream, on the redistribution size, the hierarchy starts declining in size up to the small ration shops served by trucks or rickshaws.

- *Curves*: They follow the same reverse U-shaped hierarchy, given that flows first grow in size up to national storage depots, only to sub-divide till they reach the end consumer. These curves first represent cohorts of bullock carts, then trucks, later trains. As they 'move down', they are covered by trucks once again, representing on the whole the food supply *network* infrastructure.

'Such a hierarchical configuration of networks takes the form of superposed sets of connections: from the minute meshes of local road networks whose sides can be measured in hectometres in dense areas, to the very wide meshes of faster networks, whose sides can be measured in hundreds of kilometres' (Bonnafous 1994: 329). The problem is that a network is often characterized by an inequality of spatial and informational access for the actors involved, depending on their location with reference to the nodes. Contrary to the notion of a 'market' according to the conventional economic theory, and even to that of the 'field' of the geographer, 'the discreet nature of nodes and links in the networks leaves the interstitial areas apart' (Dupuy 1994: 148). The spatial balance that the PDS attempted to establish could not help but be imperfect, leaving imbalances behind, at least at local level. We shall see that these exist in reality at all levels.

Balancing the Economic Scales

(a) *State Intervention in the Agricultural Production Market: The FCI*

The food policy has two objectives. The first has remained unchanged since the early days of Independence: ensuring low and stable consumer prices through the PDS and intervention in the open market and, in particular, through the availability of safety stocks. The second is a more recent aim—that of increasing national food grain production by ensuring remunerative prices to producers and thereby encouraging the greater use of inputs. At the national scale, agricultural production has to be raised; at the farm level, farmers must be freed from the yoke of loan sharks, who buy their produce at low prices immediately after the harvest (Fig. 2.7).

The Ministry of Consumer Affairs, Food and Public Distribution[17] is the key ministry for the food policy. Its Food Department under it is in charge of procurement, storage and imports. The PDS, consumer protection as well as domestic trade, fall under the Civil Supplies Department, today linked to the Food Department. The Ministry runs three public–sector companies—the Food Corporation of India, the Central Warehousing Corporation (CWC) in charge of storage, and Hindustan Vegetable Oils Corporation Ltd. For its part the Ministry of Agriculture plays an essential role, implementing agricultural policies that have a direct impact on the food situation. The Directorate of Economics and Statistics works under it. Its pre- and post-harvest estimations are supposed to guide the authorities despite their often-doubtful validity.

Taking over from the Food and Warehousing Corporation, the Food Corporation of India (FCI) was set up on 1 January 1965. The law that gave birth to it affirmed, as a reflection of the dual objective of the food policy, that it should be guided by the 'interests of the

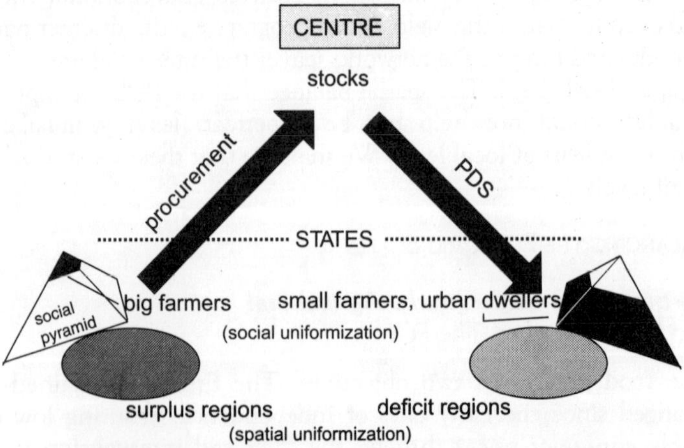

Figure 2.7: The Indian food mechanism—an ideal view

producer and consumer'. Thanks to the transfer of the executive functions of the Food Department in 1969, it became the only central institution to be given charge of the purchase, storage, transportation and distribution of wheat and rice. Procurement, which rarely achieved 1 per cent of the net food grain production before the Corporation was set up, was never to fall below 5 per cent and exceeded 9 per cent by 1971. It has offices in the Union states, and owns warehouses (15 million tonnes of its own in 2000, along with 14 million leased from the CWC and different State Warehousing Corporations) and processing units (rice mills). At the end of 2003, it had 55,000 employees—not to speak of unskilled workers (71,000 persons in 1986). Moreover, it provides several consultancy services to the public with regard to food processing. It is all the more important as it sub-contracts a part of its activities to similar corporations set up in different states. Thus, the latter set up and manage public procurement centres that are increasing in number with the increase in productivity gains.[18]

The Agricultural Prices Commission was set up in 1965.[19] Its role was to recommend floor price levels, which would then be fixed by the government, in accordance with three highly ambitious objectives: encouraging farmers to intensify production; optimizing the use of land, water and other resources, in particular by trying to influence the choice of crop rotation; and, finally, taking into consideration the effects of prices on the cost of living and salaries in the economy on the whole (Dandekar 1994). The first objective became more important after the first oil crisis, given the rise in the cost of inputs. In 1977, the decision was taken to fight the 'scissor crisis' officially, along with the deterioration of the terms of trade between agriculture and other economic sectors. Indeed, the change in the name of the institution was symptomatic: in 1985, it was called the Commission for Agricultural Costs and Prices (CACP). As it also tries to take international conditions into account, particularly world price levels, its task proves extremely delicate, as it constantly tries to please both consumers and producers. Initially, at the start of the Green Revolution, the latter had found favour, but self-sufficiency was soon to make it possible to define food grain prices generally at a lower level than world prices.

In any case, the CACP's role is merely advisory in nature. Agricultural price levels are actually fixed by the government. So the political, and not just the economic, situation is the reason why the state fixes prices that are higher than those advocated by the Commission. Two prices are defined (Acharya 2001), the minimum support price and the procurement price.

This first, an intervention price, is normally supposed to be announced before the sowing season.[20] It theoretically makes it possible to prevent a fall in prices in the open market in the event of overproduction or a decrease in consumer purchasing power. Price support operations had already been conducted on a large scale in 1953–5, but they were always temporary in nature. Henceforth, the minimum price dogma was institutionalized. Combined with a relatively closed Indian economy until the 1990s, support prices made it possible to reduce price instability.[21] The State is committed to ensuring compliance with the floor price by purchasing from the market in order to make prices move up. It is also committed to purchasing all the grain offered by farmers at that price. It is not calculated as a minimum price claimed to prevent only significant falls in price, but a rather generously calculated price, taking all agricultural costs into consideration, including those of inputs produced on the farms themselves, and whose estimation at market prices unquestionably tend to lead to an overestimation of production costs. At least in high productivity regions, this price functions more as a support price than a floor price—as an incentive to invest rather than mere insurance.[22]

The procurement price comes into operation when the government decides to purchase from the market so as to constitute its stocks. This price, which must normally be announced before the harvest, is theoretically lower than the open market price, but higher than support prices. Its level varies according to the state's needs to replenish stocks, and depending on the outcome of the harvest. Hence, during the agricultural crisis of the early stages of the Green Revolution, the procurement price for wheat rose from Rs. 540 per tonne in 1966–7 to Rs. 760 the following year. From being lower than total production costs in the 1950s, it later became markedly higher, providing for an average margin as high as 52 per cent in 1967–8. As land productivity increased at the same time, the rise in farmers' income was remarkable, up to the first oil crisis. The margin fell to less than 4 per cent in 1977–8. For wheat, the procurement price has often remained below world prices since 1974, at least until international prices fell at the end of the last century. The case of rice was even more remarkable, since till that time, the procurement price had always remained below world prices, which made it a fairly highly taxed cereal[23] (Bhalla 1994). In any case, because of the isolation of the Indian market, at least since the late 1970s to 1991, the CACP and the government practically never took world price levels into account to fix domestic prices. Their reference was rather the national open market, in order to try and influence its development.

Figure 2.8 shows a correlation between retail and procurement prices, supporting the stand taken by those who blamed inflation on state purchases. From another perspective, Indian prices fell in constant monetary units throughout the 1980s, without the farmers benefiting from the rise in world prices in 1995–7. There were barely any variations in Indian prices, particularly retail prices. The public food system allowed for a certain degree of levelling, which in the long term could be deemed to have benefited all the sections of the society.

In the beginning of this century, the minimum wheat and rice prices were below CIF import prices, which were themselves quite low. This enabled India to escape certain liberal reforms that the WTO was promoting, since it was easy to show that its agriculture was not subsidized at all, but rather taxed (Bhalla et al., 1999). The

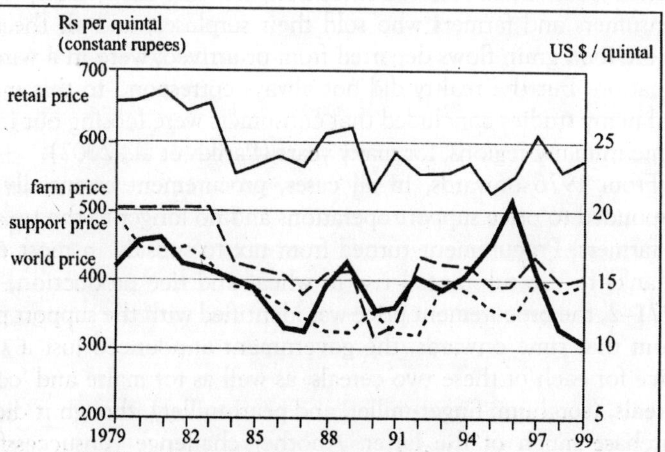

Indian Prices in Rupees. World wheat price in dollars (HRW FOB US Gulf)
Sources : Mahendra Dev et al., 2004 ; cimmyt.org.

Figure 2.8: Wheat price trends (1979–99): India and the World

Aggregate Measurement of Support of Indian agriculture remained negative: it was still—25.6 per cent in 2000, according to Gulati and Narayanan (2003). All this despite the considerable subsidies for inputs, which could not compensate the low agricultural price levels (Dorin and Jullien 2004). In 1992, the government began to dismantle the support system for fertilizers, but urea, which accounted for half the consumption of fertilizers, was still offered at a statutorily notified sale price in 2008.

In the absence of imports, by 'sucking up' food grains for supplying the PDS the state ran the risk of shooting prices up in the open market to levels higher than those that would have prevailed otherwise. To fend off this danger, the procurement price had to be fixed at levels that would offer an incentive to raise overall production. In addition, PDS prices would have to be fixed at levels that were not too low, so that demand did not exceed public stock supplies. This was a dangerous game—fixing high procurement prices was like treating one disease with another, and running the risk of offering production incentives that were lower than incentives to sell to the state would lead to inflation in the open market. Besides, the spatial dimension is an additional parameter. The public system could easily push prices upwards because of procurement, but only in areas of overproduction, while pushing prices downward in deficit areas, thanks to redistribution. On this basis, many of the consumers and farmers who sold their surpluses, and all the areas where food grain flows departed from or arrived, were in a win-win situation. But the reality did not always correspond to this model, and many studies concluded that consumers were loosing out in this game in many regions, for many years (Parikh et al., 2002).

From 1976 onwards, in all cases, procurement essentially corresponded to price support operations and no longer to the taxation of farmers. Procurement turned from tax to subsidy in most cases. Thanks to the substantial rise in wheat and rice production, as of 1971–2, the procurement price was identified with the support price. From that time onwards, the government announced just a single price for each of these two cereals, as well as for maize and 'coarse' cereals, (sorghum, finger-millet, and pearl-millet), though it did not purchase much of the latter. Another challenge (unsuccessfully) taken up by the Commission was the prevention of highly imbalanced crop rotations favouring certain plants, which meant that

that the price policy had to cover all the major crops throughout the country (Krishnaji 1990). Thus other crops benefit from the single support price, often only from the 1990s onwards (which does not mean that the state never purchase them, but it demonstrates its lack of interest in intervening through public procurement). Such is the case with barley, the four main types of peas, sugar cane, cotton, jute, groundnuts, soya bean, sunflower, sesame, *niger*, rapeseed-mustard, safflower, copra and tobacco. On the whole, 24 crops, which account for more than 88 per cent of the value of agricultural production and 80 per cent of the agricultural area.

Until the 1970s, the central government had to deal with the divergent interests of the various states. In the Chief Ministers' conference, which oversaw the fixing of prices, the deficit states generally tended to limit the price hikes, that surplus states normally asked for. But with food grain self-sufficiency and the expansion of the distribution network, there were fewer and fewer voices criticizing price increases. The government also had to take into account farmers' claims. Indeed, farmers' movements were no longer limited to small farmers or the landless demanding agrarian reforms and better land distribution, but rather movements by farmers' unions calling for a rise in farm prices (Varshney, 1994). Until the end of the twentieth century, their main argument was the gap in procurement prices in relation to world prices—meaning a net taxation of agriculture to the benefit of other sectors of the economy. The surpluses drawn from agriculture to enable industry and the service sectors to grow were yet another example of an 'urban bias' at the expense of rural areas. In the 1970s, Sharad Joshi, one of the most prominent farmer leaders of Maharashtra, even went so far as to affirm with Gandhian overtones that the oppression of the rural areas constituted the struggle of the real India against urban India, *Bharat* versus *India*. That was when farmers' representatives found their way into the CACP, in which their numbers grew.

In fact, procurement operations are essential to explain how agricultural growth is maintained in high surplus regions. There is no doubt that without these guaranteed outlets, productivity would not have gone up as much in Punjab or Andhra Pradesh. Acharya (1983) goes so far as to say that the reason Bihar, Karnataka, and Bengal did not experience similar growth was because large-scale procurement was never used there. However, this could be seen as taking the effect as the cause. If these states did not see much procurement, it was because there was no surplus to sell, not the reverse.

In the early days of their establishment, the FCI and the Agricultural Price Commission set up a 'national food budget' with the help of the Planning Commission. To 1977, a quantified objective was planned for procurement, most of the time. It was broken up into monthly 'food budgets' for each state, defining procurement and allocating food grain quotas in accordance with their production forecasts and needs (and any restrictions imposed on product movement). The FCI regional offices were alerted so that they could make the required quantities available. However, the Food and Public Supply departments of the states tended to underestimate their production and overestimate their food needs. Self-sufficiency made it possible to do away with this exercise (which greatly resembled the one currently carried out to allocate and manage urea).

The FCI and its counterparts in the states were assisted by 'cooperatives' (apex marketing societies) and even private traders. Food grain procurement methods changed with time, depending on the state (which was generally free to choose the method it wanted) and crops concerned. In 1967–8, for instance, it was done as in the Fig. 2.9.

Today, on the contrary, the procurement method most often corresponds to price support interventions. As early as 1976–7, 84 per cent of the wheat was purchased on the basis of this system. However, forms of public procurement varied according to the crops.

For wheat, the state purchases directly from farmers, through brokers, or else at regulated markets where auctions are handled by the administration.[24] Henceforth, sales to the state are completely free, except in years where transport restrictions are imposed, when open market prices are much higher than procurement prices. However, a distinction must be made between the official situation and the actual one 'in the field'. Officials who are in charge of food grain purchases often use far more coercive methods than those stated in legislative documents. The case of Karnataka, studied by Mooij (1999) is one example, where procurement objectives are defined in advance and the administration is ready to use all possible means to achieve these objectives.

Procurement	*Functioning*	*Areas concerned*
Monopoly procurement	The state enjoyed a monopoly over purchases from farmers	Assam and Orissa (rice and paddy), Maharashtra (*idem* and sorghum)
Levy on farmers	Farmers had to sell part of their produce to the state, depending on the size of their farm holding, extent of irrigation, etc.[25]	Andhra, Bihar, Kerala, Gujarat, Bengal (paddy), Madhya Pradesh (wheat), Uttar Pradesh (wheat, paddy), Mysore (paddy, millets).
Levy on rice millers and traders	Rice millers and traders had to sell a part of their stocks to the state.	Andhra, Bihar, Haryana, Punjab, Madhya Pradesh, Bengal (husked rice), Uttar Pradesh (husked rice, millets).
Pre-emptive right	At the end of the day, the state procured from regulated markets	Punjab, Haryana (wheat)

Source: According to Dandekar, 1994, pp. 258–9.

Figure 2.9: Procurement methods in 1967–8[26]

Since 1977, levies on farmers themselves ceased completely for all crops (except some time in Maharashtra and Bengal) because of abundant stocks, the unpopularity of the method, and its ineffectiveness. Henceforth, wheat procurement takes place around May-June plain, from where the state purchases almost the entire produce. There is practically no intervention from the private sector, as public prices are fixed too high to their liking, but also, in some years due to the 'lack of railway wagons which are earmarked on priority for the FCI for grain movement and partly to some other obstructions at the executive level' (Chopra 1988: 344). In the field, however, commission agents often buy to indebted farmers their harvest for fertilisers, seeds or some loan—with a huge profit sometimes—and illegally resell the grains to the procurement agency.

For rice, first and foremost, a levy is imposed on rice mills—a percentage of their husked production, varying according to the state: between 75 per cent for Punjab, Haryana, and Orissa and (in some years) nothing for Gujarat and Maharashtra (Fig. 3.4). This mode of procurement became popular in the 1980s, with the emergence of large modern rice mills (two to four tonnes per hour), which made it relatively easy to collect levies, as the grain was concentrated. Further, it was advantageous for the state to handle rice, as it was less voluminous and, in particular, easier to store than paddy. Despite it all, the system is more constrictive than the one for wheat.

The FCI also purchases paddy directly from the farmers sometimes (Fig 2.10) and sends it for husking to rice mills working under contract or owned by the FCI itself (in Punjab, Haryana, Andhra Pradesh, Tamil Nadu). Finally, it is also possible to levy traders, although that has become rare, given their number and the distortions introduced in the market. Further, a trader's aim is to maximize his turnover by turning his stock around. Imposing a levy based on his turnover would mean going against the logic of trade itself and would oblige merchants to raise their margins.

The general framework remains one of a particularly segmented national market, with more or less temporary barriers erected by certain states and for certain products to date, thereby facilitating

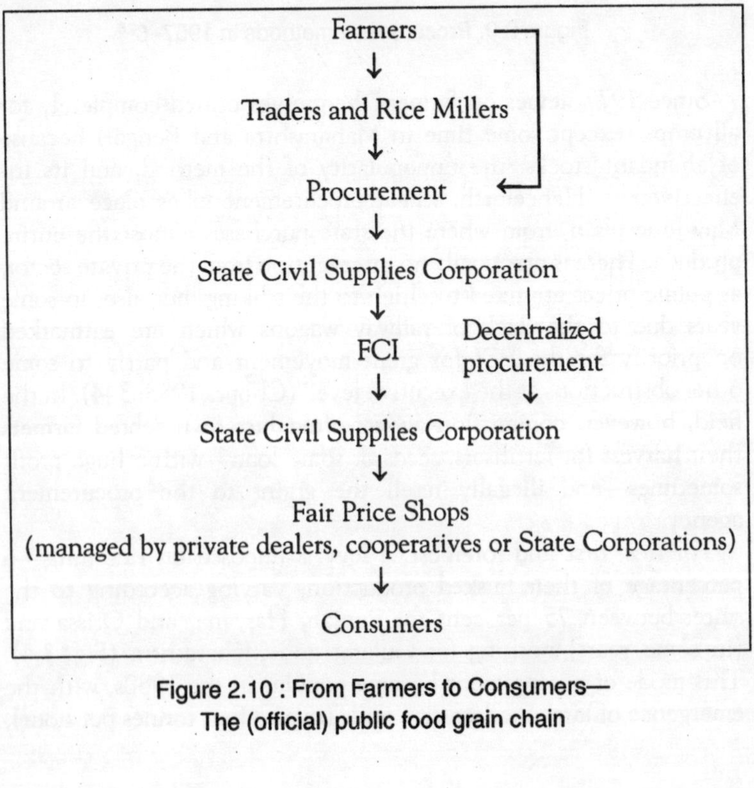

Figure 2.10 : From Farmers to Consumers— The (official) public food grain chain

procurement or limiting price hikes. The Green Revolution was not a 'food' revolution, nor a commercial revolution, in the sense that many of the food policy tools remained unchanged as compared to the ones used before 1965. Further, the government's logic changed slowly as the food grain trade balance became less and less negative. It was only after 1976 that India entered a period that continues until today, characterized by issues of managing abundance rather than shortfall. 1979–80 was a symbolic year in this connection, as it was probably the first in which the nation did not face a difficult food situation despite a poor harvest—proof that the battle for food was gradually distancing itself from the struggle for agricultural advance.

There is no longer any need to narrate the developments of the food system year after year. It can be observed till 1980 with the help of Figure 2.11. Maximum controls were achieved in 1973, when, after two bad years in a row, the too optimistic cessation of imports under PL 480, and the exports to the young Bangladesh out of political compulsion, it was decided to nationalize wholesale trade. After all Indira Gandhi had won the elections two years earlier on a resolutely leftist programme. Furthermore, the tense situation on the food availability front pushed for asking a loan of 2 million tonnes of wheat from the USSR, willy-nilly affirming in which geopolitical block India now had friends. The nationalization of rice was however limited to an announcement, since the ubiquitous character of its production made the imposition of controls difficult. On the contrary, the nationalization of wheat had been in effect since April 1973. Single-state zones were formed, and even reinforced, in Bihar, Rajasthan, Madhya Pradesh and Uttar Pradesh through restrictions on movement within these states. Only retailers had the right to purchase directly from farmers. The Essential Commodities Act was used to ensure the administration's control over marketing circuits. Four thousand new purchasing centres were set up in cities as well as in rural areas; state officers and even non-officials were requisitioned for the enormous procurement exercise. Yet this proved to be disappointing as wheat production had been very average. Some farmers chose to stock up their harvests since the procurement price was deemed too low, but also, as per the terms of the Food Department's annual report, 'acute shortage of different consumer goods gave rise to a general psychology of shortage among the masses and encouraged large-scale hoarding of food grains not

Year	Type of harvest	Measures undertaken
1966–7	Poor	8.7 MT imports; single-state zones for procurement of wheat, rice and coarse grains
1967–8	Good	MSP defined for 5 cereals; restrictions on movement withdrawn, except for paddy from Punjab-Haryana
1968–9	Good	Market prices fell, procurement prices were raised.
1969–70	Good	Increased procurement, decreased imports and distribution, movements authorized.
1970–1	Good	For the first time, procurement higher than PDS requirements. Movements authorized, credit to merchants facilitated, statutory rationing limited to Bombay, Calcutta and Asansol.
1971–2	Poor	Decreased procurement, increased distribution. Stocks enable disappearance of forced sales imposed on wheat producers.
1072–3	Poor	2 MT imports, restrictions on inter-district movements. No more than 2 kg of food grain distributed per week.
1973–4	Poor	Nationalization of wheat wholesale trade.
1974–5	Poor	End of nationalization, but maintenance of single-state zones except for millets. Levy of 50 per cent for wheat merchants in surplus states. Maximum wheat price published by certain states.
1975–6	Good	Restrictions on inter-state movements for wheat. Levy on wheat replaced by public purchases from the market (Punjab, Haryana) or levies imposed on farmers.
1976–7	Good	Decision to stop food grain imports. Larger rice zones defined.
1977–8	Good	End of restrictions on inter-state wheat movements. End of rice zones. No imports. Distribution under the Food for Work programme.
1978–9	Good	Idem. Procurement corresponds to price support operations, even if levies remained.
1979–80	Poor	Despite a mediocre harvest, stocks make it possible to maintain the situation.

Source: After Dandekar (1994) and Chopra (1988).

Figure 2.11: From deficit management to the management of abundance, 1966 to 1980

only by the producers but also by the traders and consumers' (Dandekar 1994: 265). Traders began to hoard their stocks notably by storing them at farmers' houses. The demonstrations by wholesalers and opposition parties, the general dissatisfaction in Punjab-Haryana, and malfunctioning within an FCI plagued by union drifts and corruption, explain why the system was not repeated the next year. It was replaced by a simple levy of 50 per cent on merchants and cooperatives in Haryana, Punjab, Rajasthan, Uttar Pradesh, and Madhya Pradesh. That is how the sole attempt at nationalization in the agricultural field ended.[27]

It is obvious that such instability in measures, a consequence of the inter-annual instability of harvests, could only impede the initiatives of private actors, traders or farmers, notably as far as investments were concerned. The Agricultural Prices Commission regularly warned the government against a zigzag policy, exactly as right from the early days of Green Revolution it protested against prices that were often fixed at levels higher than what it had advocated. To govern is to anticipate, but it also means meeting expectations in the short term. No doubt the short term, synonymous with hunger as well as electoral defeats, governed many a political choice made in Delhi.

Even after the 1960s, the state found it difficult to transform a policy of restriction with regard to the private sector into a more positive policy of encouragement. As far as food grains were concerned, traders could not have access to credit from commercial banks (nationalized in 1969); railway wagons were given for private transportation only once FCI needs had been met, which often forced private traders to use road transportation, which was more expensive over long distances. However, the situation changed markedly once self-sufficiency was achieved. Controls became more lax. In fact, in 1976, the centre enjoined the few states that selected PDS beneficiaries according to socio-economic criteria to abandon these practices. 1977 marked the end of food zones (at least as far as restrictions imposed by the centre were concerned), and 1986, the end of licences for flour mills.[28] In fact, even during crisis years (the 1987-8 drought, the 1977 wheat deficit and the 2003 food crisis), there was no longer any need for drastic measures by the central government to prevent famine in certain areas. Often, provincial states may close their borders, but this is generally only a temporary measure. Generally speaking, stocks are adequate and the machinery is effective enough to ensure that the significant pockets of undernutrition do not experience excess mortality that is too visible. Unless of course, these are isolated areas in peripheral states, populated by tribals and lacking proper links with India's centre of gravity through material infrastructure as well as culture or politics. The Kalahandi region in Orissa is a sad example.

In fact, the state is less and less concerned about obtaining food grains and more and more about how to get rid of them. Before 1964, Delhi had never purchased more than 2 per cent of the net food grain production. But state procurement reached 8 per cent in 1970, 13.5 per cent in 1981–5 and 17.2 per cent in 1996–2001 (Fig. 2.2). In 2000–1, the State bought the majority of rice and wheat sold in India. The following year, it even procured 80 per cent of the wheat sold, so much so that the term '*de facto* nationalization' of trade began to be used more frequently. This cannot but discourage private investment in a storage, transportation, and distribution infrastructure, so badly needed in India.

It was felt that reducing controls meant reducing frauds. But in fact, it was only the nature of fraud that had changed. In the past, people avoided selling to or giving the state the grains they had produced. In 1974, for instance, when the traders had to sell part of their purchases from the markets (*mandi*) at a fixed price, they managed to cheat

> in connivance with the government officials but also by secret agreements and collusive deals with big landlords and farmers. Wheat sales outside the mandis were the order of the day. . . . In certain cases, as consumers were allowed to buy up to 5 quintals of wheat on their ration cards without being subjected to levy, fictitious deals, ostensibly in the name of consumers, were also made to evade the levy. . . . The prices fixed by the government did not take into account the quality of wheat. The traders exploited this loop-hole by buying inferior stuff from the market and delivering it as levy wheat. As single state zones were allowed to stay and the inter-state movement of wheat was allowed through permit, there was considerable stepping up of smuggling of grain from the surplus states to deficit states, with the connivance of anti-smuggling staff of the governments. The policy, as it developed, gave an upward impetus, quite unexpected, to the prices of cereals. (Chopra 1988: 195–6)

Indeed, there were frauds in the quantity, quality and destination of food grains, and these combined to produce results that were far from convincing.

As of 1980s, for the most part people want to sell to the state by any means possible, so long as procurement prices are higher than market prices. Traders pass themselves off as farmers. There are even sales of rice bought from PDS shops to the procurement! Thus, leakages remain significant, as we shall see, and the illicit flows are no less significant than in the past—only the direction changed.

(b) *State Intervention in the Consumer Market—The PDS*

The FCI's PDS is responsible for maintaining price stability and facilitating the availability of food for the poor, both under normal and deficit conditions. Historically, it was also its responsibility to compete with the private sector, accused of being filled with incorrigible speculators. However, it must be observed that apart from very large cities, which often remained exclusively under statutory rationing in the past, open markets prevailed.

The central government defines the issue price for each product, even for each quality of rice. The lower the issue price, the higher the purchases by households from the PDS, and the lower the prices in the open market. Apart from these medium-term interventions, the issue price can even smooth out the inter-seasonal instability of markets in the short term.

In the beginning, there was practically no subsidization of the issue price.[29] However, gradually, as the volume of public stocks to be sold increased, and out of real social concerns, systematic subsidies were introduced for the products to be distributed. The difference between the issue price and the overall procurement cost (procurement price + transport + storage costs) corresponds to the amount of the central consumption subsidy, i.e. 10–12 per cent during most years between 1970 and 1980.

However, this is not the final price. A state can, in fact, add its own subsidy or, on the contrary, include its own taxes and management costs in the price finally offered to the consumer. In fact, while it is the central government's responsibility to procure food grains and transport them to central warehouses, it is for the states to send food grain from the warehouses to the final consumers via their Food and Public Supply Departments.[30] In 1986, of the 10 major states, only Andhra Pradesh and Tamil Nadu offered prices that were lower than the federal price for rice, and Himachal Pradesh fixed its wheat price at the same level as that of the centre

(Tyagi 1990: 42). All other states imposed prices that were higher than the federal price (up to 33 per cent higher for rice in Orissa). It is true that many of them fixed their prices in accordance with local food habits: the rice-eaters of Andhra had their wheat heavily taxed, unlike Himachal's wheat eaters who had to pay more for eating rice.

Andhra Pradesh was the first state to establish a subsidy system, which was reinforced in 1983. Tamil Nadu and Karnataka, governed by parties other than the Congress, fell in too and offered more advantageous prices and monthly quotas to poor households. Although there were not many states that followed a similar policy until 1997, fairly considerable price differences emerged very soon between the different regions. These differences were far from being due to transportation costs, as shown by Map 2.8 that illustrates the PDS sale prices for 1994.

The two-tier subsidy system varies in degree according to the product sold. The PDS essentially offers wheat, rice, sugar, edible oils and kerosene. In some states and in certain seasons, other products could also be distributed (coal, clothes, etc.). Such a diversification was introduced during the 1971 war to provide supplies to Bangladeshi refugees. Other cereals were almost never made available through the PDS, because the quantities procured from farmers were too low and never crossed state borders. Thus, in 1999, the FCI allowed Madhya Pradesh and Maharashtra to distribute the 30 tonnes of pearl millet and 283 tonnes of sorghum that it had purchased there, within their own borders.

The Green Revolution played an important role in the development of the PDS, since one of the driving forces for productivity was state procurement. But once the state had purchased a product, it also needed to sell it. Thus, the PDS purpose was as much productive and economic as it was charitable and social. Increasingly, it was wheat produced in India that constituted the bulk and later the totality of sales. Rice was offered regularly for distribution once national production had reached an adequate level. From being temporary and urban, the PDS became permanent and universal.

Indians consume 35 to 40 per cent more rice than wheat. However, the national production/demand ratio is much lower for rice than wheat, while recourse to possible rice imports suffers due to the limited world market. Thus, distribution long remained focused on wheat, particularly during the PL 480 import period. In 1964, wheat accounted for 83 per cent of distribution. On the other hand, procurement concentrated on rice for a long time, in an unsuccessful attempt to try and limit the imbalance. From a wheat/rice/secondary cereals ratio of 21/63/16 in 1951, India gradually shifted to 9/73/18 in 1965, with several years showing no wheat procurement at all. Procurement proportions balanced out later with wheat production taking off and a reduction in imports. Parity was achieved for the first time in 1970 (wheat/rice/secondary cereals ratio at 47/45/7). In the 1980s, wheat tonnages were even slightly higher than those of rice. The proportions reversed in the 1990s (47/53/0 in 2000–1), more in tune with national food requirements (to the exception of millets): this is the proof of productivity gains in rice-growing areas.

The rise in production was just one factor leading to the increase in distribution. Another explanation of the growth of rice as compared to wheat was the choice for the first time in 1996 of a man from south India, H.D. Deve Gowda, as prime minister. Later there was the key role played by the Andhra party, TDP, between 1998 and 2004, in maintaining a coalition dominated by the BJP at the centre. Indeed, a certain readjustment in favour of southern rice-eating regions occurred, and the food system carried its stamp.

The overall growth of distribution in the early 1970s went hand in hand with high inflation in consumer prices, fuelled by the first oil crisis. Gandhian leaders such as Jayaprakash Narayan conducted a campaign on the issue. Between 1975 and 1977, Indira Gandhi set democracy aside to impose a state of emergency, which led to drastic controls over price hikes, often at the expense of human rights. In 1978, the opposition to the Congress party came to power for a short duration. Indira Gandhi's return in 1980 led to another spurt in distribution. Thus, crises and political events often resulted in the expansion of the distribution system so as to limit the nutritional impact of poverty as well as to get into the good graces of voters who could no longer be duped by the old political class.

The food crisis in the mid-1960s increased the number of PDS ration shops: 100,000 more between 1962 and 1967, as against 13,000 new ones opened between 1957 (when they were only 18,000) and 1962. Till then, in early 1960s, statutory rationing was supposed to prevail in all major cities and industrial centres, covering about 30 million persons, and mandatory distribution amounted to about 3 million tonnes per year. To this could be added 1.5 million for Kerala, 'where informal rationing closely approximated statutory rationing' (Dandekar 1994: 241). For the rest, non-statutory rationing, covering 245 million persons, could provide one million tonnes only if market prices were low or 10 million in the opposite case. As of 1976, with adequate public stocks, even without any major imports, it was possible to consider a significant increase in distribution. In 1976–7, while the state of emergency was at its peak and populism could easily go hand in hand with the liquidation of stocks, the Fair Price Shops (FPS) even offered wheat and flour without ration cards, and cash advances were offered to government officials so as to encourage them to buy!

The expansion of the PDS did not prevent its share in the net availability from falling, thanks to the increase in overall agricultural production. During the 1965–7 crisis, the PDS accounted for 19 per cent of marketed tonnages on an average, as against 15 per cent in 1988–90, though for much higher quantities distributed. Experts who predicted reduced dependence on the system thanks to the Green Revolution may, however, have been disappointed. In 1965, statutory rationing was reintroduced in all cities with a million plus population, and was only done away with officially in the 1990s in some towns in Bengal (a state both communist and industrial) and Bombay. The FPS continued to expand: 239,000 in 1979, 478,000 in 2004, some of which only function on paper. Thus, the quantities distributed per head also went up, from 12 kg in 1963 to 17 kg in biennial average 1973+1974, and 22 kg in 1988 + 1989, only to fall again during a crisis that we shall look at later (7 kg on an average in 2000–2). The quantities distributed after Independence (22 kg in 1951) re-emerged just a few years ago, but the situation was far from comparable, since the 1950s' averages concealed major disparities between the main cities and the rest of the population.

Balancing Space

(a) *How could the Entire Territory be Covered?*

'Now when grain stocks with the public agencies are ample here is the opportunity for the Government of India to see that all rural, backward, tribal, industrial, drought and flood affected areas in the entire length and breadth of the country-side are adequately served by, even saturated with, the fair price shops' said Chopra in 1988 (267).

India dealt with the issue of a regional balance in two ways. In principle, it was no doubt an important issue for the governments of a young and fragile nation. The PDS was one of the means of transforming geographical space into a united and well managed 'territory'. We shall deal in the fourth part with this concern to provide supplies to cover Indian territory through all possible kinds of flows in order to achieve spatial and national integration.

In reality, the actions taken corresponded to a series of choices made under political and logistical constraints. The choices consist of stocking up deficit areas, urban and then rural. The concern for giving mountain regions a special status and instituting special measures for fields other than food alone, is noticeable. These were Jammu & Kashmir, Himachal Pradesh, the future Uttarakhand, Sikkim, and the north-eastern states.[31] When the PDS seemed inadequate to deal with emergency or chronically difficult situations, programmes such as 'Food for Work' were developed and launched at the central level in 1977. Under this programme, wages were given partially in the form of food grains to the very needy, in exchange for their work on road repairs, constructing a canal, etc.

The constraints are first and foremost logistical. It may mean transporting bags of grain over more than 3,000 km in a developing country. The principal means, as we shall see, are the railways, with a particularly dense network in north India. Maps 2.5 and 2.6 show the great challenge posed by the extreme complexity of flows. For 1960–1, a year of major imports (5 million tonnes), we saw the arrival of food grains not just at the three main ports (Bombay, Calcutta, and Madras), but also Cochin, a strategic port given the huge rice requirements in Kerala. It was the volume of imports that accounted for the major portion of flows heading for the interiors. Two other elements were significant: first, the ubiquity of rice transportation as compared to wheat, much more concentrated in the northern parts of the country, given food preferences. Having said that, significant amounts of wheat imports were unloaded in Madras or in Andhra ports (Vishakhapatnam), for consumption in major southern coastal towns, since half a loaf was better than no rice. For want of an adequate international rice market and adequate national production for distribution in the entire country, southern people had to resign themselves to eating a few wheat chapattis.

The enormity of wheat imports explained the tonnage transported, contrasting with limited rice flows, which were mostly

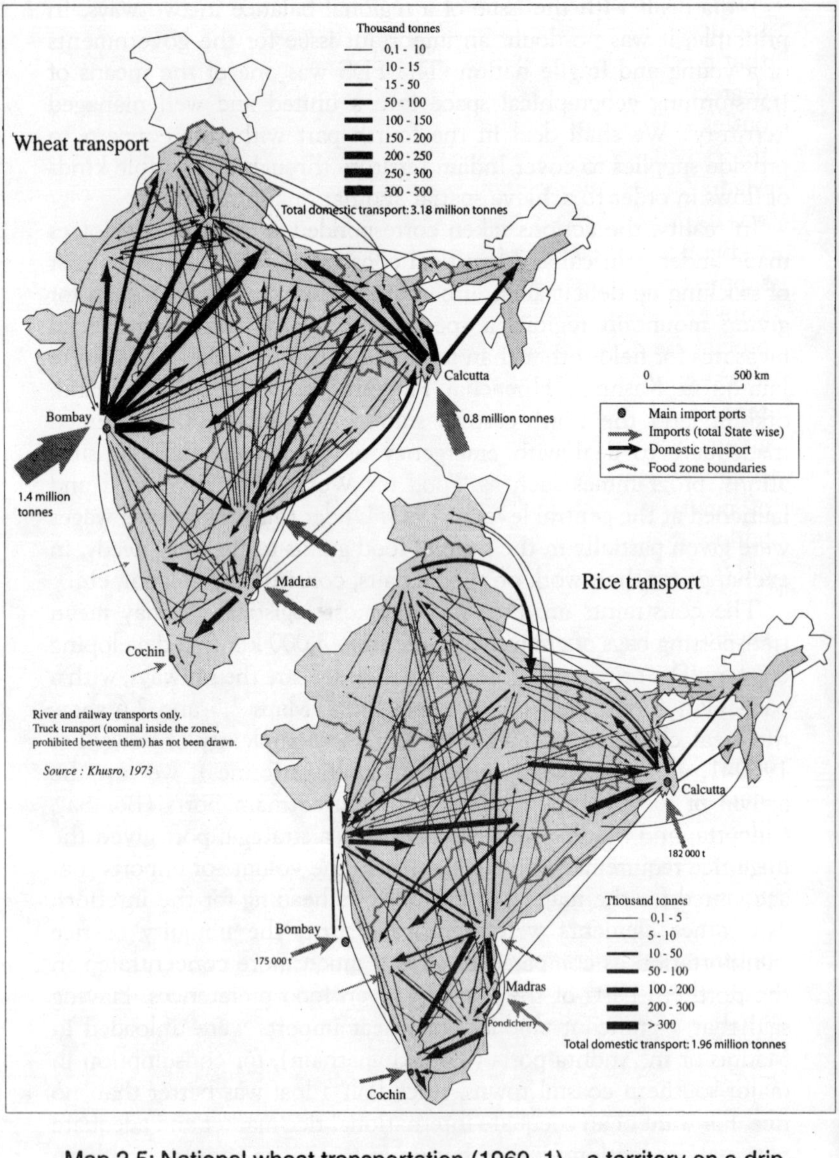

Map 2.5: National wheat transportation (1960–1)—a territory on a drip

Map 2.6: National rice transportatin (1960–1)—supplies to major cities a priority

supplied through the meagre national production. This also explains the dominant direction of wheat flows—from coasts to the interiors that needed supplies, while rice flowed in all directions to different degrees. The new port of Kandla (Gujarat), replacing Karachi as an outlet for Punjab, clearly did not enjoy the same importance as the Bombay port. The maps show how Bihar seemed to be fed by Madras, much more than Calcutta—proof that the railway system was used to somehow compensate for the congestion of the ports.

Besides, rice supplies has always been more scattered than wheat supplies. This can be seen in the two other maps (Map 2.7) on state procurement in the early 1980s. For reasons of climate, wheat procurement was concentrated in the northern half of India, as it was a winter crop. Punjab alone already accounted for 64 per cent of food grain purchases. The rice map is much more even, given a partial readjustment represented by Tamil Nadu and particularly Andhra Pradesh, and here Punjab accounts for 44 per cent of purchases. Indeed, the entire Indian territory contributed to building up rice stocks, though to different degrees. The situation did not change fundamentally subsequently.

If Punjab dominates the food map so extensively, it is surely because of its high agricultural productivity, as well as for climatic reasons. Indeed, it is part of the only region capable of producing both rice and wheat. Whatever the reason, the fact that the government does not purchase from the entire territory sufficiently shows the failure of its ambition to support prices. As we shall see, market integration in the four corners of the country is far too limited for rice procurement in Punjab to have repercussions in Maharashtra or Orissa. If the state does not intervene there, market prices can easily fall below the legal support price level.

Finally, the constraints on national integration practices are political in nature.

(b) '*Cooperative Disputes*'[32] *between the Centre and the States*

The Indian Constitution grants to the states the duty 'to raise the level of nutrition and the standard of living' (Art. 47). Agriculture and the taxes associated with it, as well as land issues, also fall within the states' purview according to the Seventh Schedule of the Constitution (Singh 1973). However, the latter remains fairly ambiguous, since the Concurrent List defining the subjects falling

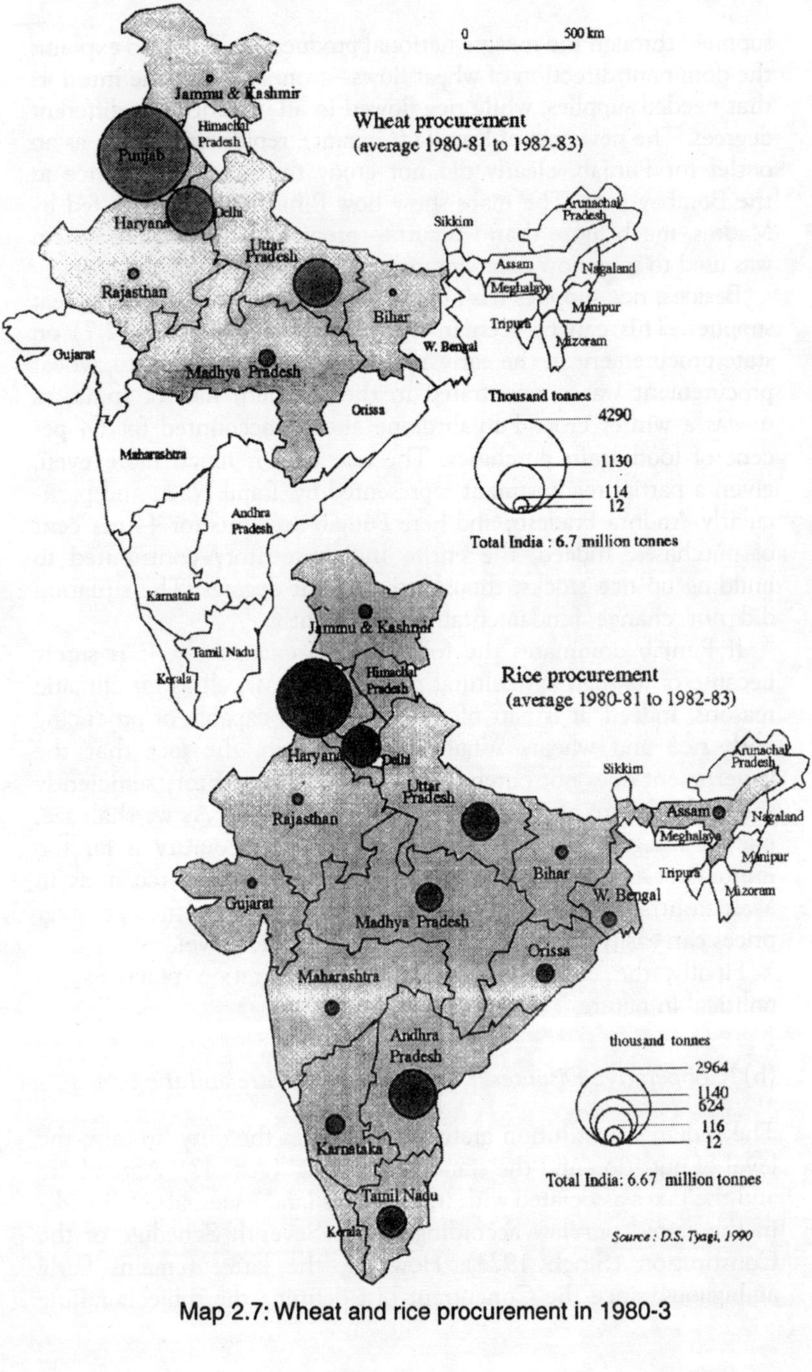

Map 2.7: Wheat and rice procurement in 1980-3

within the purview of both the centre and the states also mentions the 'production of . . . foodstuffs', which is nothing but agriculture. Moreover, Article 249 of the Constitution gives the central Parliament the power to 'legislate with respect to a matter in the State List in the national interest', without the notion of 'national interest' being defined more explicitly. As we have seen earlier, the Essential Commodities Act stems directly from this ambiguity.

In 2001, the states financed 68 per cent of public expenditure on 'agriculture and allied services' as against 32 per cent by the centre, and as much as 88 per cent on 'power, irrigation and flood control' (Rangarajan Srivastava 2004). Such ratios are deceptive, since a large portion of state budgets actually come from central grants. In fact, the states are greatly handicapped by the chronic lack of resources (in 2000–1, they only collected 41 per cent of revenue receipts, thanks above all to sales taxes).[33] Property taxes have not been revised for a long time and there are no taxes on farm income, except for plantations. In the 1990s, the states' own resources only funded 36 per cent of their expenditure (Kannan et al. 2004). Thus central transfers are essential. Finally, the federal system is relatively centralized and while the 'principle of subsidiarity' in India can be mentioned, it largely exists by default: the states enjoy freedom only in sectors that the centre does not seek to control. Among agricultural subsidies alone, those affecting food and fertilizers stem above all from the central budget, while water and electricity subsidies are paid by the states.

There are, however, three factors that undermine the great powers conferred upon the centre by the Constitution and the poverty of the states—factors that qualify, distort, filter or even cancel central decisions before they can actually be implemented in the field. Indeed, this is a form of entropy that prevents the centre from being a demiurge state, with three tiers and two dimensions (Figure 2.12).[34]

The first factor of entropy is the plural aspect of decision-making at the centre, where internal disputes can take place. Grossly speaking, in the case of the food policy, there is the Ministry of Food, seeking the lowest prices possible, as opposed to the Ministry of Agriculture, seeking to increase farm prices at the risk of making food prices rocket, and the Ministry of Finance, looking at what all this would cost (Nawani 1995). If we were to add the Ministry of Trade's own logic with regard to import-export, to say nothing of

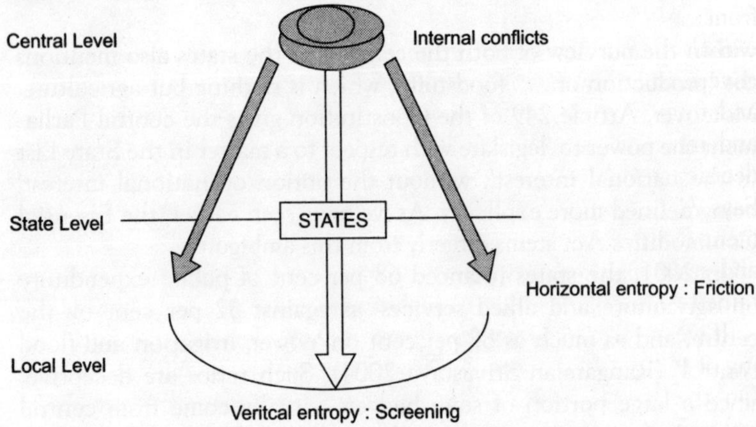

Figure 2.12: The dual entropy of governments

differences of personal, partisan, or ideological opinions, we would see that as in any other government, there is here a high degree of heterogeneity in what is called the 'central government' too.[35]

The second factor of entropy has to do with the vertical dimension: from Delhi to the district level and then to individuals, there are several filters that can negate decisions taken at the federal level, engendering major transaction costs, not just because of the corruption and malfunctioning specific to bureaucracy, but because the Constitution recognizes a large number of powers and counterpowers. Administrative and political personnel are well entrenched in the four corners of India—the result of a development model that was meant to be both planned as well as democratic. But their omnipresence paradoxically makes it difficult to implement decisions from the top. 'It should be recognized that India consists of 26 governments, one at the centre and the rest in the States' wrote Guhan (1995: 73). Three new states have been created since then and the seven Union Territories enjoy some autonomy. Federal transfers are not targeted, thereby making it difficult for the centre to control their use by the states.

The third factor corresponds to horizontal entropy engendered by distance—not institutional distance as in the preceding case, but physical distance. This has three components—simple geographical distance, since connecting the Nagaland hills to the capital is far from easy; secondly, political distance, because the same Nagaland can also face extensive disturbances, 'ethnic struggles', or merely a government ideologically opposed to the government in Delhi;[36] and finally, socio-economic distance, when local cultures, values, and interests are too different from the general norm for central decisions to correspond to regional requirements and potentials. Says Acharya (1983: 214), 'Food represents that sensitive department of administration where the delicate framework of the centre and state relations enshrined in the Constitution has to be maintained with utmost care, thought, and ingenuity.'

If we were to examine centre-state relations in the very functioning of the food machinery, we would observe the same ambivalence. On the surface, the centre enjoys undisputed primacy over the states. Price proposals by the Agricultural Prices and Costs Commission are discussed by a chief ministers' assembly, but it is the federal government that takes the final decision. Quality norms—and for long, the quantities to be purchased—are also fixed by the centre. Pending distribution, 'operational stocks' are partially in the hands of the states, but safety 'buffer stocks' continue to be administered solely by the FCI.

Before the FCI was set up in 1965, the states were the primary actors in procurement, under the supervision of the Food Department in Delhi, which delegated Regional Directors of Food to the states. When they purchased food grains for their own needs, the latter asked the State Bank of India for credit, but when they wished to add to federal stocks, they received an advance from the centre (Varshneya 1969). Such practices continued even when the states set up their own food offices, miniature versions of the FCI called Food and Civil Supplies Corporations. Only some of these offices (Andhra Pradesh, Himachal Pradesh, Madhya Pradesh, Tamil Nadu, Punjab, Kerala, Karnataka, Bihar) survived food grain abundance. Yet even today they carry out procurement on credit, since it is the FCI that reimburses the bulk of the expenditure. But the latter also has supervisory powers over them and only reimburses what it deems legitimate. Thus the states are not completely free to fix the various taxes on markets, commissions to intermediaries and other charges that come up in the purchase and storage processes under the procurement system. If they fix them too high, they run the risk of not being reimbursed fully by the FCI. Needless to say, discussions are often bitter, given the states' budgetary difficulties and their need for fiscal resources, and also given the FCI's efforts to cut costs in the face of criticism about its lack of effectiveness.[37]

In fact, till the 1980s, most states were faced by a serious dilemma: 'to collect grain for distribution in needy pockets within the state itself but also to establish their bonafide earnestness with the Government of India, with a view to being able to get reasonable allotments of cheaper grain from the central pool' (Chopra, 1988: 236). The fact that until 1976 the centre often added a bonus for the states, proportional to their procurements, was an additional incentive. Nevertheless, New Delhi kept wary about the importance of a national feeling in these states, which were suspected of regionalism.

In fact there was a major difference between surplus states in which procurement did not raise problems (being in the interest of the farmers) and deficit states that were barely self-sufficient and therefore any procurement—no matter how limited—could only be achieved by coercion. In times of scarcity, it was not easy for the central administration to convince the states to stick to the principle of national solidarity rather than meet the requirements of their own population. In fact, many chief ministers did their best to deliver the least possible amount of food grain to the central pool so as not to generate any deficit in their own state to the benefit of the other regions. In the 1950s, Tamil Nadu and Andhra Pradesh used to impose a levy of no more than 10 or 20 per cent on rice millers. Until the 1970s many states distributed the food grains they themselves had procured among their own populations, without delivering them to the federal government. In 1967–8, for instance, up to 68 per cent of wheat procurement was carried out for the benefit of the states and only 32 per cent for the central pool; up to 60 per cent of the rice procurement was also for the states themselves (Chopra 1988). These percentages fell with the increase in the FCI's authority.

But the latter did not have the means to control the entire system directly. 'The extent to which the FCI is permitted to operate in the markets for purchasing stocks varies from state to state ; and within the state, from grain to grain. [In the early 1980s], in Andhra Pradesh, Madhya Pradesh and Rajasthan, procurement of rice, as well as price support purchases of paddy, are almost handled by the FCI. In Punjab and Haryana, the state agencies handle 65 and 80 per cent of wheat respectively, the balance being left to the FCI.

In Uttar Pradesh practically all the rice procurement is done in the first instance by the state agencies' (Acharya 1983: 224–5). It was obviously in the latter case that the states could play their cards more easily.

Since the FCI did not itself enjoy institutional power over the states, it could only count on the centre's authority to carry out its task. Furthermore, theoretically, it had no power over food grain transportation between states—in the first instance, the latter remained responsible for procurement operations carried out within their borders. 'While the food policy is laid down by the central government, it is implemented by the states' (Acharya 1983: 219). Every cog in the machinery, as small as it may be, is vital to the system for functioning. . . .

Other practices used by the states were made possible by the confusion that reined between stocks purchased for the states' own needs and stocks procured for the FCI. Thus, some states sold a part of their stocks to other states at open market prices, thereby making a profit, while using the food grains provided by the PDS for local consumption (Acharya 1983). (Incidentally, we shall see that these practices were no different from individual practices at the local level, where PDS shop managers engaged in similar misappropriations of food grain by selling it on the open market.) A part of the problem was resolved once self-sufficiency was achieved. The states found it much easier to rely on central stocks rather than ensure the replenishment of their stocks by themselves. Their budget lightened and consumers lost nothing, since federal distribution was now increasingly subsidized. Only the FCI's expenditure went up, because it now had to pay for more food grain to be distributed.

However, other problems arose—for instance, the quality of food grains. In times of abundance, the centre has the means to be more punctilious about what it purchases. Surplus states do not want the centre to be too strict with regard to procurement quality norms, while deficit states curse the food grains supplied under the PDS, which are sometimes barely edible. Food grain quality proves to be both a major issue and a pretext. That is why it is a legal practice for state corporations not to pay the exact procurement price to farmers if the food grain delivered is not of standard quality. But that does not prevent such corporations from sometimes providing the same food grains to the FCI by passing them off as conforming to standard, in order to obtain the full procurement prices and pocket the difference. The states may declare, though often with good reason, that the FCI has delayed taking possession of the food grains and that they have deteriorated in the interim. The states then claim both the full procurement price as well as reimbursement for additional storage charges (Acharya 1983). Their recriminations are much sharper if they discover that the food grains later delivered by the FCI for distribution in their states are not of the prescribed quality. The FCI would then retort that the fault lies in the procurement . . . and it all comes full circle.

Generally speaking, till the late 1990s the states were accused of dragging their feet in implementing the procurement and storage process. Totally dependent on the FCI for distribution now, most states, barring a few, lack the motivation to carry out complex purchase, transportation, and storage operations—except if their farmers push them to offer real support for their farm prices. Perhaps one of the system's main problems has been its legacy of a period when the states were mostly supplied by food grains procured within their own territory, and thus sought to achieve effective procurement. So the FCI still delegates procurement to certain states and therefore needs their cooperation, while the latter, without much responsibility or policy-making freedom now, are limited to executing tasks that are not very inspiring and yet constraining. (As we shall see below, since 1997 and the difficult starting of 'decentralized procurement', the margin of manoeuvre of some states is now much higher.)

Some states—initially governed by non-Congress parties for the most part—set up subsidy systems that were reinforced from the 1980s onwards (Tamil Nadu, Andhra Pradesh, Karnataka, and later Gujarat). PDS products were available at reduced prices and in quantities higher than those provided by the centre. This can be seen in Map 2.12—some states added their subsidies to those offered by New Delhi, while others (much more numerous) did not intervene or even imposed a tax by fixing a price that was much higher than the central issue price. The generous states adopted policies that were social, or even populist in nature. These were states that were relatively rich (or ready to be indebted) and endowed with a distribution network and a relatively effective administration, though all these criteria rather limited their number. Such measures corresponded to a new perception of the food issue. 'In the 1960s and 1970s, food policy supported industrial development and agrarian production. It was only in the 1980s that food and food programmes became an obvious element of political opportunism. In the 1970s, populist slogans meant to catch votes had to do with poverty, not with food directly' (Mooij 1999: 235). The social aspect was actually missing in the food policy until the 1980s, especially with regard to poor rural consumers who were hardly targeted by any of the measures implemented. Drawing a line between an aggressive social policy and populism is, in any case, never easy (Mooij 2002).

The fact remains that the centre was both much farther from the voters than the states, and much closer than them to international players, whether the latter were powerful countries (US), creditors (IMF), or markets (world agricultural prices). Thus, the centre tended to follow a more 'responsible' policy as against the states that could afford to be 'populist', especially since the central administration failed to restrict their strong tendencies towards indebtedness and budget deficits. So did international donors: Andhra Pradesh was the first state to sign a structural adjustment programme with the World Bank in 1999, while it had followed a costly food policy till then.

Such political choices by states often compromise the principle of national solidarity. This is because in financial terms, the states' food system is rarely viable and it falls to the central government to reduce indebtedness. During times of relative scarcity, Andhra Pradesh over-subsidizing rice and thereby facilitating its consumption among its population, even in areas where millet is preferred, is pretty badly viewed because this can reduce exports to other states, endangering food supplies to many Indian citizens.

National Integration or Regionalist Disintegration? State Rivalries

Constituencies were established only to facilitate the administration of the kingdom. But they cannot make one province foreign to another or destroy the unity binding different localities, which makes France a whole and its inhabitants one single family. (. . .) Scarcity in one area and overabundance in another would be the outcome of a mistake the government would commit by tolerating attacks on the free movement of products.

Resolution circulated among *préfets* [district officers] by the French Richelieu government, 1816. (quoted by Bourguinat, 2001, p. 141)

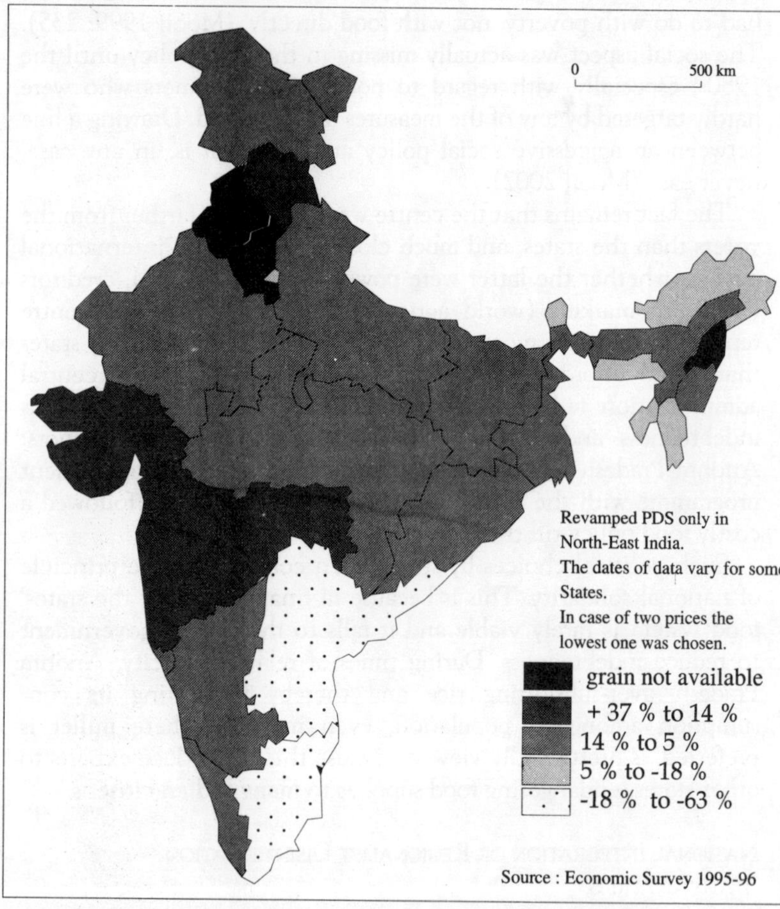

Map 2.8: Common quality rice prices in FPS in relation to Central Issue Prices (February 1994)

Such vertical conflicts undoubtedly exist in all countries. But they appear particularly significant here because of the federal character of the Indian Union, and the strategic character of food products also plays a role. During times of relative scarcity, relations between the central and local powers tended to become strained, each claiming to 'play its own game' for fear of depriving itself either in favour of the centre or a neighbouring local power. Hence, in a country as centralized as France in early nineteenth century, while prefects (district officers) were generally favourable to economic liberalism, they were divided over whether it was better to be mere cogs in the imperial and later royal machinery established in Paris (and *for* Paris above all), or to take the side of their district and ensure social peace locally (Bourguinat 2001). In 1812, Napoleon forced them to fix floor prices for wheat. Prefects who imposed a relatively lower price because they believed their department to be sufficiently well endowed saw their wheat disappear in favour of departments offering more attractive prices. So the bonus sometimes goes to those who are more selfish, and it is not always gratifying to act in the national interest.

Finally, in nineteenth century France and contemporary India, the same opposition between two perceptions of the national territory seems to exist. The first, that of Paris and New Delhi, perceives districts and states as sub-sets of the national space—mere elements in the food grain market's long food chain, parts of an integrated (or to be integrated) whole, and not territories with their own needs. The centre views districts and states only in terms of their food grain status—whether surplus or deficit. They 'have become abstract, defined by a degree of variation in relation to a norm' (Bourguinat 2001: 136). On the contrary, in the light of the second perception of the national space, prefects and more so chief ministers refuse to function merely as adjuncts to the centre. They claim to represent much more than mere squares in the national chessboard and defend the interests of the territory they command.

Thus, the tensions that emerge go much beyond the issue of food grains. It is a certain political philosophy that is at stake, 'unity in diversity'. Likewise, the efforts that were required for Paris to distribute wheat throughout post-Revolution France thereby creating a uniform territory were the same as those involved in the recent carving-out of districts or the establishment of a single system of weights and measures—all in the name of an 'integrating representation of the national space', which 'trade flows made transparent both to the eye and to more detailed analysis' (Bourguinat, 2001: 137–46). At the state and district levels, on the contrary, there are several leaders ready to take up a 'food morality' of their own, claiming that their primary responsibility is that of ensuring the well-being of the inhabitants under their charge.

Finally, the issue of relations between the centre and states is coupled with the problem of relations among the states themselves. Farmers from surplus regions have an ambivalent attitude that changes depending on prevailing prices. In the event of scarcity, or low world prices, large-scale Punjabi farmers are proud of being able to 'feed the nation'—a pride coupled with the satisfaction of selling their produce to the state at a guaranteed price. On the other hand, in the event of significant national surpluses and high world prices, the same farmers curse when the state balks at implementing the procurement price in time, and demand that they should be able to make the most of the international situation by exporting their food grain more easily. They then accuse deficit states of sponging off them. The case of Kerala was often highlighted by the powerful north Indian farmers' unions, such as the Bharatiya Kisan Union, as Kerala's paddy fields are converted to the benefit of cash crops. Especially when world prices are favourable, these export crops allow planters to make profits by making the most of cheap rice from Andhra Pradesh or even Punjab. The discontent then shifts to the centre, which is accused of favouritism. *Thanks* to its food grain deficit that allows it to plant coffee or rubber, doesn't Kerala fill India's coffers with foreign exchange?

When N.T. Rama Rao, Andhra Pradesh's charismatic Chief Minister, decided to sell a kilo of rice for just Rs. 2 in 1983, it was partly because of his refusal to feed 'outsiders' (non-Telugu states). He considered that it was much better to make the most of the state's productivity gains to galvanize the local PDS or to institute free meals in schools rather than subsidize food for states such as Kerala, although it too was governed by a non-Congress party (Olsen 1989; Venugopal 1992). Hence, Andhra Pradesh was the first state to add its subsidy to the one offered by the centre. Budget costs undoubtedly rose, since along with consumer support, production support too was offered, as the state found itself obliged to purchase food grains in excess of the quantity supplied by the FCI to feed its now vast distribution channels.

Other schools of thought conversely denounce the preferential treatment that states with high procurement prices enjoy, at least during years of abundance. The 1990s were marked by an increase in the real value of food grain prices in India, without any relation whatever to world price trends, as the government had fixed high procurement prices in order to satisfy the farm lobbies of Punjab and Andhra Pradesh. The fact that many farmers in these states were poor and depended on state procurement for their survival should not make us forget that, by the same token, the centre encouraged the perpetuation of crop rotations that were economically unprofitable, ecologically non-sustainable, and socially highly unfavourable for consumers as they pushed PDS prices as well as open market prices upwards. We shall come back to this issue later. But it may be added that in the 1980s, the harshness of New Delhi's response in the face of the claims of Sikh Khalistan militants could also be explained by the importance of Punjab (with its Sikh majority) as the nation's breadbasket.

NOTES

1. Most of the information for the 1943–91 period comes from Knight (1954), Bhatia (1991), Dandekar (1994), Dantwala (1996), Venugopal (1992) and Chopra (1988).
2. http://fcamin.nic.in/ecpbacts.htm#ESSENTIAL COMMODITIES ACT, 1955.
3. 'It is a tragic sight to see India's representatives going from one end of the earth to another—literally from Persia to Peru—with the begging bowl in their hands for food which she ought to be able to produce', bemoaned the Food Minister in 1946 (quoted by Chopra 1988: 58).
4. In those days, a distinction was made between 'ration shops' corresponding to 'statutory rationing' and 'fair price shops (FPS)' for 'informal rationing'. Today, statutory rationing has been done away with, but the term 'ration shop' is still commonly used.
5. In Bihar, which suffered a famine in August 1967, rice prices were four times those prevailing in Haryana (Drèze 1995). Cf. comparison with control measures imposed in 1984 in Kenya, described by Drèze and Sen (1989: 91).
6. Maharashtra avoided a famine in 1973 thanks to a public works system in which labourers were paid in cash, which covered 5 million people at the height of the crisis. But it was private trade that compensated for the gaps in the PDS by supplying grain that the employment programme's

beneficiaries were able to purchase (one billion workdays created in 1972–3!). The approximately 30,000 FPS were, in fact, far from able to distribute 12 kg per head per month. This is all the more remarkable since at the time, the ban on inter-state trade should have hindered the entry of grain into Maharashtra, but the state administration—which had protested the imposition of a food zone by the centre—closed its eyes to the smuggling, which was both very useful and, for some officials, extremely lucrative (Drèze 1995).

7. Hence, procurement accounted for 7 per cent of the total food grain production, a percentage that would only be exceeded in 1971–2.
8. An element in defence of the PL 480 agreement, however, may be found in this note of caution by Drèze and Sen (1989 : 25) concerning 'the temptation—to which it seems easy to succumb—to replace the old error of concentrating *only* on food output and availability by a new error of ignoring altogether the influence of output and availability on the entitlements of different sections of the population'.
9. There were four procurement prices, depending on the grade of wheat, and different prices according to rice varieties.
10. Between 1965 and 1968, wheat imports corresponded to 54 per cent of the production on an average. In 1966, the PDS accounted for more than 19 per cent of the net availability of grains, a percentage that would never again be achieved. In 1964 and in 1965, imports would account for almost three-quarters of the food grains distributed by the State.
11. In 2003, hybrid rice in India made less than 15 per cent of areas under rice cultivation. No hybrid wheat is commercially cultivated in the world.
12. Cf. Maps published in 'The socio-ecology of groundwater', http://www.iwmi.cgiar.org/waterpolicybriefing/index.asp.
13. The number of farmers was twice that of industrialists and traders in the first Lok Sabha in 1951, three times in 1957, five times in 1971 and 9 times in 1977 (Mooij 1999). As many as 52 per cent of the MPs elected in 1996 called themselves farmers.
14. At the same time, the FAO recommended stocks corresponding to 17 to 18 per cent of consumption, or 5 to 6 per cent 'reserves' (buffer stocks) and 12 per cent of 'pipeline' (operational stocks) at the world level. Indian buffer stocks were defined as exceeding this norm (around 14 per cent) in order to ensure two months of wheat distribution.
15. Intra-urban agriculture is much less developed in India than, say, in Africa.
16. As testimony, we can quote the yearbook of colonial origin, *Inter-State*

Movements/Flows of Goods by Rail, River and Air. This extraordinary document, which is the source of Maps 2.5, 2.6, 3.19, and 3.20, is presented as a matrix of 38 rows and columns for 78 products. For each of the 38 'trading blocks' (states or parts of states), inflows and outflows are noted. Thus ceased publication in 2001 as economic liberalization no longer allowed for valid statistics for most products.

17. This that has been its name since 2000.
18. In 1987–8, including the infrastructure in the states, there were 4,417 procurement centres for rice and 7,800 for wheat.
19. Its first chairman was the economist, M.L. Dantwala, who had spent almost four years of his youth in prison during the struggle against British colonisation. Achieving independence in food grains was, in a sense, a continuation of his former political struggle. His personal path was representative of the intellectual and political development of his times, which could not conceive of political independence without economic independence.
20. For the 1990s, studied by Acharya (2001), this was true for just 38 per cent of the *kharif* and 75 per cent of the *rabi* sowings.
21. 'The coefficient of variation of rice and wheat prices in India has been contained to 4 to 7 per cent during the last twenty years as against 15 to 25 per cent observed in world prices' (*High Level Committee*, 2000, §1.8).
22. Today, there is just one support price defined for the entire country. For rice, different prices had been fixed for each variety and each state up to 1979–80. It was later that the central government standardized prices by limiting itself to three categories of rice (common, fine, and superfine).
23. Since the world rice market is much smaller than that of wheat, prices are higher.
24. Procurement from regulated markets made it possible to limit price hikes, triggered by state intervention. In Punjab, where these were highly developed, the state purchased wheat on the basis of a pre-emptive system once market prices were established by solely the interplay of private actors (Dandekar 1994: 234).
25. Farmers had to sell this share to the nearest market (*mandi*), or the procurement administration was carried out from door to door. 'The police and the revenue inspector used to visit us in the night. It was procurement at gunpoint, which exists nowhere else in the world. It was just like the movies. They came like a gang of dacoits [robbers], and they left our houses after they had seized what they wanted', a farmer leader informed Mooij (1999: 76).
26. Other years experienced mere variants or combinations of the four

modes given below. However, an original form of procurement emerged in Maharashtra in 1975–6 for wheat, with sales imposed in accordance with the property tax paid by the farmer. The system was extended the following year to coarse grains.

27. In the mid-1960s, Maharashtra instituted the public monopoly of rice and sorghum procurement. For the record, Dandekar's highly bureaucratic project (1994: 280–9) must be noted, which in 1967 proposed to establish in each district an office that would hold a monopoly over inter-district food grain trade.
28. Till then, roller flour mills had to obtain administrative authorization to purchase wheat from the markets.
29. The wheat and rice issue prices remained almost always higher than the CIF cost of imports until the first oil crisis (Acharya 1983).
30. Arrangements varied extensively, depending on the period and the state. Around 1980, the FCI was responsible for managing retail distribution in Madhya Pradesh, Andhra Pradesh, West Bengal, Rajasthan, Kerala and Delhi, while it was the State Corporations' role in Haryana, Gujarat, Uttar Pradesh, Maharashtra, Karnataka, and Punjab (Acharya 1983).
31. Thus, in 1999, while the federal government did not provide for access to common quality rice by 'non-poor' households in the rest of India, the same did not hold true for these states. Further, rice was supplied to the states at a central issue price of just Rs. 7 per kg, i.e. 23 per cent less expensive than in the plains (*Hindu Business Line*, 1.2.1999).
32. Oxymoron used by Drèze and Sen (1989).
33. As Arshad Zaman (Pakistani Planning Commission member) said during a symposium in Paris in 1998: 'Pakistani Provinces want autonomy for their expenditures but they want dependence for their resources'. Such ambiguity also exist in the Indian Union—or in fact, even in the European Union.
34. This diagram does not show the powerful non political actors (merchants, business lobbies, Reserve Bank of India, etc.) who aggravate the entropy of governments—and sometimes contribute to the choice, design, and implementation of policies (Harriss-White 1996).
35. Such antagonisms are of course present even in state governments among different ministries. Furthermore, transfers and credits allocated by the centre or from elsewhere often overlap with state projects (Singh 1973).
36. It is not merely by chance that the three often communist-ruled states are three peripheral states (Kerala, West Bengal, Tripura).

37. For the FCI, transporting food grains from one state to another involves transportation costs as well as tax expenditure. In fact, each state imposes different taxes that the FCI has to pay, particularly a sales tax. The tax rose in the 1970s from 0 to 7 per cent in Haryana (Acharya 1983). The central government had to put an end to it, and in 1976 a central law imposed a ceiling on sales tax on all essential products, especially food grains.

CHAPTER 3

Assessment Time—The Persistence of Inequalities, 1991–2007

RECONCILING ECONOMIC LIBERALIZATION WITH STATE CONTROL

The structural adjustment programme signed with the IMF and the World Bank in 1991, followed by entry into the WTO when it was set up in 1995, in quick succession, reinforced a process that had been set in motion in the late 1980s—economic liberalization combined with an assumed place in globalization (Bhalla et al. 2002). Henceforth, the problem was much less the availability of food grain than the budgetary cost of the food policy. Food grain self-sufficiency had been achieved and 'comfort' imports seemed no longer very difficult to manage, given the international environment. On a more economic and financial level, two types of criticism developed (Mooij 1999a). On the one hand, State expenditure was now more rigorously scrutinized and the food system soon came under fire. Conversely, another school of thought stressed the importance of the PDS as a 'safety net' so long as structural adjustment increased poverty. While the former wished to dismantle the system, the latter sought to consolidate it. But almost no one wanted to leave it unchanged.

Starting with this ambiguous situation, it was even more difficult to make the right choices. 'The inherent "genius" of India loves compromises. India's food policy . . . was a "via media" solution between the two extremes of complete "laissez faire" of the private grain trade and the complete monopoly of that trade in the hands of the government in the public sector' (Chopra 1988: 349). The private sector has never been completely ousted. In fact, it plays the role of a partner (albeit an obedient one) of the state machinery. Indeed, some part of public stocks are stored in private warehouses, the rice-mills delivering part of their production to the state are private, as are the roller flour mills though the latter have worked with public wheat for over two decades,[1] not to speak of most FPS managers, the trucks transporting food grains and gunny-sack suppliers.

However, generally speaking, to the 1990s the government officially controlled a large part of food grain trade directly or indirectly. The centre had full monopoly over international trade. Food grain exports were generally prohibited, except for basmati rice. As for imports, they were 'canalized' through public entities. Within the country, the states aspired to control the maximum of circuits as well as transactions between producers and consumers. Thus, the bulk of the measures taken by the centre and the states were 'anti-mercantilist' in essence (Harriss-White 1996). Government trading, because of the capillarity of its extremely finely-meshed networks—or so it was claimed—linking the administration to the remotest of villages, sought to supply and siphon off farm products to and from the remotest of villages, while possibly linking them to international trade. Grants to cooperatives and the establishment of regulated markets sought to reduce the role of intermediaries between producers and consumers, so that the former would benefit from maximum prices and the latter from minimum prices.

From this perspective, the state was partly successful. If international comparisons of domestic prices mean anything, we can affirm that 'price spreads between the consumer and producer are not too excessive given the poor infrastructure and low holding power of farmers ; for example, in 1999 Indian farmers received about 30 per cent more for wheat than US farmers while Indian urban consumers paid only a fourth [at purchasing power parity] for a loaf of bread as their US counterparts' (High Level Committee 2002: § 2.3.1). On the other hand, some of the hypotheses that were not taken into consideration when the food machinery was being built were that the state's role led to rigidity and malfunctioning at least as much as integration with national or international trade, and that restrictions on private storage accentuated price fluctuations instead of reducing them.

The government faced a new problem with the diversification of marketed products and the complication of circuits due to modernization and urbanization. Further controls became necessary. Hence, a certain 'institutional fission' (Harriss-White 1996) was engendered by the large number of corporations specializing in different products (such as the Cotton Corporation of India set up in 1970), or in certain stages of the production chain (the Central or State Warehousing Corporations for storage). Coordination problems between public-sector organizations also occurred with regard to regulated markets. Currently, there are 7,000 of them all over India. But they were unable to constitute a counterweight to the abuses inflicted by private trade in rural areas, failing in particular to eliminate the need for small farmers to borrow from traders or brokers to prepare for the following year, or to obtain consumer credit.[2] It was only in 2003 that commission agents playing a key role as middlemen were prohibited in regulated markets by a Central Act.

The ever-increasing cost of these structures and their inefficacy did not prevent the food machinery from growing, obtaining more credit, or incorporating new segments. There were three factors at play: the interest of all bureaucracies in reproducing themselves; the interests of private companies or individuals, in making the most of the food mechanism through different kinds of misuse of public property; and also the well-ingrained belief among government officials that the state was responsible for organizing product flows while respecting optimal social and spatial equity. The second factor, corruption, is undoubtedly fundamental, but it well be that the third—a generous, but rather naïve ideology—still remained valid, though to a lesser degree.

On the whole, there is no question of abolishing regulated markets in India—only of developing private channels concurrently: that was the point of the State Agricultural Produce Marketing (Development & Regulation) Act, 2003, which enabled the creation of private wholesale markets competing with regulated markets. Large specialized corporations lost their influence (the Cotton Corporation only has an 8 per cent market share), but continue to remain in place, encouraged by the government to take on commercial operations regardless of their public-service functions. Sugar quotas that refineries are supposed to sell to the state at a fixed price were progressively decreased to 10 per cent of their production—but a minimum price is always guaranteed to farmers. As for international trade, in 2000 you still needed a special permit to export rice. Wheat was subject to an export quota and a minimum price (Dorin and Landy forthcoming). In 2007 exports of non-basmati rice and wheat were banned.

MIXED RESULTS

In 1999–2000, NSSO surveys revealed a major north-south disparity, with northern regions consuming less food grain overall than they produced. Another look at the map of exporting provinces in 1937–40 (Map 1.5) would show that such an imbalance existed *mutatis mutandis* even before Independence. The similarity between Maps 3.1 and 3.2 showing the state-wise production/consumption balance, whether for rice or wheat, is also remarkable. Only West Bengal and Himachal Pradesh do not enjoy the same status in the two maps. That is because the north-west produces both rice and wheat, while it mostly consumes wheat. In other words, the north-western states produce a lot of rice, but do not consume much, while the southern states eat a lot of rice without producing any wheat.

The conjunction of agriculture and food explains the importance of the north-west. The supremacy of Punjab-Haryana in terms of production and productivity constitutes the agricultural angle. The food angle is that these two states are culturally defined by *roti*—pancake-shaped bread made of wheat (*chapattis*) or, for the poorest, of maize. Given this fact, the considerable paddy production (greater today in Punjab than that of wheat!) cannot be sold in the state itself nor in the upper Ganga plain, but necessarily in eastern and southern India. Conversely, productivity in south India and the deltas, major rice producers, is not too high, and their produce is essentially consumed by the farmers themselves, or even by the farm labour paid in food grain. In fact, one-third of the rice produced in these regions is marketed, as against 99 per cent in Punjab.

At the all India level, this means that deficit states dominate spatially over surplus states. The spatial concentration of surpluses is high, especially as regards wheat. However, in the case of rice, West Bengal started producing surplus quantities, and Tamil Nadu and Andhra Pradesh are not far behind.

Thus, the procurement/distribution pair simply perpetuates an ancient situation, without restoring the regional balance. And that is not the least of the criticism that can be made for these two components of the system.

Reappraising Procurement

Procurement had taken on considerable importance (Fig. 3.1). If an estimated 40 per cent of the food grain produced is marketed, the

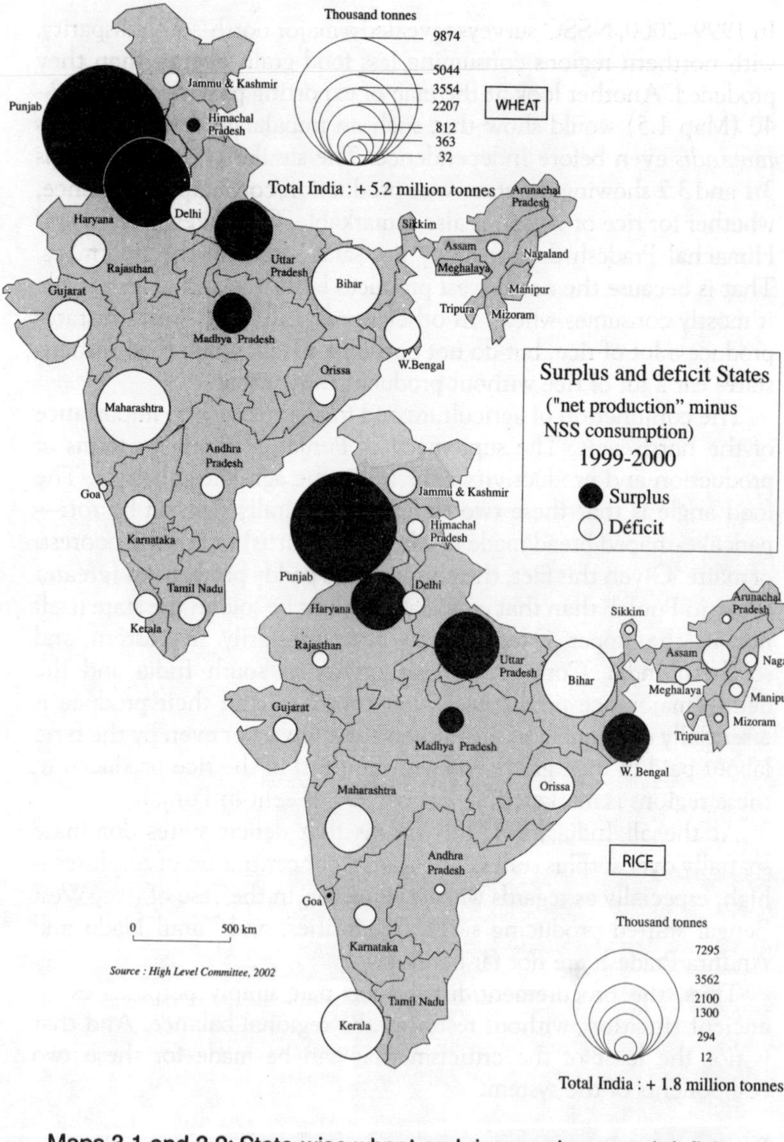

Maps 3.1 and 3.2: State-wise wheat and rice surpluses and deficits

	Percentage of procurement in net food grain production	*Percentage of public distribution in net availability*
1951–9	3.4	7.1
1960–9	4.8	10.8
1970–9	9.7	10.6
1980–9	13.1	12.8
1990–9	14.7	10.8
2000–3	22.1	16.7

Notes: net production = production less 12.5 per cent on account of seeds, losses and animal food.
net availability = net production + net exports + stocks.
Between 1978 and 1990, Food for Work programmes were included in 'distribution'.

Source: 2003–4 *Economic Survey.*

Figure 3.1: Share of public channels in food grain production and availability

state managed until recently to procure almost half the tonnage on the market. (Procurement dropped in 2006 due to the liberalization of markets and sales by farmers to private companies.) So it is easy to see that a dual problem of concentration is being reinforced.

(a) *Concentration in Time*

Inter-annual contingencies remain marked. Fig.2.2 highlights deficit as well as surplus years (from 1979 onwards, and then 1985, 1996, and 2000–3 in particular), which were also cumbersome for the state because it was difficult to get rid of large stocks without losing money. The fact that for wheat and rice, support and procurement prices are identical, obliges the administration to make costly purchases in surplus years. When public stocks of the preceding year are considerable, private traders fear that these food grains will be dumped on the markets and do not purchase much the following year, which further increases state stocks, creating a sort of a vicious circle (Tyagi 1990).

Intra-annual concentration makes that almost two-thirds of India's food grains reach the market from the kharif crop, against one-third from the rabi harvest. The establishment of high procurement prices only consolidates the trend. In Punjab, in 1961–2, 52 per cent of wheat arrivals were concentrated between April and

June. In 1970–1, the figures stood at 70 per cent, and at 92 per cent in 1979–80, as against an average of 70 per cent for the whole of India (Tyagi 1990). For rice, the market influx period is October to December, but there is less concentration in time because of climatically heterogeneous production zones, since rice has to be processed in various stages and because of the existence of various modes of procurement.

Overall, the seasonal concentration obliges the FCI to purchase and store wheat 45 days after the harvest, with purchases of around 300,000 tonnes per day. It may be said that the glutting of circuits is paradoxically reinforced by the stability of prices, often fixed for the entire year. If the wheat procurement price could vary according to the season instead, would the FCI still have to manage its wheat procurement for the whole year in just six weeks? The idea of establishing a season-wise price seems wise, as it would encourage farmers to store their harvests themselves. The USA, with its system of marketing loans, and the European Union both grant a bonus for farm storage that farmers receive when they decide to sell. But India (like Australia) takes the risk of getting the state to support the entire storage cost. Reform was rejected for technical reasons, but also by arguing that small farmers could not afford to wait and sell their produce after the harvest, and that such a measure would only benefit rich farmers and traders (Acharya 1997). For the moment, it is in the farmers' interest to get rid of their harvest as soon as possible, and although there may not be any figures available in this regard, we may well believe that farm storage is limited to meeting self-consumption needs. As a result, a greater weight has to be borne by the public budget, because the procurement infrastructure rapidly becomes saturated (staff, purchase centres, trucks, roads, railways, and temporary or permanent storage areas).

The FCI still does not have enough capacity in terms of economic intelligence and market forecasting. Despite a unique network covering the entire country, it does not have essential data to better plan its operations, although many private operators do have such information. In any case, there are many parameters that it cannot control, particularly the rules of the institutional game determined by the state, and its procurement tools.

Thus the impact of public stock management on market prices is far from adequate. While it manages to eliminate the worst highs and lows in price curves, it is incapable of avoiding all the high-price crises, essentially because of a short-term policy. The barely satisfactory rice and wheat situation is still worse for other food grains. Tyagi (1990) rightly condemned two factors: continued market segmentation which prevented local price variations from having any repercussions on the regions (we shall see that the country's general under-development, and the maintenance of politico-administrative barriers between states are at fault); and the low capacity of FPS unable to distribute large product quantities even when the state pushed them to do so. A third factor too could be added—the low purchasing power of poor consumers, who cannot afford to purchase large quantities even in these shops.

(b) *Concentration in Space*

With a few rare exceptions, state procurement took place in the regions where the Green Revolution had taken well, thereby encouraging an increase in agricultural investment and productivity. Conversely, regions that were lagging behind were unable to benefit from the procurement 'vacuum cleaner'.

Spectacular progress had been achieved in some regions (Singh 1997; Landy 2002). Between 1966–7 and 1976–7, rice production in Punjab increased sixfold and wheat production 3.5 times. However, many other regions, not content to have been left as they were, tended to deteriorate further. Thus, between 1962–5 and 1970–3, the annual growth rate of the per hectare production value was 5.2 per cent in Haryana and 6.1 per cent in Punjab, but 0.2 per cent in Bihar and just –1 per cent in Orissa. Between 1960 and 1987, the per capita food grain production only rose in the northern region, while the three other regional groups experienced a fall in the ratio (Byres 1998) (Map 3.3). Thus while the Green Revolution marked a period of overall agricultural growth, there was an increase in regional differences. Until the 1980s the country was split into three parts: high growth wheat (and rice) producing regions (Punjab, for instance), low growth, purely rice-growing, regions (Bengal), and the central or semi-arid regions, where coarse grains continued to predominate. The Green Revolution's inequalities were as much crop-based as regional. These regional differences were paradoxically aggravated by the late development of rice, given that the high growth of rice took place in states that were already producing wheat, such as Punjab. Initially, rice did not 'catch up' in terms of space.

It was in the late 1970s that the situation changed somewhat, if Bhalla and Singh (2001) are to be believed, as according to them inter-regional differences decreased (Figure 3.2). But agricultural growth rates remained low in Bihar, Assam or Orissa, although they were among the poorest.[3] It would seem that only West Bengal managed to pull through. But let us note that protectionism in favour of oilseeds—now ended—and the good monsoon in the early 1990s were probably major factors for positive growth. Bhalla and Singh's optimism might be excessive.

In any case, Map 3.3 needs to be discussed. First, it must be borne in mind that the statistics presented at state level are extremely rough. The mediocre situation of a state as large as Maharashtra obscures major differences between the developed west and the poor east, with limited irrigation. Further, the mapped variable—per capita production—is just another average, barely concealing socio-economic contrasts. Over the entire period, Orissa's production was higher than the national average, while it was also in this very state that the majority of hunger deaths probably took place in India. Finally, the significance of this ratio is reduced considerably, given that it is hardly correlated with the development level or even the overall agricultural productivity. Pitting the north against the south, the ratio also indicates the marked agricultural diversification in south India, with the substitution of food grains, particularly rice, with cash crops. Thus, it would correspond more to the needs the public food system has to meet—which in fact transfers food grain overall from north to south—at least if low per capita production states, such as Bihar, were not 'overlooked' by the distribution system.

In all cases, it may be inferred from these maps that the procurement venues will remain the same. Figure 3.3 confirms the continuance of this type of concentration, as do Maps 2.7, 3.4 and

	1962–5	*1970–3*	*1980–3*	*1990–3*
Variation coefficient in percentage	49.9	56.0	51.2	50.2

Source: Bhalla and Singh 2001.

Figure 3.2: Inequalities in agricultural yields between districts in India (35 crops)

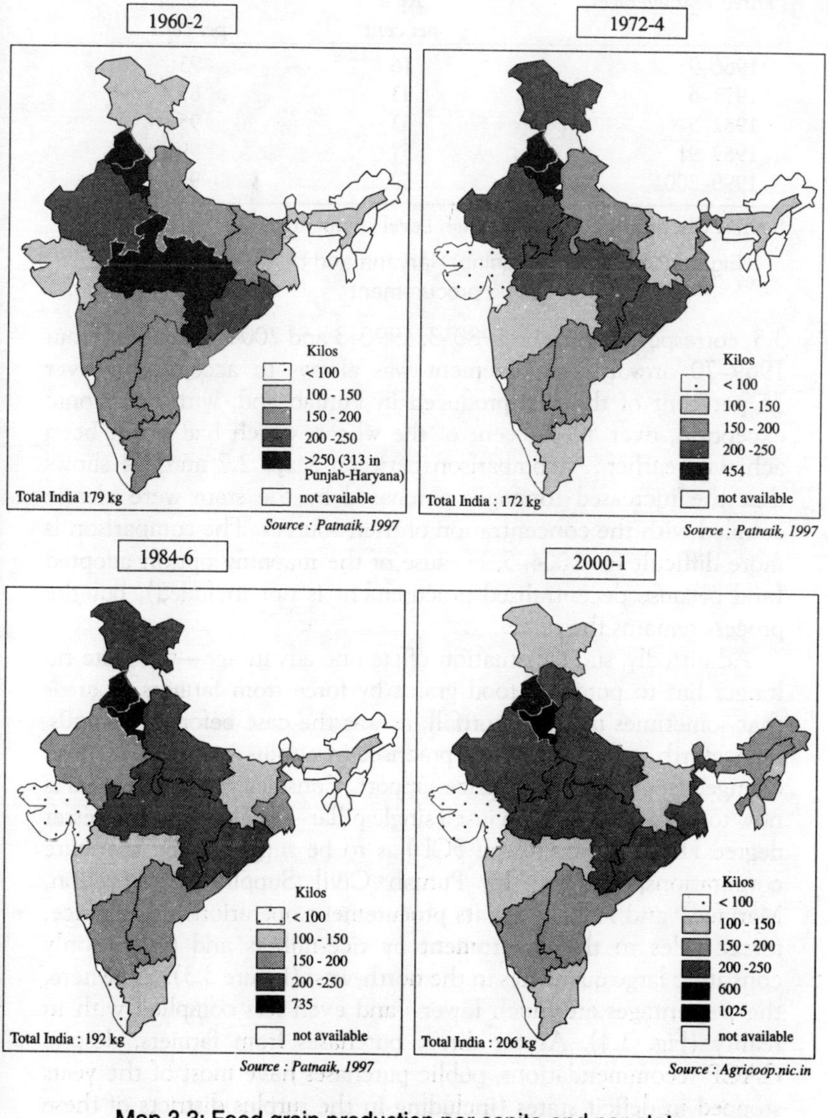

Map 3.3: Food grain production per capita and per state (three-year average)[4]

(Three-year averages)	Rice per cent	Wheat per cent
1966–9	16	93
1973–6	43	85
1982–5	53	95
1989–91	57	99
1999–2001	50	95

Source: Chopra 1988: 394, and High Level Committee.

Figure 3.3: Share of Punjab, Haryana and Uttar Pradesh in total procurement

3.5, corresponding to the 1980–3, 1990–3 and 2004–5 periods. From 1969–70 onwards, procurement was always to account for over 75 per cent of the rice produced in Punjab and, with occasional exception, over 50 per cent of the wheat, which had never been achieved earlier. A comparison between Maps 2.7 and 3.4 shows that the increased tonnages purchased by the state were clearly coupled with the concentration of their sources. The comparison is more difficult for 2004–5, because of the mapping option adopted (and because decentralized procurement is not included), but the process remains the same.

Admittedly, such a situation offers one advantage—the state no longer has to purchase food grains by force from farmers in areas that sometimes faced a shortfall, as was the case before the 1960s. Henceforth, procurement was practised in surplus areas, as the status changed from farm tax to price support. Consequently, the system is now too strongly based on just a single pillar—Punjab and, to a lesser degree Haryana, where the FCI has to be supported by the state corporations, namely the Punjab Civil Supplies Corporation, Markfed[5] and Hafed,[6] for its procurement operations. As for rice, forced sales to the government by rice-millers and traders only constitute large quantities in the north-west (Figure 3.3). Elsewhere, the percentages are much lower—and even less complied with in reality (Fig. 3.4). As for direct purchases from farmers, despite CACP recommendations, public purchases have most of the years stopped in deficit states (including in the surplus districts of these states), although they had been fairly common in the 1960s.

Andhra Pradesh's recent ascendancy as far as rice supplies are concerned is much less the outcome of increased production than the crucial role played by the Telugu Desam Party, in power in the

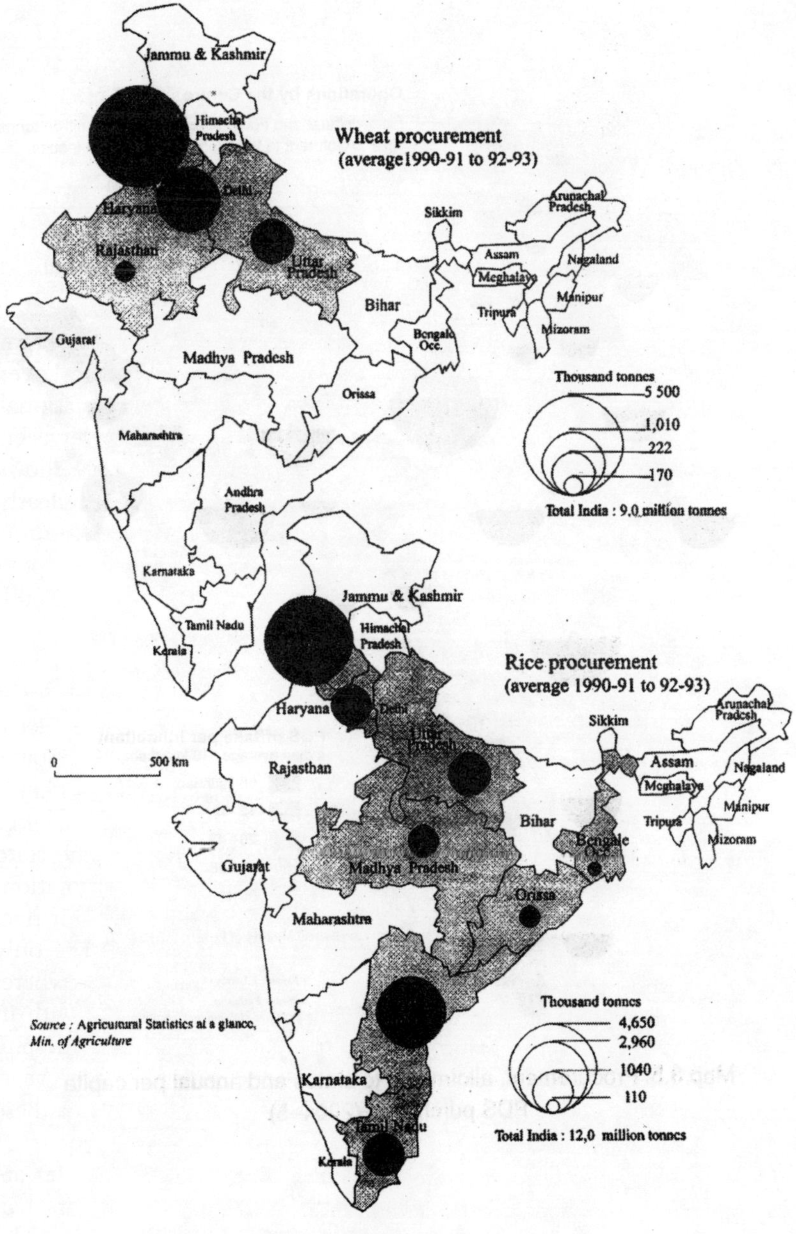

Map 3.4: Wheat and rice procurement (1990–3)

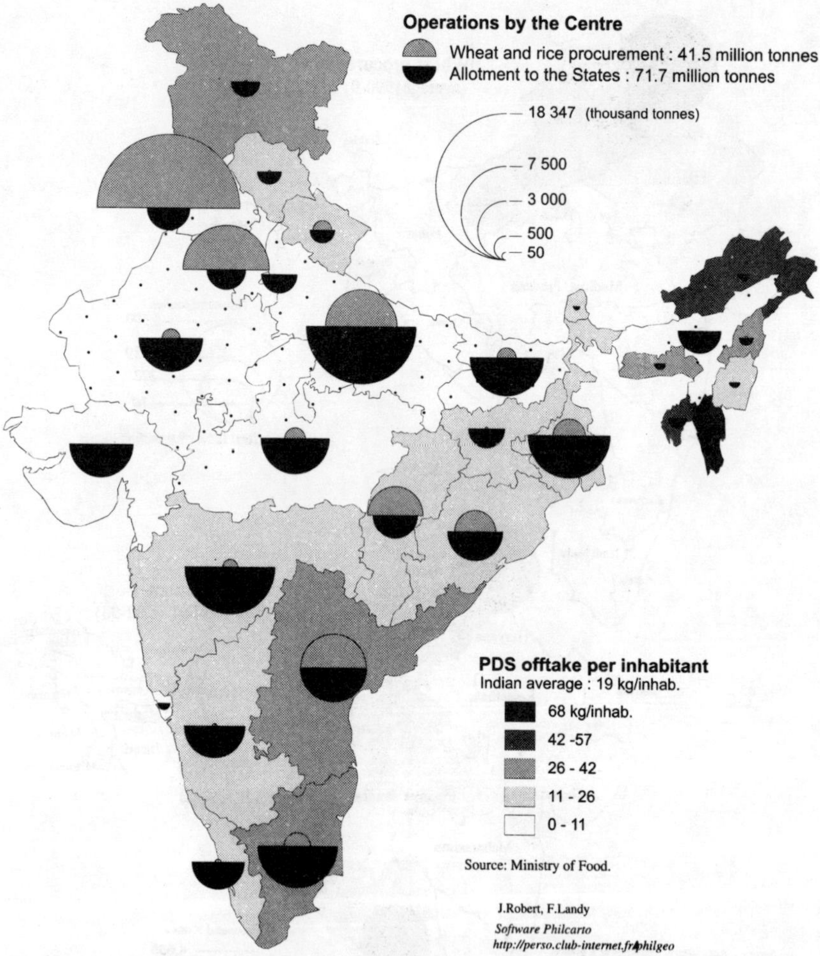

Map 3.5: Procurement, allotments to states and annual per capita PDS purchases (2004–5)

State/Territory	*Category imposed*	*Taxation percentage*
Punjab	Rice-millers and traders	75
Haryana	Rice-millers and traders	75
Orissa	Rice-millers	75
Chandigarh	Rice-millers and traders	75
Uttar Pradesh	Rice-millers and traders	60 in the west, 40 in certain eastern districts
West Bengal	Rice-millers	50
Madhya Pradesh	Rice-millers and traders	30 (raw rice)
Andhra Pradesh	Rice-millers and traders	50
Assam	Rice-millers and traders	50
Tamil Nadu	Rice-millers and traders	50
Bihar	Rice-millers and wholesalers	40 on rice-millers, 25 on wholesalers
Karnataka	Rice-millers and traders	33.3
Rajasthan	Rice-millers and traders	50
Pondicherry	Rice-millers and traders	10 (20 transport levy)
Gujarat	Rice-millers	10
Maharashtra	Rice-millers	30
Delhi	Rice-millers and traders	75

Source: Department of Food, *Annual Report 2003-04.*

Figure 3.4: Official sale percentages of rice to the state (rice levy) imposed on rice-millers and traders (*kharif* – 2003–4)

state till 2004 and part of the coalition at the centre between 1998 and 2004. Henceforth, the FCI agrees to procure rabi rice, which increased Andhra Pradesh's share in total rice procurement from 14 per cent in 1970–1 to 30 per cent in 2000–1.[7] The fact that the TDP is dominated by the Kammas—a caste of paddy farmers from the delta regions—is not unrelated to this development. On the contrary, the growth in rice production in West Bengal was not followed by corresponding FCI purchases, and compensations granted to the state on account of decentralized procurement were deemed lower than those conferred upon others. The presumed reason was the communist government in power in Bengal, at that time firmly in the opposition (Raghavan 2004).

If procurement were an effective tool for supporting prices, we might find it deplorable that 80 per cent of the zones sown with cereals in India only account for 10 per cent of state purchases. Only farmers cultivating 20 per cent of the total wheat area and 30 per cent of the total rice area actually benefit from support prices (Raghavan 2004). At a time when procurement was a means to ensure safety stocks, its implementation in only a few regions was justified so long as they had significant surpluses. After all, the concentration of surpluses in a single region facilitated procurement operations, easier than having to collect food grains from all over India. But once the nature of procurement changed to a support price operation, theoretically, the government should have been able to intervene in any part of the national territory so long as there was a risk of deflation. Procurement in its new avatar should have been ubiquitous and not spatially concentrated. However, the opposite occurred. Formerly procurement was implemented in most states, although with variable intensity, because it was necessary to make use of all the means available and collect each and every grain available to feed the nation. Today, it is limited to a few states, given their productivity gains and the degree of saturation of public stocks. Henceforth, there are entire regions in India that are not covered by the official guarantee of support prices.

In fact, how would it possible to ensure compliance with the floor price if the administration does not intervene through its purchases? Market controls *vis-à-vis* private buyers prove to be clearly inadequate to ensure compliance with the law. In May 2001, the price per quintal of wheat flour was Rs. 570 in the Hapur *mandi*, in Ghaziabad district near Delhi, and Rs. 595 in Delhi itself, while the support price was Rs. 610.[8] On the other hand, this price was respected in Haryana and Punjab, although at the village level many small farmers had to sell their harvest at lower prices to private traders to pay off debts contracted at the start of the crop year. Yet rice and wheat appear privileged, because there are no mechanisms for other crops, making it mandatory to respect support prices—apart from sugar cane and cotton in certain states. One can understand why the efforts made by the Commission on Agricultural Costs and Prices to promote a diversification of crop rotation by increasing the floor prices for pulses (of which India imports 10 per cent of its consumption) or oilseeds (half of oil consumption needs are met by imports) proves fruitless.

In any case, the minimum prices are defined for the whole of India, without taking regional differences in production costs into account. The general idea is that a single price allows farmers to cultivate the optimal crop area, thanks to the law of comparative advantages. Regionally defined prices would encouraged inefficiency (in high production cost regions), not to speak of the issue of border controls, which would have to be set up to prevent smuggling. Having said that, in the early years of this century, the minimum rice and wheat prices are defined much above production costs in most regions,[9] and as far as effectiveness is concerned, their utility is questionable, discouraging any agricultural diversification in Punjab, in particular.

Storage procedures and locations are an important issue linked to procurement and all the more difficult to manage since they have to take into consideration the problem of distribution. At the end of 1967 the Green Revolution was well on its way, but the public sector storage capacity only amounted to 4.4 million tonnes, less than 5 per cent of food grain production. Two-thirds of this capacity was located in five states: Andhra Pradesh, Gujarat, Tamil Nadu, Maharashtra and West Bengal, where the major import ports were located, that are also the largest cities (Map 3.6). The areas from where food grains originated had very few warehouses. The success achieved in food grain self-sufficiency soon made it possible to re-design the storage map (Cummings 1969). But where should the new depots be located? Near production areas where procurement could be concentrated? Or in regions with appropriate conservation conditions—particularly Punjab, which had a semi-arid climate? Or should they be located near consumption areas, the cities, from where further distribution in times of food emergencies was easier? Map 3.7 shows that the first two options were basically combined in different degrees. The first, favouring procurement areas, was the most encouraged, with high capacities in the Upper Gangetic plains, which created a remarkable contrast with the 1968 map. Ports had lost their prevalence (low capacity in Gujarat, despite the presence of Kandla, a major outlet for Punjab), which proves that India's commercial maritime infrastructure remains ill-adapted to the new situation where exports dominate. As for deficit regions, they have limited storage capacities in relation to their requirements (north-east and, particularly, Kerala), which means that there is adequate confidence in the infrastructure's effectiveness with regard to responding to emergency high food demands.

India is lucky to be a wheat and rice consumer, since these cereals

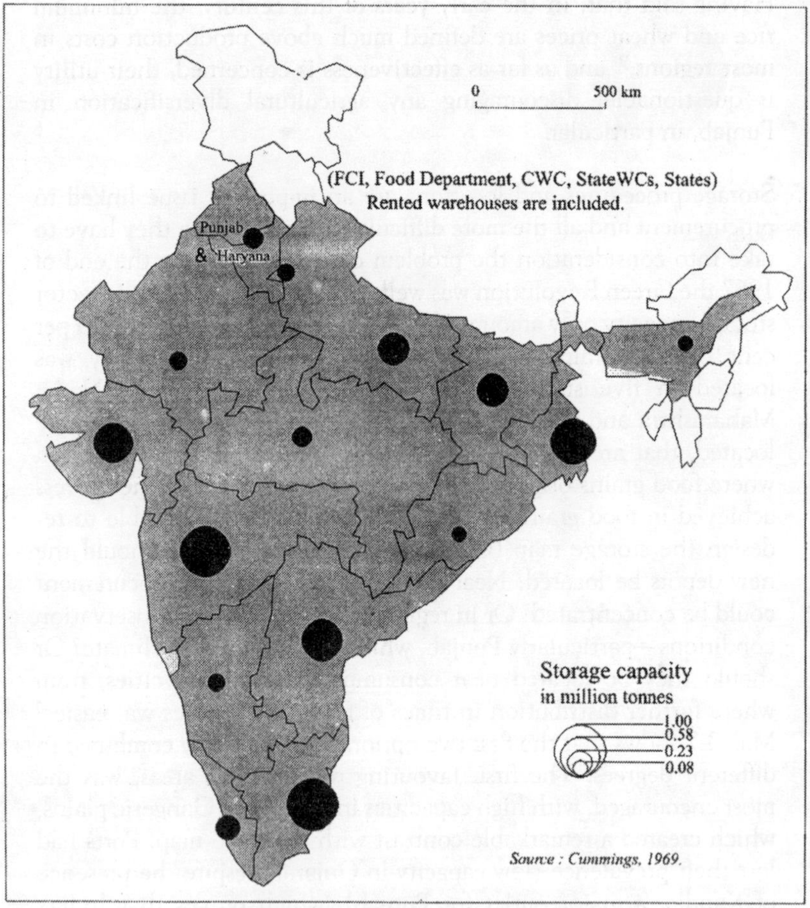

Map 3.6: Public storage capacity in 1968

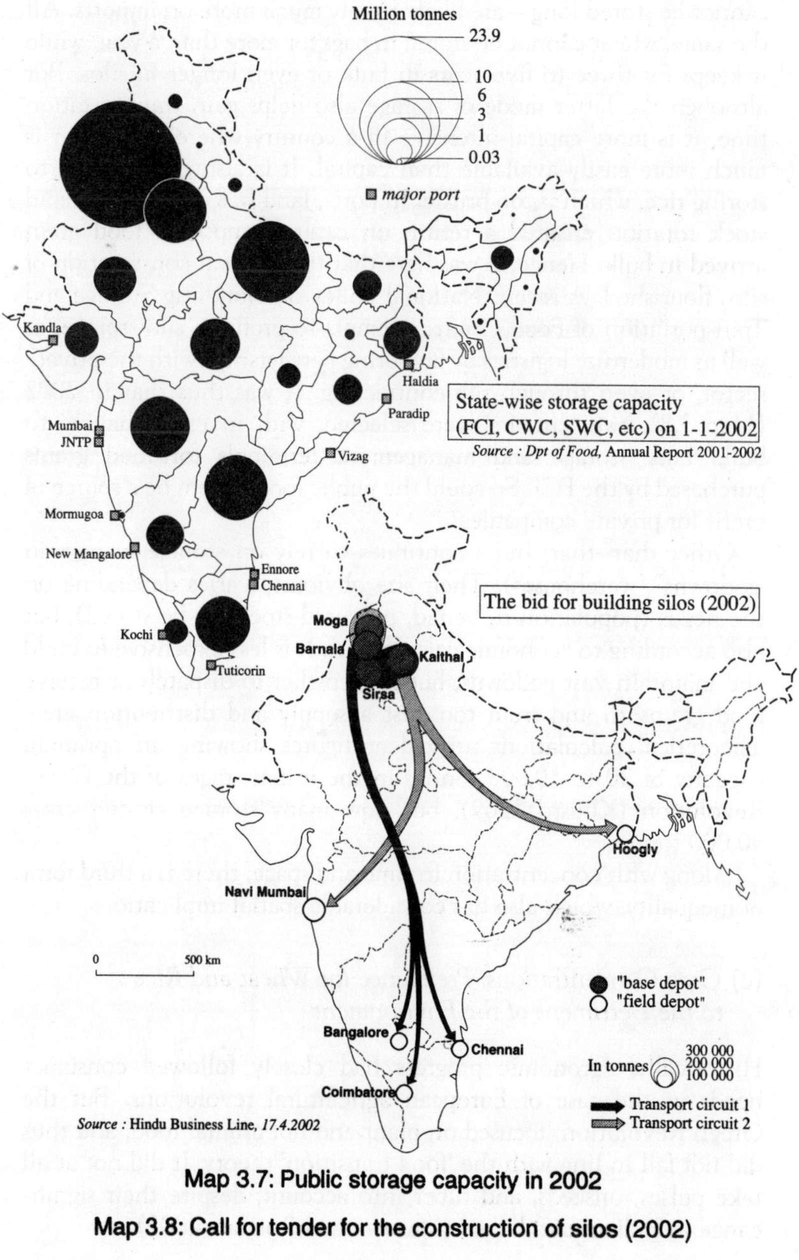

Map 3.7: Public storage capacity in 2002

Map 3.8: Call for tender for the construction of silos (2002)

keep relatively well: the maize-consuming countries—this cereal cannot be stored long—are likely to rely much more on imports. All the same, wheat cannot be stored in bags for more than a year, while it keeps for three to five years in bulk or even longer in silos. But although the latter mode of storage also helps gain transportation time, it is more capital-intensive in a country where manpower is much more easily available than capital. It is also not adapted to storing rice, which is too brittle. In ports, land was expensive, rapid stock rotation ensured a return on capital, imported food grain arrived in bulk. Hence, it was here that the vertical construction of silos flourished. A recent National Policy on Handling Storage and Transportation of Food Grains attempts to promote silo storage, as well as modernize logistics by favouring partnerships with the private sector, or even through sub-contracting. It was thus that in 2002 (Map 3.8), two 'circuits' were selected, with investors having to build bulk storage and management terminals for food grains purchased by the FCI. So could the public food system be a source of profit for private companies?

Other than that, India continues to rely on storage in bags in 'godowns' (warehouses). Their size obviously varies depending on the needs (population to be fed, procured stocks to be stored), but also according to economic calculations. It is less expensive to build and maintain vast godowns, but it is costlier to dispatch or receive food grains to and from too vast a supply and distribution area. Theoretical calculations arrived at figures showing an optimum capacity of 20 to 30,000 tonnes in the initial stages of the Green Revolution (Khusro 1969), but now many storage centres cross 40,000 tonnes.

Along with concentration in time and space, there is a third form of inequality, which also has considerable spatial implications.

(c) *Crop Concentrations: Preference for Wheat and Rice to the Detriment of the Environment*

Historically, agronomic progress had closely followed consumer needs in the case of European agricultural revolutions. But the Green Revolution focused on plant and not animal food, and thus did not fall in line with the 'food transition' theory. It did not at all take pulses, oilseeds, and tuber into account, despite their significance in Indian food habits (Mazoyer and Roudart 2002).

At the start of the Green Revolution, the opinion was that it was better to lay stress on wheat and to a lesser degree on rice, because international research centres had created improved varieties for distribution. (Developed countries were interested in crops such as wheat, temperate in origin, for a long time, and they had funded the bulk of research.) Moreover, a tradition of irrigation and intensive agriculture would facilitate the spread of new High Yield Varieties. Wheat is cultivated in winter, which is a dry season with a few crucially important showers, and often needs irrigation. Similarly, rice had already been cultivated in canal-irrigated areas. Wheat also had the advantage of being cultivated in a cold and generally cloudless season, with fewer pests and a lot of sun to improve yields. The granary was Punjab, where farms were relatively large because of recent agricultural colonization, which facilitated the modernization of crop systems. Finally, wheat and rice could be stored longer, while coarse cereals are more fragile and cannot be purchased in bulk by the FCI to supply national food stocks.

Today, India is the second biggest producer of wheat and rice in the world, with 12 per cent and 21 per cent of the planet's crops respectively, corresponding more or less to its demographic weight (17 per cent of the world population) (Charvet 2004). But we can also see that such reasoning can have pernicious effects. Maps 3.9 and 3.10 of food grain flows also shows 'virtual water' flows, since it is irrigation that enables the production of agricultural surpluses that are later transported by FCI to deficit regions.[10] The over-use of water in Punjab, which has caused soil salinization and water-logging, was advantageous for the states that were PDS beneficiaries. In 1997, 11 million ha in India were suffering from salinity. In Haryana, the Kurukshetra district saw the ground water level fall by 48 cm per year between 1974 and 1994 (Dorin and Landy forthcoming). Incentives for double or even triple paddy crops in the deltas made farmers dependent on dammed rivers (such as the Krishna and Kaveri) whose flow had become increasingly erratic because of draw-offs, making bad monsoons even more difficult to bear.

Wheat and rice dominate while other cereals decline, with the result that the latter are absent from the PDS, although they constitute staples for many rural inhabitants. Only finger millet in Karnataka and sorghum in Maharashtra are (very rarely) available. Upon its establishment in 1965, however, the FCI had been

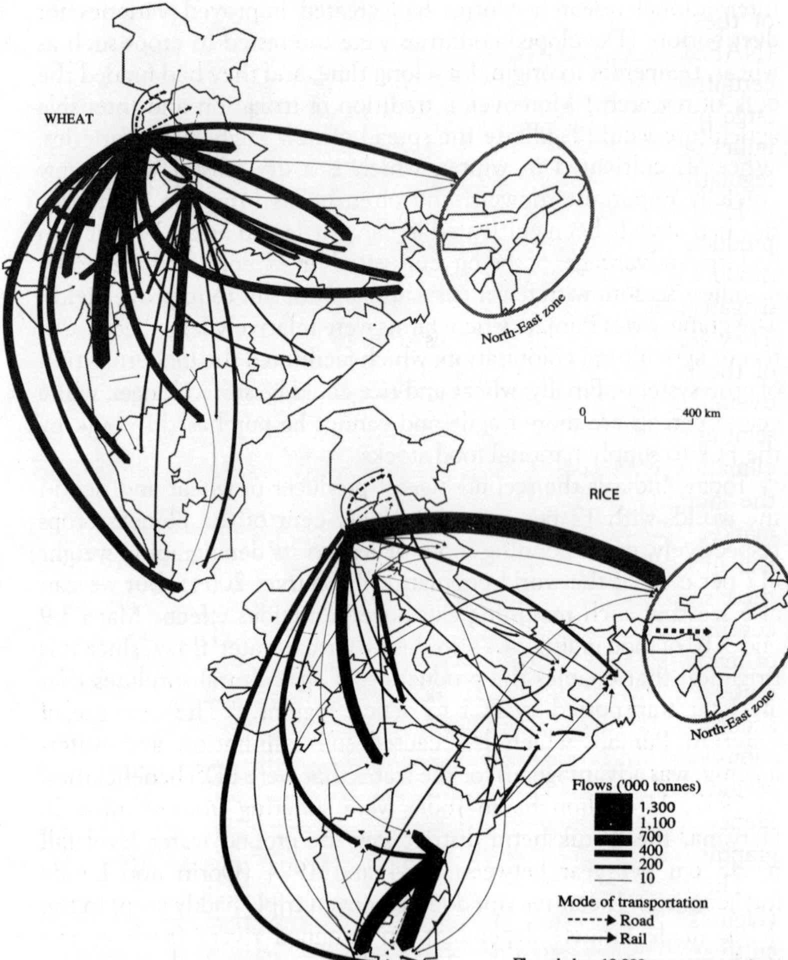

Maps 3.9 and 3.10: Wheat and Rice Transportation by FCI in 1999–2000

entrusted with the procurement of all food grains, including secondary cereals. Since 1980, the latter became the responsibility of the National Agricultural Cooperative Marketing Federation (NAFED) also subsequently entrusted with pulses, oilseeds and certain vegetables. The centre has not, however, purchased them in large quantities, and neither have the states. It may be said that millet producers are the losers in the food policy, with market prices regularly falling below the minimum support prices.[11]

However, this needs to be qualified, given that a number of producers of coarse cereals such as pulses (beans, lentils) do not produce enough for their own consumption, particularly in non-irrigated areas, and depend on the market for a part of their food. They are not necessarily interested in high prices. Therein lies one of the primary factors behind the low procurement—the limited overall production of these cereals and pulses, mostly confined to semi-arid central India where cultivation is not so easy because of climatic conditions. But other reasons were the scarcity of irrigation, the late advent of High Yield Varieties for millets on the Indian market, and the lack of response to chemical fertilizers due to the lack of water and HYV. If the state had intervened in a major way in these small markets, it would have lead to price hikes untenable for consumers. Another reason is the absence of the spatial integration of markets. Indeed, the narrowness of surplus production zones is quite remarkable (not to speak of their location, which shifts in accordance with the monsoon). Equally remarkable are the consumption areas, since these millets constitute the staple diet of small regions and are often scorned by consumers from the rest of India. Hence, all this together would lead to extremely complex geographical circuits.

The situation of pulses is comparable to that of coarse cereals (Figures 3.5 and 3.6). While yields rose slightly, the area under cultivation stagnated and since imports did not increase proportionally, the per capita availability declined considerably. The situation of oilseeds is better because of the upturn brought about by the 'yellow revolution' in the 1980s, which saw the emergence of a protectionist policy to promote sunflower, rapeseed-mustard and soyabean production (Dorin 2002). On that account, India seemed to follow world trends, marked by a 50 per cent increase in oilseed yields in twenty years (Charvet 2004). However, this did not prevent it from becoming the world's primary oilseed importer.

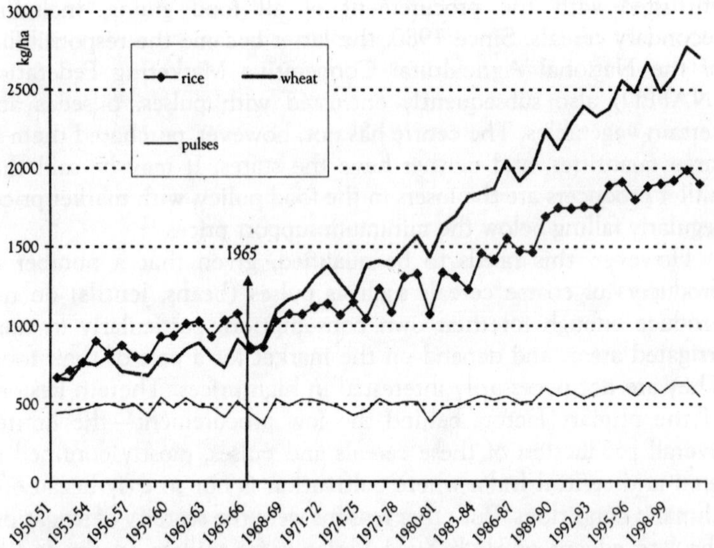

Figure 3.5: Yields of wheat, rice and pulses (1950 to 2003)

(Three-year averages)	*1950–1 to 1952–3*	*1999–2000 to 2001–2*
Wheat		
Production (million tonnes)	6.7	26.4
Yield (quintal/ha)	6.9	27.5
Rice		
Production (million tonnes)	21.6	89.3
Yield (q/ha)	7.1	19.9
Coarse cereals (millets)		
Production (million tonnes)	17.0	29.8
Yield (q/ha)	4.3	10.7
Pulses		
Production (million tonnes)	8.7	12.6
Yield (q/ha)	4.5	6.0
Per capita availability (g/day)	60.8	32.3
Oilseeds		
Production (million tonnes)	5.0	23.3
Yield (q/ha)	4.4	8.6

Source: http://agricoop.nic.in/statistics2003

Figure 3.6: Highly differentiated crop-wise agricultural growth

Tyagi (1990) strongly qualified the admission of failure in the field of pulses, by observing that a good portion of these was used as forage. However, the introduction of tractors has reduced the need for draft animals, and certain compound feed purchased on the market then became an integral part of the livestock diet. He also observed that these pulses—a source of protein—could be replaced by meat, vegetables, and fish—other foods whose growth could not be denied. Therefore, the fact that the per capita availability of pulses was halved would not be so serious an issue. Objections can be raised, however. If pulses are very expensive, fresh meat and vegetables are even more so. Only eggs could constitute an economically convincing food replacement. But it remains to be proven that all poor Indians would be happy with one hard-boiled egg instead of their bowl of dal (pulses in curry) with rice or chapatis. For the moment, statistics show the opposite, as Indians consume less than two eggs per month.

Overall, it was the two ends of the public food system that added up to facilitate the growth of wheat and rice in the food bowl. Then, not just public purchases, but also redistribution by the PDS promoted them.

Reappraising the PDS

Theoretically all Indian households have the right to a ration card (actually a booklet) per family, where the names and ages of the family members are registered along with a photo of the registered holder. As far as wheat, rice, oil, kerosene, and sugar are concerned, the quantities available each month vary depending on the number and age of the people mentioned in the ration card, but also according to the estimated household income. The prices also vary. (The system depends on the rules adopted by the concerned state.) It is the family's responsibility to go to the PDS shop where it is registered and pay cash for what it wants to buy —once a month for kerosene, more frequently for the other products. The shop manager notes the quantities sold in the booklet.

This is the ideal situation. However, we might recall our analysis of the limited food and nutritional growth throughout India. Famines still take place locally and malnutrition remains chronic. In all this, the PDS is admittedly a partial failure. The stocks in June

2002, which had reached 65 million tonnes of food grains, accounted for the food rations of half the Indian population for a year, which is indeed scandalous. With 8.1 million tonnes of food grains distributed by the PDS in 2001–2, the ration statistically corresponded to 22 grams daily per person!

However, this average hides major disparities, since only the poor try to purchase FPS food grains whose quality is deplorable. Besides, the share of purchases carried out under the PDS is far from negligible, although it is true more for sugar, oil, and especially kerosene, rather than for food grains (Figure 3.7). In addition to its direct effects on consumption, the economic impact of subsidized distribution has also to be taken into consideration, as it tends to reduce prices in the open market and therefore promote consumption.

However, such an assessment would be too general and makes a less aggregated perspective necessary. If we were to take up the same analytical grid that we used for procurement, we would make the same observations regarding a high level of irregularities.

(a) *In Time*

The seasonal concentration of PDS purchases is less marked than that of procurement. It is not as if there was no issue of bridging the gaps, but rather because the state does not manage to take variations in requirement into consideration. The quantities allocated barely vary: sugar quantities sometimes double during the Diwali festival season, but it is quite rare for the food grain quotas allocated to increase during periods of food vulnerability, mostly at the end of the rainy season. In the best of cases, it is the Food for Work programmes or, even more rarely, free emergency food distribution, that take over from the PDS.

	Rural (%)	*Urban (%)*
Rice	16	13
Wheat and flour	8	7
Sugar	35	37
Kerosene	71	53

Source: NSSO.

Figure 3.7: PDS share in household purchases (1999–2000)

At the national level, there is only a slight increase in PDS sales at a time when agricultural prices reach their peak, before the harvest, when the difference compared to the prices offered in subsidized shops is at its maximum. Some have denounced this as an unresolved problem, given that on the contrary, public purchases tend to make open market prices shoot up (Timmer 1989) by 15 and 35 per cent according to different Indian studies. If subsidized public distribution fails to compensate for the hike in open market prices, poor households are the losers. However, this criticism seems unjustified, given the space and time gaps between purchases and sales. Today, the state only engages in procurement in areas and times when the prices are, on the whole, lower.

As far inter-annual variability is concerned, increases in the tonnages distributed during the drought years cannot compensate for the decrease in availability due to problems of under-production. In 1987–8, food grain production fell by 15 per cent in relation to the preceding year, but PDS redistributions only rose by 3 per cent. (The percentage was lower, whereas its base in tonnes was even much lower at the start than the production base.) In 2002, India was able to fight drought better, since it led to a historic distribution record (22.5 million tonnes of cereals in 2002–3).

(b) *In Space*

Before coming to the spatial disparities in the PDS, we must remember that the system did not come up within a totally empty space. In particular, cereal needs are not identical from one state to another (similarly, oils, and sugar). The per capita cereal consumption decreases everywhere in India, but significant gaps remain between Kerala and Orissa (Map 1.7) Per capita food grain production is rising, but Map 3.3 clearly shows that the national average is the outcome of two contrasting situations: stagnation, or even the worsening of the ratio in most states, particularly in the south, versus the enormous growth in Punjab. If we were to estimate that Indians consumed 136 kg of food grain per year (NSSO 1999–2000), considering losses and the use of grains as seed and feed, this would amount to 170 kg per person and per year that needed to be produced to meet the people's needs. This ratio was not achieved by states as populated as Tamil Nadu, Maharashtra, Bihar, or Kerala of course—a situation already confirmed by Maps 3.1 and 3.2 on the 'production less consumption' balance.

Another challenge for the PDS relates to the type of rice consumed. Kerala (and West Bengal, another long-standing deficit state) eat parboiled rice, while the main exporting states (Punjab, Haryana, Andhra Pradesh) produce and consume raw rice. Thus, in these surplus states, some of the rice-mills started parboiling rice, prompted to do so through federal subsidies. The centre was concerned about providing fresh supplies to deficit states as well as containing the amount of broken rice and loss of quality, which a new technique made possible.[12] Thus the bulk of rice from Andhra Pradesh is now parboiled rice, intended for Kerala. We can see that constraints of specific types and qualities of products lie hidden behind the gross tonnage and percentage figures that the FCI is obliged to consider if it wishes to meet consumer needs some of the time. (However, it hardly distributes enough parboiled rice.)

Maps 3.11 and 3.12 illustrate the changes in the degree of dependency *vis-à-vis* the PDS. In 1973–4, the PDS mostly met the cereal consumption needs either of communist dominant states (West Bengal, Kerala) and highly urbanized states (Maharashtra, Gujarat) . . . or both at the same time (Bengal). In 1988–9, their lead dropped—proof of the gradual extension of the system to other states and to rural areas, and also an outcome of the decline in statutory rationing in major cities. The national average increased from 15 to 18 per cent. Dependence on the PDS remains very variable today. According to NSSO, in 1999–2000 rural households purchased 5.2 kg of grains from the PDS, and the city-dwellers 4.1—a dependence of about 9 per cent and 7 per cent respectively, if the base were a monthly requirement of 11 kg of cereals per person. Thus, dependency reduced as compared to the situation in 1988–9 (true, 1999–2000 was a year of very low distribution). In reality, dependence was almost nil in Punjab and Haryana, while it was 42 per cent in Kerala and 30 per cent in Tamil Nadu. Himachal Pradesh, Jammu & Kashmir, and Andhra Pradesh were just behind.

It is natural that the PDS does not operate in Punjab, in view of local overproduction. But if we were to take into account the volume of agriculturist population and local production in the various states, distribution did not correspond to the proportion of the poor population or middle-income groups (Swaminathan 2000; Bhalotra 2002). Maps 3.5 and 3.13 show the south Indian

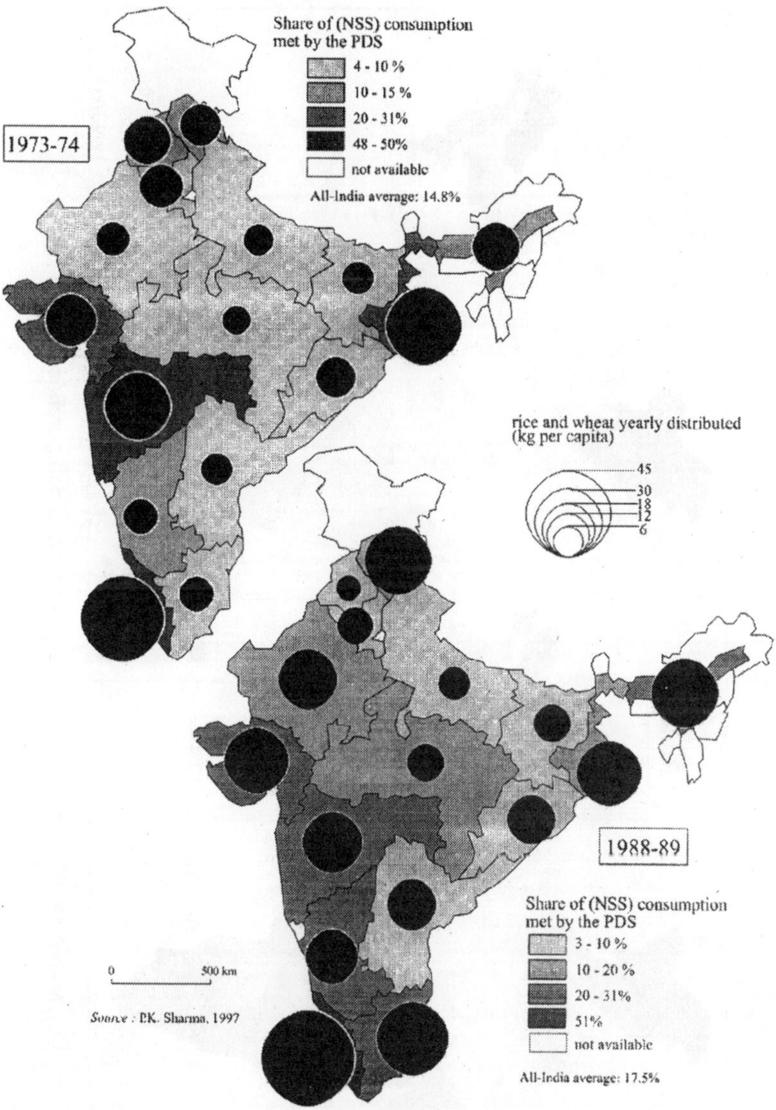

Map 3.11: State-wise dependency on PDS in 1973–4

Map 3.12: State-wise dependency on PDS in 1988–9

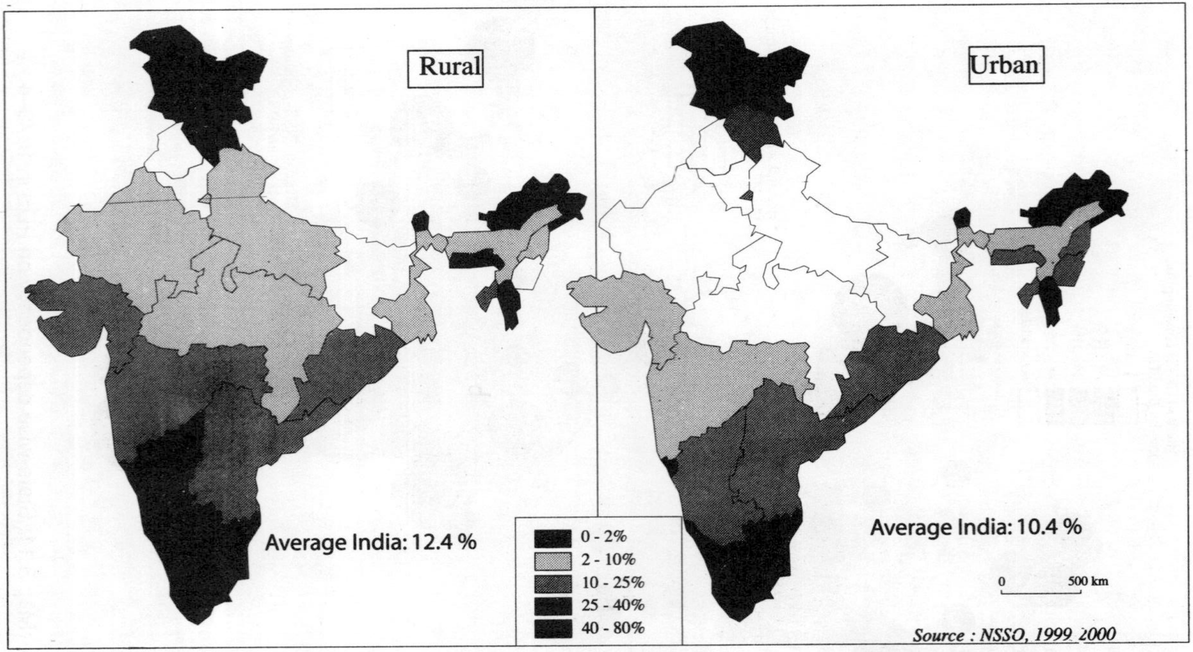

Map 3.13: PDS share in household wheat and rice purchases (1999–2000)

advantage, where the PDS functions rather well, but also that of the Himalayan north-east region. On the contrary, very few purchases take place in the Indo-Gangetic plain, in spite of great poverty. Central India is also very little represented. Thus, there is no correlation between dependence on the PDS and the poverty of the population or state food deficits (Fig. 3.8).The fact that very poor states barely use the PDS is merely a sign of their poverty, given that administrative and infrastructure deficiencies do not make it possible to distribute food grains suitably. Apart from this fundamental reason are economic factors such as the fact that food grains are more expensive in southern rather than northern markets, including Bihar, a deficit state (High Level Committee 2002). But the main problem is perhaps political in essence.

First external factors: The communist government of West Bengal frequently accused the centre of not allocating it enough rice—this was, however, visibly not the case in 2004–5 (Map 3.5). Conversely, subtle strategies come to light, such as that of Chandrababu Naidu, the former Andhra Pradesh Chief Minister. Maintaining a certain uncertainty *vis-à-vis* his support to the ruling coalition, he was able to bargain. Central favours were obtained, particularly in the matter of food, to the envy of other states (rice allocations for the Food for Work programmes, for instance). In more fundamental terms, states such as Jammu & Kashmir or Tripura are favoured in certain years by the FCI, due to their strategic and

	Percentage of below poverty line population	*PDS quantity purchased per households per month*	*Percentage of rural households purchasing rice or wheat from PDS*	*Percentage of urban households purchasing rice or wheat from PDS*
Bihar	42.6	0.6 kg	5.4	1.0
West Bengal	27.0	2.0 kg	17.5	5.0
Tamil Nadu	21.1	12.8 kg	75.2	27.6
Kerala	12.7	19.0 kg	37.1	47.6
India	26.1	4.1 kg	32.4	10.4

Source: Planning Commission and NSSO.

Figure 3.8: Poverty and rice purchases in traditional consumer states (1999–2000)

politically sensitive character. It is also in the name of regional planning that certain regions are favoured, thereby following the Planning Commission's directives regarding the Centre's allocation to the states. It is notable that Bhutan, an independent Himalayan country, also benefits from public stocks (20,000 tonnes of unsubsidized cereals in 2003–4). The strategic role of Bhutan is important, notably because it is used as a 'base camp' by several regionalist militants from north-east India.

Internal factors: Traditionally, leftist states have long seen high per capita PDS usage rates, often those with a communist government—Kerala, West Bengal, and Tripura—given their governments' efforts to have made the best use of the system. Likewise, the reason the southern states use the PDS more is because their governments have been adding their own subsidy to the one provided by New Delhi's since the 1980s. For 1994, Map 2.8 on price variations in PDS shops as compared to the prices announced by New Delhi is eloquent, with differences ranging from –63 per cent (in Andhra Pradesh) to +37 per cent in Himachal Pradesh, whose government, short of finances, heavily taxed the PDS.

If we take a look at Maps 3.14 and 3.15 on total PDS purchases, we come across a field that is less social and nutritional than logistical in nature. Indeed, what matters for the FCI or the railways is the gross tonnage to be transported, not the ratios per capita. For rice, purchases are undertaken in the traditional areas of consumption (coastal and southern regions), with Bihar–Jharkhand being under-represented. Overall, this corresponds to a crescent centred in the eastern half of the country. As for wheat purchases, they correspond to a second, westward crescent—these are regions that traditionally consume wheat, but Punjab–Haryana are hardly visible, since prices in the open market are low overall and discourage PDS purchases. On the other hand, West Bengal and Bihar enjoy a noticeable presence, probably because of urbanization (Bengal) and wheat arrivals through the FCI, which compensated for the low rice procurement here.

On a different scale, inequalities in terms of distribution are no less obvious. Consider how many isolated, badly connected villages exist in the states that nonetheless appear to be doing well. In Dharavi, 'Asia's biggest slum' in Mumbai, with more than 500,000 inhabitants, there were just 128 ration cards in September 2003.[13]

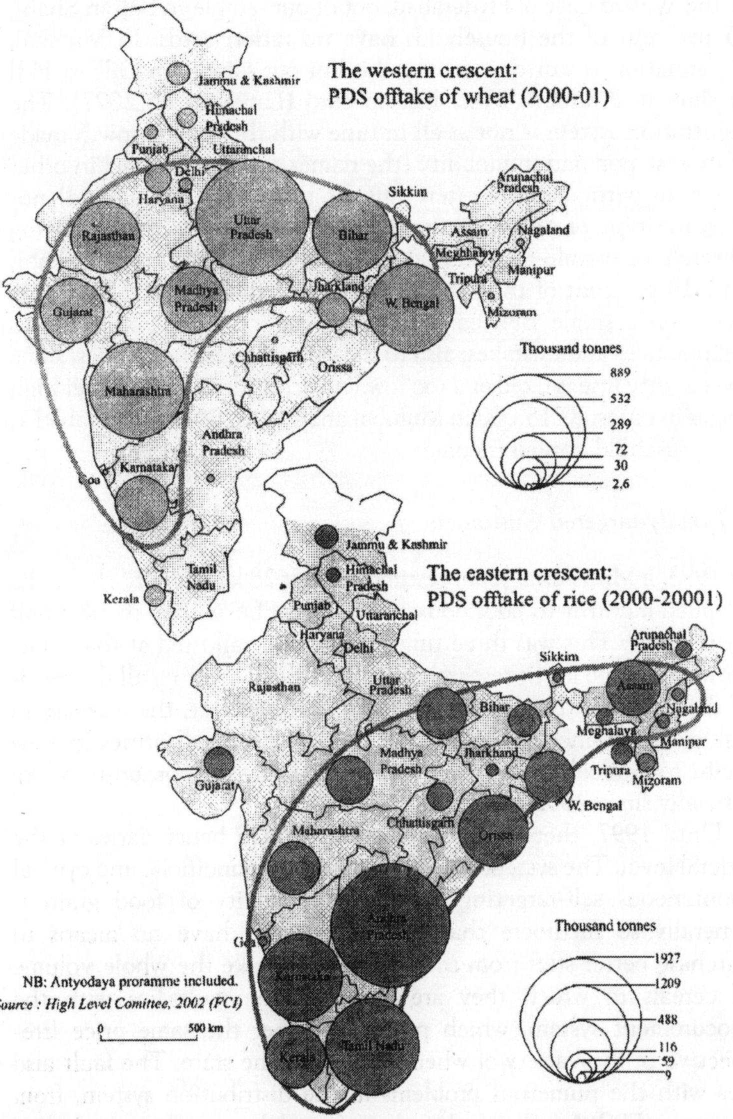

Map 3.14: Western crescent—wheat purchases from the PDS (2000–1)

Map 3.15: Eastern crescent—rice purchases from the PDS (2000–1)

In the Walled City of Hyderabad, out of our sample in Sultan Shahi, 15 per cent of the households have no ration cards. In Mumbai, the situation is worse since one-third of our sample in Gilbert Hill (a slum in Andheri West) has no card (Landy et al. 2007). The registration system is not at all in tune with the urban growth made of intense population mobility (the names of wives married in other states, in particular, are often difficult to include in the card) nor with the type of people living in slums (a majority of them being illiterate or unable to read Marathi). Furthermore in Sultan Shahi, only 18 per cent of the cards are BPL, and in Gilbert Hill there is not even a single BPL card. Such a situation is not only due to malpractices and mistakes, also to the official rules themselves, since the poverty line is fixed at a too low level considering the rather high wages in cities: Rs 15,000 in Mumbai and Rs 11,000 in Hyderabad as the household annual income.

(c) *Badly-targeted Customers*

In 1993, a Ministerial report estimated that 28 kg of grains should be supplied monthly to poor households if the PDS wished to meet half their needs. This was three times the volume allotted at that time. However, some leftist researchers still dream of meeting all the needs of the destitute through public distribution. In fact, the increase in public stocks since the end of the 1990s led the authorities in New Delhi to gradually raise the quotas issued to the poor, up to 35 kg officially since 2002 to today (2008).

Until 1997, there was no selection of PDS beneficiaries at the federal level. The system relied on more or less unofficial and cynical spontaneous self-targeting. Indeed, the quality of food grain is generally so mediocre that only those who have no means to purchase better stuff from the open market take the whole volume of cereals to which they are entitled. The fault lies with the procurement system, which pays the farmer the same price irrespective of the variety of wheat he sells to the state. The fault also lies with the numerous problems in the distribution system, from storage to FPS. Another fault is that of fraudulent practices, including sorting PDS qualities and removing good quality cereals from legal circuits. While half the paddy purchased in Punjab–Haryana is of 'superfine' quality, very little of it is found at the end of the chain. It disappears, only to reappear on the open market and quite often in rice-mills. Thus, it was understandable that in Bombay, some slum-dwellers bought rice from the PDS shops, sorted it, washed it and then resold it to make a bit of a profit. With such massive quality-related problems, PDS cereals were not exact substitutes for the cereals available in the open market at the same price (Ramaswami and Balakrishnan, 2002).

> 'RAT DROPPINGS IN WHEAT FLOUR TO BE MADE ILLEGAL: New Delhi—The government is finally ensuring that wheat flour is free of rat droppings. The rule which allows five piece of rat excreta and hair in one kg of cereals and pulses under the Prevention of Food Adulteration Act is being amended through a gazette notification.'
>
> *The Times of India, 6.3.2000*
>
> (This was about cereals in general, not just those transported by the FCI in particular.)

In some states, coarse cereals were distributed to make self-selection even more effective, given that it was often the rural poor who appreciated them. However, these were just occasional practices, because only limited surpluses were available for these cereals and because in rural areas, the rich barely ate less of these cereals than did the poor (Suryanarayana 1995a).

Thus there are three levels of failure: few PDS clients are poor, few of the poor are clients, and few poor clients buy a lot.

Few Clients are Poor

Before implementing the targetting procedure at the central level in 1997 and even later, it was common for well-to-do households to purchase products from the PDS despite their quality—in order to give them or sell the same to their domestic employees, for instance.[14] According to Ahluwalia (1991), the poorest four deciles (40 per cent households) purchased less than half the foodgrain sold by the PDS. Even today, depending on the products, the four last deciles only account for 45 to 55 per cent of PDS users, and purchase about 45 per cent of all the cereals transiting through the PDS. The rural poor do not even buy as much as 17 per cent of sugar. Overall, 40 per cent of the food grains, i.e. 6 million tonnes approximately, transit through the PDS in favour of the 'non-poor'.

However, some of the states had prematurely implemented a dual pricing policy depending on the degree of poverty. In the 1980s, these were Andhra Pradesh, Tamil Nadu, Gujarat, Karnataka, and Tripura. As for Himachal Pradesh, it granted special prices for high-mountain areas. Overall, it is logically in the states where the PDS functions the least badly that the poor use it the most (Swaminathan 2000).

Few of the Poor are Clients

Since 1997, the central government has been restricting subsidized distribution to households below the poverty line. These had first to be identified. The risk in any selection of beneficiaries was that too rigorous a filter left out a large number of the poor.

We shall see how the selection of beneficiaries was increasingly challenged in the name of the 'right to food' of every Indian citizen. Having said that, even when the PDS was not 'targeted' as such, many poor households lacked access to it. Indeed, a major obstacle is the availability of cash at the time of purchase. On days when the FPS are open and well-stocked, households have to have the cash to buy enough for the month, which is a major challenge for families accustomed to living a hand-to-mouth existence. In Orissa, in the poor Kalahandi region that Sarap and Mahamallik visited (2004), the official monthly allocation of 20 kg of rice per family did not meet even half the family's needs. Most households could not afford it. Many borrowed money from local moneylenders to buy their rations from the PDS! Thus, there appears to be a major lacuna in the food system. Despite subsidies, it acts more with regard to supply than demand, physical availability rather than economic access. Reaching the people downstream—intervening too late so to speak—it does not increase the purchasing power of the poor sufficiently and their entitlement remains highly limited.[15] The PDS is only effective, in the enhanced availability of food grains it offers. In that, it satisfies the logic that has governed its birth, shaped as it was by years of scarcity. But it is much less legitimate in the post-Green Revolution period, when at least in most regions the problem shifted towards the issue of demand and a minimum, guaranteed, and regular purchasing power.

The food policy tackles only the issue of food supply, by providing cheap food grains that are as physically and economically accessible as possible to the poor. But it would be more effective were it combined with a proper demand policy, i.e. one that tackles poverty by enabling an increase in income. Some commentators denounced the fundamentally charitable character of the present policy, which makes it possible to give out alms in the form of food without taking the risk of land reforms or truly redistributive measures. Others rely on expected results of poverty alleviation programmes such as the Integrated Rural Development Programme and its follower, the Swarnajayanti Gram Swarozgar Yojana, which are not very successful.

PDS ration cards are not given automatically to households. They are issued on the basis of a procedure that is both complicated on paper and leaves room for arbitrariness in practice, except in the rare effective states such as Kerala (Mooij 1999a). Apart from an identity photo and proof of residence—difficult or even impossible to get as far as the very poor are concerned—one often needs to spend a lot of time and even bribes to satisfy the officials. And it is not possible to make do with identity cards, because they are still very rare in India. In fact, it is rather the opposite: PDS cards are used as identity cards—for most of administrative procedures.

Few of the Poor Clients Buy a Lot

Many products are not always available—either the shop is closed, or it has not received the necessary deliveries (kerosene, for instance, is only available once a month). In early 2006 only kerosene was available in Mumbai, since cereal price was so little subsidized that there was no demand for it. For people working as day labourers, often away from their place of residence, for women often condemned to stay back in villages and walk miles away from where they live in search of water and firewood, the uncertainty with regard to the schedules and dates of the opening of the FPS would explain why in a tribal district in south-east Uttar Pradesh, 73 per cent of poor card-holders do not buy food grains from the PDS (Shankar 2004).

Thus, according to estimations for the end of the 1980s as given by Sharma (1997), poor households only gained the equivalent of two days of work per month through the PDS. According to Radhakrishna et al. (1996), in 1986–7, even considering non-food items, the poor saved only Rs. 2 to 3 per month through this system (i.e. less than 3 per cent of their monthly expenditure). Among them, those living in rural areas gained only 35 calories per day (or 2 per cent of their energy intake), and city-dwellers only 12 calories (i.e. a 0.7 per cent gain). The situation improved thereafter, with the continued extension of the PDS. In 1999–2000, the rural poor saved a little less than 6 per cent of their total consumption expenditure thanks to the PDS, but poor city-dwellers only 2.5 per cent. The corresponding Maps 3.16 and 3.17 clearly show the north-south contrast. Tamil Nadu's success, with savings of over 7 per cent, needs to be highlighted. Herein lies the entire issue—however limited is the PDS, it does have a slight impact on malnutrition, particularly that of children (Bhalotra 2002). Could it be reformed or should it be done away with at the risk of throwing out the baby with the bathwater?

It was this observation that governed the two successive reforms to ensure a targeting of the PDS towards the needy: the first made a spatial selection, the second a social selection.

The Revamped PDS was launched in 1992 to offer higher tonnage at cheaper prices in 'drought-prone areas', deserts, tribal zones, certain mountainous regions, and urban slums (24 per cent of the FPS came under the RPDS in 1995). It did not work too well, since the promised quantities were not always available and, in any case, the selection of blocks included areas that were not the poorest.

Above all, in 1997, the central government decided to implement what already existed in certain states: a socio-economic selection of PDS beneficiaries.[16] The Targeted PDS enabled households Below the Poverty Line or 'BPL households' to receive 10 kg of cereals per month at Rs. 3.50 per kg of rice and Rs. 2.50 per kg of wheat. The issue price was defined at half the economic cost in 2000, which meant that henceforth, BPL households had access to food grain at a lower price than the one they had paid under the previous single price system. The quota gradually increased to 35 kg in 2002, given the availability of stocks.[17] On the other hand, households above the poverty line (APL) were only entitled to prices that were not very advantageous, even defined as being equal to the economic cost in 2000–1, which *de facto* almost excluded them from the system, given the low quality-price ratio of PDS products.

The Revamped PDS was abandoned. Even though 'non-poor' households in mountainous states (Jammu & Kashmir, Himachal Pradesh, the north-east, Sikkim, Uttarakhand) continue to benefit

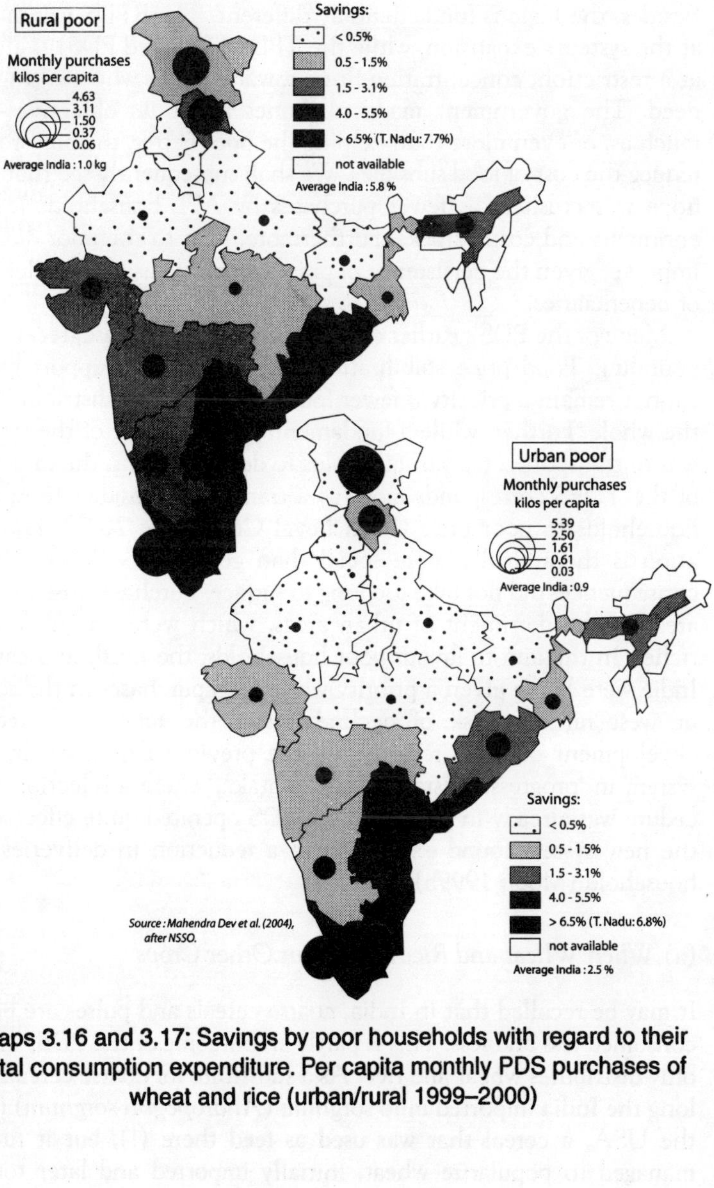

Maps 3.16 and 3.17: Savings by poor households with regard to their total consumption expenditure. Per capita monthly PDS purchases of wheat and rice (urban/rural 1999–2000)

from the same conditions as poor households, the targeting is now no longer based on geographical factors but socio-economic ones. Besides, the logic is fundamentally different. The RPDS was aimed at the system's expansion, while the TPDS (Targeted PDS) is aimed at a restriction, concentrating flows towards those who are truly in need. The government made no bones about its objectives—as much as, or even more than helping the poor better, the aim was to reduce the cost of food subsidies. We shall subsequently see that this hope was crushed, as fewer purchases by APL households led to enormous and costly stocks. Furthermore, help to the poor did not improve, given the persistence of practical problems in the selection of beneficiaries.

Many of the PDS's earlier objectives have, in any case, received a pounding. Food price stabilization and agricultural support prices cannot remain a priority if fewer food grains are now distributed on the whole. Further, while a fundamental *raison d'être* of the system was to transport cereals from surplus to deficit regions, the targeting of the TDPS corresponds more to a transfer of subsidies from rich households to poor ones (High Level Committee 2002). Equalization is theoretically more social than geographic. Space-related consequences did not take too long to surface. Purchases rose in rural areas to the detriment of urban areas, which were on an average richer. In the aim to favour poor households, the north and east of India were being given a priority while PDS purchases in the south or west ran the risk of decline, given the relative degree of development of these regions and the previous expansion by the system in 'progressive' states. In Karnataka, where a selection procedure was already in place and the PDS operated quite effectively, the new system found expression in a reduction in deliveries per household (Mooij 1999b).

(a) *When Wheat and Rice Drive Out Other Crops*

It may be recalled that in India, coarse cereals and pulses are being consumed less and less. This is partly an outcome of the PDS, which only distributes wheat and rice. As a substitute for coarse cereals, for long the India imported milo sorghum (*Andropogon sorghum*) from the USA, a cereal that was used as feed there (!), but it finally managed to popularize wheat, initially imported and later totally self-produced. Coarse cereals were distributed on a large scale only during the mid-1960s crisis (279,000 tonnes in 1967, i.e. a quarter of PDS distribution). The substitution by wheat and rice definitely had deplorable nutritional consequences since these cereals were not as rich in mineral and vitamin content as coarse cereals. The negative impact on local biodiversity was also remarkable, with many of the varieties traditionally cultivated tending to disappear (Srinivas and Thaha 2004).

However, PDS products brought about some food security, which did encourage some farmers to abandon rain-fed cereal production, which was not so 'profitable' in favour of cash crops such as oilseeds, whose selling prices had become quite advantageous during the state-supported 'yellow revolution' (Sagar 2002). In a way, the PDS presented farmers the opportunity to generate income that they would not otherwise have earned as they could not afford to take risks. However, today, oilseed and cotton prices are at their lowest, even though producers had neither experienced nor ever foreseen such a decrease in prices. This time, the PDS was hard put to providing a substantial safety net. Should the PDS system be held to blame for the many suicides by farmers that the media have never failed to publicize at the start of the twenty-first century?

Perhaps not, since this was not a game with just two pieces (PDS wheat or rice, *vis-à-vis* local cereals)—it had three pieces to it. For there to be a change in crops, a substitute for the local crop had to be available, one that was sufficiently profitable to allow farmers to abandon the local crop in its favour, despite prevailing food habits. PDS rice only competed with Kerala rice because more profitable cash crops were available there.

In fact, New Delhi's objective is rather clear: the expansion of the consumption of cereals of which India is a large producer, thereby reducing the diversity of regional consumption patterns in favour of the sole wheat–rice duo—or, better still, just wheat, whose considerable surpluses till 2005 are supplemented by ease of import. It was from 1953 onwards, in particular, with imports playing their part, that the central government subsidized wheat consumption in the south (Chopra 1988). In 1991, in the southern Karnataka rural areas, which consume finger millet, it was compulsory for those purchasing one kg sugar from the PDS to buy a kilo of wheat too (Landy 1994). And all this despite the fact that millets were practically unavailable in urban restaurants. Another sign was the expansion of roller flour mills in traditionally rice-eating states. In the 1970s, the industrial capacity increased in regions that could be described as pioneers, particularly in the south, unlike wheat-producing states, where it was harder to get a permit to set up flour mills and which received four times less grain for grinding from the FCI than other states (Acharya 1983).

On the national chessboard, the long arm of the federal government was now reallocating the pawns. Ever since it managed to build up buffer stocks, New Delhi felt that it had the upper hand. Thus, Map 3.1 showed the extent of wheat deficits in several states, demonstrating the spread of this cereal outside its traditional consumption basin—the entire south of India and the entire region up to Bengal and Bihar has become substantial consumers. Overall, wheat appears to be the only national-level crop, at least from the perspective of the network and the policy set up in its favour. Rice retains a certain regional dimension[18]—while the other food grains only enjoyed a local dimension for the most part.

(b) *The Urban Bias: A Comparison with China*

The advantage given to cities over rural areas had certainly been marked, giving rise to criticism of the 'urban bias', expounded by Lipton (1976).[19] Priority to wheat and rice over other cereals could thus be considered one of its features. Since the system worked thanks to foreign aid to a large extent, it has been argued that the (mainly urban) Indian taxpayers were contributing relatively little to its funding, unlike farmers who were receiving little subsidized grain but had to sell a lot at a taxed price. Above all, the origins of the PDS were urban. The 1943 commission had recommended the statutory rationing system (PDS public monopoly) for all major cities and its subsequent extension to the entire urban population, but it only suggested much more lax distribution in rural areas, for obvious practical reasons. Maps 2.5 and 2.6 on rice and wheat flows for 1960–1 illustrate the imbalance in their own way. The rice flows are particularly eloquent, given that imports entering the country in Calcutta or Bombay were hardly redistributed in the hinterland. The bulk was used for feeding the mega-cities, which means that Madhya Pradesh itself was being somewhat bled in favour of several cities in West Bengal and Maharashtra. It was only gradually that FPS were opened in medium-sized cities and then in rural areas (with some reverse movements, as in 1967, for instance, when rural distribution was completely forsaken because of low stocks). Indeed, the rural areas were almost abandoned in the event of any cereal scarcity, when actually public distribution would have been all the more necessary there. In the early 1980s, 85 per cent of PDS sales were undertaken in urban areas (which only accounted for 23 per cent of India's population).

The situation has changed a great deal since. At the end of the 1980s, only two-fifth of PDS shops were to be found in rural areas, but the percentage reached 80 per cent of the shops in 2001 (with 72 per cent Indians living in villages). It is also necessary to relate to the actual needs of urban and rural households. Ahluwalia (1993)—highly criticized—recalled that if people in rural areas did not seem to use much of PDS, it was essentially because a section of them consumed their own agricultural production. And what is more, according to the 1993–4 NSS round, cereal prices in rural areas were 16 per cent lower than in the cities.

The situation in rural areas is heterogeneous, since the most developed are the best supplied by the PDS network. How many landlocked villages are deprived of FPS? How many shops never receive any supplies or never open, as they are not easily accessed or serve a clientele that is deemed to be economically unviable? Admittedly, there are inequalities between cities and villages, but these no longer draw on a deliberately selective policy. So we cannot really speak of an 'urban bias'. In fact, long-term trends stand testimony to the massive efforts made to fold rural areas into the bosom of the nourishing state. All the more so since a financial approach would establish that the FCI functions with public credit whose fiscal origins are above all urban. Property taxes exist practically only in cities, farmers do not pay income tax, and commercial taxes are levied essentially on urban companies and consumers. If we oversimplify, we could say that cities fund an infrastructure that largely benefits the rural areas.

A comparison with the Chinese distribution system sheds light on the matter. Both countries sought to stabilize their populations in rural areas, in order to contain the extent of the rural exodus, but the modalities and the initial situations were evidently different. And it all happened at a totally different scale in China. Wheat and paddy production these exceeds 300 million tonnes—not including maize—i.e. almost 60 per cent more than India (for a population over 30 per cent larger). The 'special reserves'—the equivalent of

India's buffer stocks—amounted to 65 million tonnes since 1997. The State undertook 85 per cent of the marketing of cereals, and usually purchased 100 million tonnes per year, i.e. five times the PDS tonnages (Aubert 1999). However, the gradual dismantling of the system from 1992 onwards or, more precisely, its decentralization at province level, makes any statistical estimation difficult at the national level, and the Indian PDS now enjoys a wider scope than its Chinese cousin (Zhou and Wan 2005). In 2000 procurement was wound up in Eastern China, and in 2004 in the whole country.

In any case, Chinese distribution had never been universal and was always limited to urban areas. More precisely, it was limited to citizens who were legally registered as such. In fact, since 1958, there is a residence certificate (*hukou*) for each individual, which carries the description 'agricultural' or 'non-agricultural' as well as the locality of registration. Non-agricultural *hukous* offered several advantages, particularly a free supply of different food products (according to the type of locality, borough or large city). In times of maximum restrictions in China, the *hukou* was almost the equivalent of the Indian ration card, both from the point of view of food supplies and as an identity card.

Initially in China, people in rural areas, most of whom had an agricultural *hukou*, were prevented from staying in cities, except if they were covered by a specific work contract. The restrictions were gradually reduced with the establishment of a provisional city residence certificate in 1985, and in the 1990s it became possible to get a non-agricultural *hukou* after living in a city for a specific duration or after the purchase of (costly) property—the situations vary according to provinces and cities. Above all, a stigma remains associated with the bearers of an agricultural *hukou* in cities—a feeling of indignity that added to the various material humiliations to which they are subjected (absence of social security, expensive credit or credit that is impossible to get since they can leave at any moment, separate canteens in companies, etc.) (Thireau and Hua 2003).

Indeed, China's agricultural growth, its entry into the WTO, and the fall in world cereal prices could be considered factors that played a fundamental role in the relaxation of the system. It gradually became easier to supply food to city-dwellers, irrespective of whether they had an agricultural or non-agricultural *hukou*. The gradual extension of the PDS to the whole of India was due to comparable reasons, particularly because of Green Revolution gains. A more fundamental comparison concerns the policy adopted regarding rural exodus. One of the *hukou* system's objectives was to limit cities from growing into mega-cities, a problem that also existed in India. However, the reasoning used was almost completely opposite. The Chinese one was restrictive—not all urban dwellers were full-fledged citizens to enjoy the same rights, since migrants were stigmatized as transitory dwellers. Thus, it was expected that people would be discouraged from leaving their villages and moving to the towns. But the Indian reasoning was positive: food supplies to rural areas were facilitated and, since the Green Revolution, were used to support agricultural prices. China contained the pull of its cities, while India contained the push or repulsion from rural areas. Truly, the food policy is a very convenient tool for regional planning.

The fact that India is a democracy, unlike China, prevents it from adopting an authoritarian policy. Universal suffrage introduces a factor of rigidity in the mobility of its population, as the government cannot displease its voters, even if this means giving up any means to better distribute the population in the national territory. (This was a bit like the III French Republic in the nineteenth century, which could not encourage the rural exodus and the proletarianization of farmers and rural craftsmen too brutally, despite its industrialization needs, because of the early introduction of male universal suffrage. Indeed, French industrialists were forced to take recourse to foreign immigration.)

(c) *The Prevalence of Fraud*

The fact remains, however, that the functioning of the Indian system is far from satisfactory, given the number of fraudulent practices. Indeed, the extent of fraud is statistically perceptible at the national level. In its annual report, the Ministry of Food does not hesitate to publish the number of ration cards (198 million in 2001) along with the number of households that exist in India (194 million), clearly revealing that there is a significant number of bogus cards. In 2003–4 a Planning Commission survey estimated that 47.5 per cent of BPL cards were bogus (Saxena and Mander 2005). Another example has to do with the extension of PDS shops. In 1977 the number of FPS per capita was highest in Assam and Meghalaya, followed in particular by Kerala, but also by Punjab, strangely enough. There were much fewer shops in the crescent formed between Rajasthan and Uttar Pradesh, as was the case in Tamil Nadu. Instead of the official norm of one FPS for 2000 inhabitants, there were just 0.84 in India. Now there are 0.9 FPS per 2000 inhabitants in 2002. While the north-east remained in favour, Bihar or Punjab continue to enjoy the enviable position that neither corresponds to official PDS distribution tonnages or to the quantities declared during NSSO consumption surveys. Thus, the number of FPS is absolutely theoretical; many such shops only exist on paper. Unfortunately these figures have a high symbolical value, enabling the Indian state to delude itself about the realities of its food grain policy.

If we limit ourselves to statistical estimates, an official report by Tata Economic Consultancy Services sponsored by the Parliament estimated that 31 per cent of rice and 36 per cent of wheat did *not* reach the expected beneficiaries in 1997.[20] The proportion rose to 50 per cent in the north-eastern states as well as in Orissa, Bihar, and Punjab. It appears that obviously the PDS purchase figures published in NSSO surveys are far lower than the FCI official data. According to the Planning Commission, in 2003–4 37 per cent of food grain leaked out of the system (not even taking into account the BPL grain diverted to APL households!); Bihar lifted only 44 per cent of food grain allocated by the central government, and only 8 per cent of the allocated grain reached poor households. Meanwhile Tamil Nadu lifted 101 per cent [*sic*] of what had been allocated, out of which 85 per cent reached the consumers (Saxena and Mander 2005).

Indeed, the locations and times that particularly favour frauds and leakages can be distinguished both for procurement as well as for distribution as such (Figure 3.9).

At the start of the chain, millers or traders are able to bypass procurement operations, while they are obliged to sell a portion of their rice to the authorities at a fixed price in most states. Ministry of Food officials are themselves sometimes the first to indulge in illegal practices, not always in the general interest (Mooij 1999a). There are fewer frauds in high-surplus states like Punjab. Here, since market prices are lower, public purchases are looked upon favourably.

In mid-chain, police enquiries revealed, some public warehouses had 'false bottoms', with a hidden door at the back for secretly

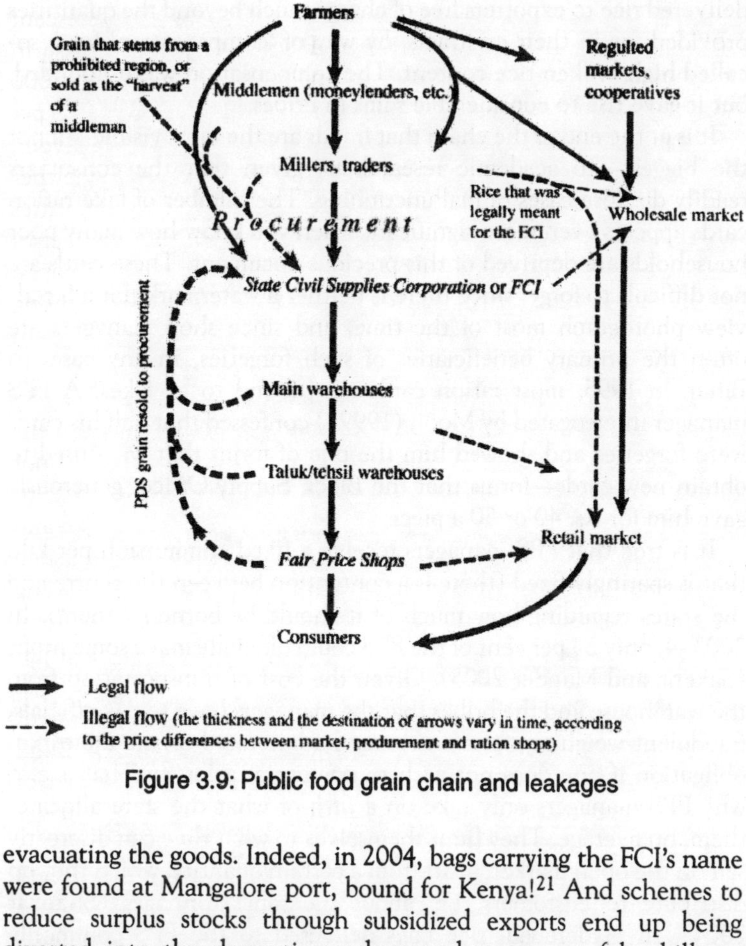

Figure 3.9: Public food grain chain and leakages

evacuating the goods. Indeed, in 2004, bags carrying the FCI's name were found at Mangalore port, bound for Kenya![21] And schemes to reduce surplus stocks through subsidized exports end up being diverted into the domestic market: traders present false bills to benefit from export subsidies.

During the breaking of loads (loading and unloading), 70 kg-grain bags can 'disappear' to end in the open market or in 9 tonne-trucks. There are fewer leaks when products are transported by train. Hence, in 2003, food grain exports by road were banned. Indeed, many traders who had bought cereals from the state at highly subsidized prices for purposes of export preferred to divert some of their trucks to the more lucrative domestic market. The same year, another scandal came to light involving senior FCI officials who had delivered rice to exporters free of charge much beyond the quantities provided for in their contracts, by way of 'compensation' for a so-called high broken rice content. The compensation was unfounded, but it gave rise to considerable sums in bribes.

It is at the end of the chain that frauds are the most visible—if not the biggest—to academic researchers, given that the consumers readily disclose cases of malfunctioning. The number of fake ration cards appears even more significant when you know how many poor households are deprived of this precious document. These cards are not difficult to forge, since there is neither a watermark nor a facial-view photograph most of the time, and since shop managers are often the primary beneficiaries of such forgeries, in any case. In Bihar, in 1995, most ration cards were found to be fakes. A FPS manager interrogated by Mooij (1999b) confessed that half his cards were forgeries and showed him the pile of forms that were used to obtain new cards—forms that the Block Supply Officer generously gave him for Rs. 40 or 50 a piece.

It is true that FPS managers receive a fixed commission per kilo that is sparingly fixed (there is a contention between the centre and the states regarding how much of it should be borne by them). In 2003–4, only 23 per cent of the FPS could officially make some profit (Saxena and Mander 2005). Given the cost of transportation from the warehouse and the bribes that the managers have to pay officials, fraudulent weighing, false entries and adulterated oil are almost an obligation if one does not wish to operate at a loss.[22] That is also why FPS managers only take on a *fifth* of what the state allocates them, on average. They limit themselves to what they can discreetly sell on the open market, apart from a certain quantity, which they do distribute to customers, i.e. about the same tonnages (Shankar 2004). In Hyderabad, rice bags delivered to the FPS commonly contain 2 to 4 per cent less grain than what is invoiced, as warehouse officials deduct their tithe. It is easy for the FPS Dealers Association to assert, 'We are cheating the people because we are cheated. The whole system of rationing is based on black marketing.'[23]

In addition, there are other situations that are difficult to describe as frauds. For instance, in around 1990 in what is currently Uttarakhand, FPS managers openly raised their selling price, since the FCI did not reimburse transportation costs between shop and public warehouse, unlike the practice in other mountainous regions (Nawani 1995). In more general terms, the state was unable to integrate FPSs within the more diversified network of cooperatives, which were nonetheless provided for in the Third and Fourth Five-Year Plans (Chopra 1988). Indeed, their highly specialized activities—a legacy of the times when these shops operated only during crisis situations—is no longer suited to long-term operations.

It is no use having more Food Inspectors for checking ration shops or lorries: the more inspectors there are, the greater is the scope for bribery. Low-level or high-level officials of the Ministries of Food and Railways, central or state administrations, politicians and notables, millers, merchants, private carriers—an entire series of actors intervenes at different levels of the chain. The multiplicity of controls means that most frauds are not necessarily individual or group initiatives, but the outcome of understandings between several actors and groups, each covering for the others in exchanging bribes. Each of these understandings is a link uniting those who commit the offence with those who are supposed to prevent it. All the links put together constitute what could be called the chain of corruption.

This has a significant vertical dimension. For most actors, it means extorting illegal revenue not just for the direct accumulation of wealth, but also to pay back debts, for instance, those contracted to obtain their post (Wade 1982). An official who has to wait several years and pay several bribes before obtaining a lucrative post with the State Civil Supplies Corporation has to find some money to pay off his expenses, get some reimbursement for this investments and cash in the interests—not to speak of all his friends and relatives, who would call him selfish if they failed to receive any largesse from him, now that he had obtained the coveted post. It is up to him to demand money from those under his domination, who do the same at their level—which leads to cascading corruption. In caricature (except perhaps in Kerala, thanks to an educated population and its political conscience), it could be said that everyone corrupts everyone else and everyone is corrupted by everyone else—from paddy buyers to senior officials. The only special cases are those at the ends of the chain. At one end, the top official, Minister or Chief Minister, had to spend a lot of money to obtain his post, but often owes nothing to anyone. He or she is the ultimate winner. At the other end, the farmer or the consumer suffers while getting nothing in compensation from any actors at lower level. Hence, they lose out twice.

It may be noted in particular that the administration (especially the State Civil Supplies Corporations) often has an extremely ambiguous attitude towards private actors. On the one hand, it is in competition with them, because of its purchases and its subsidized sales: different interventions that have a strong influence on the market. The administration is also in charge of implementing the regulations that are enacted within the framework of the Essential Commodities Act. At the end of the 1980s, major merchants in Karnataka, all-powerful that they were, found it difficult to sway the government and make it relax some of its controls (Mooij 1999a). The Act was highly useful in obliging merchants and millers to deliver their quota of levy rice to the state—working almost like blackmail. If the rice was not delivered, they were charged with non-compliance with the Act with regard to other practices in which they may have indulged.

On the other hand, the administration functions in line with the private sector, since for the most part it carries out the bulk of its procurement through the intermediaries such as millers, and food grain transportation is sub-contracted to private haulers, just as storage is sometimes sub-contracted to private operators. This kind of 'out-sourcing', which is not new, but which can only become more marked with the push for liberalization, presents a difficult dilemma for the Corporation. 'How do you compete with, or develop into an alternative to, your own subcontractors ?' (Mooij 1999: 182). This dilemma is often resolved with illegal arrangements and rigged invitations to tenders. Convictions under the Essential Commodities Act are very rare as compared to the number of offences noted, and the harshness of the Act seems yet another means to extract fresh bribes for officials and politicians, rather than a desire to facilitate the control of food grains in the name of public interest.

From all these perspectives, the state is definitely a 'mercantile state' (Harriss 1984). It takes on a large part of the marketing of food grains either directly (FCI) or indirectly (taking over of regulated markets), plus it is found to be closely associated with the trading milieu, even going so far as to fall under its domination. In Tamil Nadu, while it is the state that drafts the rules and laws, their implementation is rendered impossible by the power of the big traders (Harriss 1984). By the same token, the issue of the privatization of these public corporations, highly bureaucratic in nature, becomes meaningless: 'Private appropriation is much more a problem than the public character of the Corporations' (Mooij 1999: 189).

We cannot describe here the attitudes of different states in the face of such problems. Some of them do not react at all, since it is in the best interest of a large number of decision makers to retain the *status quo* (on Bihar, cf. Mooij 2003). Others like Andhra Pradesh introduce coupons, hoping to make leakages more difficult: the card-holders give a coupon to the ration shop keeper as a proof of purchase.[24] Andhra Pradesh also tries to establish greater transparency by trying to 'promote awareness' among the citizens so that they may demand their rights. It is the federal government that follows the most active policy, undoubtedly because it costs it little, given the fact that the system is decentralized. In 2001, a PDS (Control) Order was published pursuant to the Essential Commodities Act, which obliged the states to identify all households below the poverty line within three months, to update the list of ration-card holders every year, as well as to follow a drastic policy for improving the functioning of ration shops. The FPS had to report every month to the district collector, who had to send the state a summary, with the aggregated statistics being dispatched to Delhi. Rations had to be offered for sale at least once a week. At the same time, the centre reiterated that 'the PDS is the joint responsibility of the Central and the State Governments. The Centre is responsible for procurement, storage and transport of food grains up to the FCI depots. Distribution of these food grains is the primary responsibility of the States.'[25] Thus it was easy to pass the buck to the states as far as malfunctioning was concerned.

It was in the same spirit that the central Minister of Food published a 'citizen's charter' that stressed the duty of transparency and proper functioning of the PDS, at the launch of the Targeted PDS, in 1997 itself. In the text, the name of the concerned state was left blank, leaving it to the concerned government to replicate the 'model' as best possible.[26] Shop timings, time limits within which consumers' complaints had to be addressed, the establishment of vigilance committees at all levels (from the shop to the state administration)—everything was provided for in the greatest detail in order to regularize PDS operations. But at that time, the least that could be said is that the charter did not prove to be very effective. In Bihar, political parties control these committees

(Mooij 2003). In Hyderabad, Circle Food Advisory Committees do meet every quarter, without elected representatives being invited for fear of excessive politicization of assessments—though not without pernicious effects. As for local shop committees, they do not seem to exist in reality. In the absence of in-depth reform or any real social change, it would be difficult to see how such measures could lead to any results at all, not to speak of negative results, since the greater the number of controls, the greater the number of ways to get around them.

LIBERALIZATION, WISE CAUTION, OR CONFUSED VACILLATION?

Between a Food Policy and an Agricultural Policy

It ought to be appreciated that a policy of having a fixed buffer stock and distributing regular amounts of cereals through the PDS can work very effectively when imports constitute a dominant proportion of the buffer stock content. However, when the situation changes to one where a sizeable proportion of the buffer stock emerges from domestically produced cereals then the system of management of the food economy would have to be modified. (Tyagi 1990: 135–6)

Given the size of the country, the degree of instability in food production, the nature of price elasticity in the demand for food grains, and the low per capita income and its skewed distribution, it is imperative for the Government to continue to intervene in the marketing of food grains. (Ibid.: 181)

These two extracts from the same publication explain how the complexity of the situation can force an expert to give fairly contradictory opinions. The crux of the problem stems from the inadequacy of the mechanism once constituted to deal with shortages, which at present has to deal with excess production. It comes as no surprise that the FCI is facing problems in selling its stocks—and no longer in inventory investment.

It would be appropriate then to distinguish between an 'agricultural policy', a 'rural policy', and a 'food policy'. The latter relates above all to the consumption-production duo, by integrating urban and rural areas. This was the policy implemented in India thus far, and by the Common Agricultural Policy (CAP) created in 1960 when Europe wanted to be self-sufficient in cereal production. However, the CAP is now tending to become a more integraded 'rural' policy, not so much because production surplus is mounting, but because the WTO is threatening to dismantle the system if its objectives are not environmentally sound or 'multifunctional'. (India is still quite far from designing such a policy, given that it is not constrained to do so by the global context. Yet the environmental degradation it already faces ought to set it thinking along these lines.) As regards these two types of policies—'rural' and 'food'—the 'agricultural policy' appears to be the minimum. It deals with agriculture *per se*, and does not consider it a tool serving other more general purposes as do the first two. Priority to the production function was the case of the CAP in 1970–80. Today, this is the path preferred by some decision-makers and experts in india, although it gives an impetus to exports at the risk of dismantling the food system. Already, it is all happening as if the nation were giving precedence to farmers—at least to those who market their produce—by buying their surplus stock whatever be the situation, in spite of probably having to raise PDS prices in order to restrict budget expenditure (by which consumer subsidies are reduced). There is a risk that the food policy may be put on the back burner in favour of a 'single' agricultural policy.

The Vicious Circle of Food Subsidies, or how to Satisfy Exporters Alone

The PDS is no longer only a tool to offset crisis, but well and truly an instrument of economic policy; not only a means to fill empty stomachs, but also a vehicle for increasing agricultural output. Therefore it is not surprising that it finds itself a victim of its own ambitions. In a nutshell, the situation prevailing at the very beginning of this century can be described as a vicious circle, whose functioning could not be broken by political reforms, but by deficient monsoons since 2002, which paradoxically helped in lifting public stocks that had piled up (Ramaswami 2002), and later by the rise of world prices.

As in the case of most vicious circles, it is difficult to pinpoint the origin of the imbalance (Fig. 3.10).

(a) Let us start at the top of the model. A *regular hike in procurement prices* was necessitated by increased productivity and

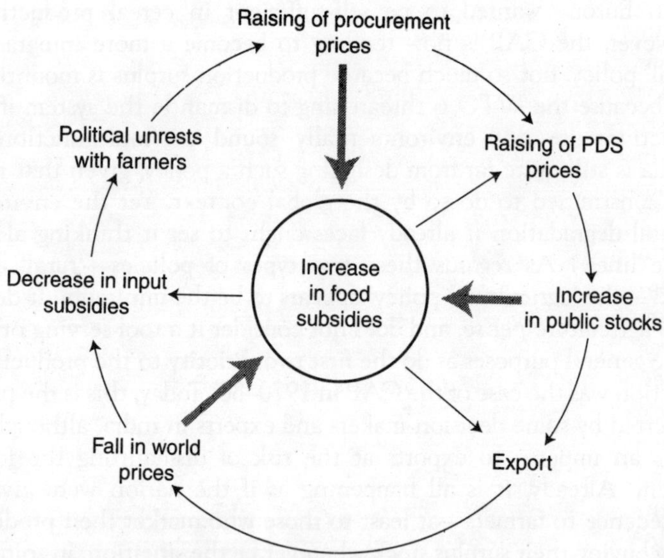

Source : Dorin and Landy forthcoming.

Figure 3.10: The vicious circle of food subsidies (1998–2003)

excess production situations that could make market prices plummet. To be fair, we should remember that for a long time agricultural procurement prices in India had remained extremely low. Even in 1993–4, whereas the support price in India was just 105 dollars a tonne, it was as high as 149 dollars in Pakistan and Egypt, 253 in Morocco, 133 in the EU (intervention price) and 147 in the United States (target price) (Charvet 1996). However, between 1996–7 and 2000–1, the wheat support price increased by 63 per cent and the paddy support price by 39 per cent. In the same period, wholesale prices rose by 27 per cent and 31 per cent respectively, whereas the global market price fell (in rupee terms) by 17 and 22 per cent.

For years and decades India's surplus farmers, the much reviled 'kulaks', sold grain, without complaining, to the Food Corporation of India at half the global price when global price was high, thus ensuring cheap food for urban areas. Now, when the global price has crashed, they have a moral right not to be abandoned to unfair competition from heavily subsidised foreign grain, and a right to be given enough price support to prevent their total ruin. (Patnaik 2004a: 25)

The CACP fixes the intervention price every year based on agricultural production costs. But it has not rid itself of the habit of arriving at a figure within the framework of a closed economy, which is not suitable for this century. Its computing methods are thus questioned by some experts, who are trying to pressure it to take the impact of global prices much more into account in deciding domestic production costs. But the CACP only has a consultative role. At the end of the day, it is the government that announces the procurement price, which has consistently been higher than the CACP's recommendation.[27] (Moreover, as a general rule, the price is announced only after seeding operations are over, which makes its regulatory effectiveness debatable.) From the beginning of the Green Revolution, some experts pointed out the danger of support prices being construed as a production incentive instead of a simple insurance against risk that partially covered production costs (Cummings 1969).[28] On the whole, in spite of the enormous inventory management costs, it was reckoned in 2000 that rice farmers gained 60 per cent of the FCI's total cost through the Minimum Support Price—a far from negligible amount (even if all rice farmers do not get the MSP, which however is the minimum legal price).

The state was forced to purchase all the grain offered for sale, even when global prices were low and public stocks were high. Potential private buyers were discouraged, which further impelled producers to sell their produce to the state, consequently increasing the system's inventory and budgetary expenditure. In 2000–1, it was estimated that 80 per cent of the wheat harvest in the market was procured by the state: thus, the private sector found itself practically out of the picture. Fraudulent dealings were encouraged: when the procurement price was much higher than the PDS sale price, sometimes both rice and wheat meant for PDS consumers were in reality resold to the State in the guise of procurement. The loop turned full circle through this kind of 'recycling', at the expense of the FCI, as Figure 3.9 also shows.

(b) Downstream, *PDS prices could not help but increase*, even if the state did once try to bear a large part of the swelling costs, only to delay the far from popular decision. The decision opted for in 1997 was to compensate for the strong rise in costs through a system that would be more advantageous for BPL families. Despite these low prices over a long period of time, however, these families have bought less and less during the previous few years—though not as little as APL families, of course. Apart from the problem of ration-card availability, it may be seen that the consequences of a dwindling APL clientele made PDS shops unviable—some of them even closed down, leaving BPL families 'high and dry'.

(c) Whenever PDS sale prices rose to keep pace with free market prices, *public stocks began to pile up*. That was the case when prices rose by 40 per cent between 1991 and 1994, taking the inventory to 37 million tonnes in June 1995. The same case arose in 1997, when prices for non-poor families were fixed at a higher rate and they simply stopped buying from the PDS. This has also been the case since 2000, when wheat and rice stocks even peaked to 65 million tonnes in 2002, which was nearly double the official standard—15 to 25 per cent of global stocks, according to certain estimates. In fact, in 2001 food grains sold through the PDS even fell to 1978 levels! In 2001–2, whereas a third of the wheat and a quarter of rice produced were bought by the government, redistribution accounted for only 30 per cent of procurement. The lack of customers forced the FCI and other stock holding agencies to store grain bags in the open air, which hastened their spoilage and made sales all the more difficult. This in turn resulted in a further inventory increase. In 2002–3, three million tonnes were 'unaccounted for' according to the government audit—they had either rotted or were stolen.[29]

(d) *Exports increased but difficulties persisted*, and not only because of a slump in global market prices at the end of 1990s. 'The psychological impact of stocks in the country's own warehouses is much greater than that of foreign exchange "reserve" searching to locate food grains in world markets' (Dantwala 1996: 284).

It was, in fact, a twofold problem, structural and due to specific circumstances. Structurally, there was a fundamental imbalance, only partially alleviated by years of continued agricultural growth: India consumes 30 to 40 per cent more rice than wheat. But the Green Revolution bore fruit above all in the wheat belt, a cereal that was also easier to import. It would have been better (had the option been feasible!) to concentrate on rice, which has a much narrower international market.

On the other hand, during the previous years, the problem lay almost as much with rice as with wheat, in a situation where it was difficult to export surplus production. However, export liberalization had been strengthened at the end of the previous century. In 2001 private players were authorized to buy wheat from the FCI for export and exports were totally liberalized by 2002, with the removal of the ceiling on exportable tonnage. From that time onwards, the Ministries of Agriculture in Punjab and Haryana have their own 'WTO cell', with a brief to keep a watch on the economy. This should be seen as the emergence of a growing awareness, no doubt provoked by the piling up of stocks, about 'thinking global', beyond the domestic market, as well as an appreciation of the difficulties involved in keeping track of the vagaries of global market and non-tariff barriers.

In 2002–3, seven million tonnes of rice and 5.5 million tonnes of wheat lifted from public stocks were exported. The following year, it was 3 and 7 million tonnes. India became the second largest rice exporter in the world, and the seventh largest wheat exporter. But the result was far from satisfactory, for the foreign currency earned through exports came at a very high price indeed. After this, the government depended on private players to absorb the surplus stock, apart from institutional exporters like the public sector STC and MMTC. These traders sometimes purchased produce at the same subsidized price at which the PDS sold to 'poor' BPL households, sometimes at even lower rates. Also, they often circumvented the 'first bag in–first bag out' principle and obtained the latest harvest to reach the warehouse, thereby leaving the FCI holding old grain. The subsidies offered to these exporters contravened the WTO directives, and India was accused of dumping. Finally, a part of the grain receiving export subsidies found its way back to the domestic market! In 2000–1, the FCI sold 1.6 million tonnes of wheat for export purposes, but in reality only 700,000 tonnes were actually exported (Chand 2005). It was absolutely scandalous that India subsidized foreign consumers instead of alleviating the suffering of its poorest citizens.[30] True, a part of the stock exported in 2003 had been procured in 1998, and it could have been exported only at a heavy discount. But it may be argued that this stock could have been distributed to a section of its population living in a drought-prone area who were hard pressed to make ends meet and fill their stomachs.

Of course, these subsidies indirectly benefited farmers. They provided an outlet for stocks and thereby maintained domestic purchases. However, there is a crying need for a long-term policy. The way things are going, it is as if India has already entered certain cycles, more or less dependent on changes in global market prices, marked by periods of abundant stocks and exports alternating with relative shortages and buffer stock imports (with the last such imports occurring in 1997 and in 2006 and 2007). In the first case, India is subsidizing white meat consumers in developed countries or cereal consumers in poor countries; in the second case, it is importing the same cereals that it has not found use for a few months earlier, sometimes at higher prices. The media often overlook this, underlining the transitory situation and forgetting the reverse situation that existed five years earlier: minimum levels into government stocks in 1997, maximum in 2002, and once again, a low level in 2004 that lead to wheat imports in 2006–7.

Why had India to wait for global market prices to rise in order to save the system? Prices started rising again since 2003 bringing back the situation to 'normally': in general, before the end of the 1990s, India's domestic cereal prices were lower than global market prices (Nayyar and Sen 1994), in spite of the high subsidies enjoyed by farmers and exporters in developed countries. This could be explained by a cheap Indian labour force and a generally low cost of production in a relatively closed economy. The rupee exchange rate took care of the rest—one dollar was worth Rs. 48 in 2001, against less than Rs. 8 twenty years earlier.

But the depreciation of the rupee was not the deciding factor explaining the rise in cereal exports. The 25 per cent devaluation in 1991 had no clear impact on the trade balance (Figure 2.2). Indian agriculture is too fragile not to be heavily dependent upon the vagaries of the monsoon, and not much can be expected from a rise or fall in global market prices or fluctuating exchange rates (Patnaik 1997). For instance, in 1995–6, wheat exports rose to 2 million tonnes due to a favourable price differential—food grain stocks rose to 34 million tonnes. But in the following year, the conjunction of high demand for PDS cereals (whose prices had remained unchanged since 1994) and meagre procurement (farmers did not find the support price very profitable) led to a relative wheat shortage. India was forced to import 2 million tonnes of wheat at a higher rate in 1997 (Landy 2004). This scenario appeared again in 2006 when international traders such as Cargill competed for wheat procurement while the FCI was continuing disposing of its stocks (Raghavan 2006). The liberalization of wholesale markets launched in 2003 allowed Indian and foreign global traders to bypass public procurement by offering higher prices to farmers, depleting the national stocks and forcing the authorities to import 5.5 million tonnes of wheat in 2006. India is still a greenhorn in the high stakes of the global trade game. Even if it were more experienced, it must not allow itself to run the risk of depending on real or expected changes in global market prices to define its agriculture and food policy.

Not only exporting food grain is difficult, competition from imports also threatens national production. Since non-tariff barriers were abolished in 2001, import duties are the only official tool that help restrict the entry of food products. On the other hand, these tariffs remain relatively low, which prompted the High Level Committee on Food Grains to demand that the 'tariffs inclusive of cost of imports do not fall below the economic cost of supplying peninsular India with grain purchased at MSP in north and east India' (High Level Committee, 2002, §3.4). The tariff ceilings approved by the WTO allow the government a fairly wide margin of manoeuvre in this matter.

India still remains a rookie player not only due to its lack of commercial know-how, but also due to infrastructural shortcomings. Its ports continue to function in the light of past needs, facilitating unloading rather than loading. Structurally, they have remained ports for imports. In 1995, the waiting time was one month to export food grains from Kandla, totally inundated with 2,000 tonnes a day. The Navi Mumbai Nehru Port is not very different (whereas Kochi and New Mangalore are actually under-utilized today). A modern machinery to clean and sort food grain would also bring a lot of relief, given the bad quality of grain unloaded from trains.

For the final problem has to do with quality. In mid 2001, Indian wheat did not find any takers for more than 110 dollars FOB per ton, that is 50 dollars cheaper than American or Australian wheat. Only the Middle East, South Asia and Africa accept Indian quality on the whole—Iraq refused to accept three successive cargos containing excessive inorganic matter.

(d) On the whole, the *food subsidy bill kept rising.* The food subsidy corresponds to the difference between the state's economic cost and the FPS issue price. The figure varies, according to different sources. However, most of them agree to a sum of a little less than 1 per cent of the GDP (High Level Committee, 2002).[31] Thus, it was far from the goal set by the Enquiry Commission on Food Grains, which asserted in 1957 that the PDS ought to operate on a no profit-no loss basis.[32] Therefore, almost all analysts view the 1 per cent subsidy as rather excessive. However, it is actually justifiable, given the nutritional needs of one-third of the population. It may also be recalled that agricultural subsidies alone in OECD countries stood at 1.3 per cent of the GDP in 2001. On the other hand, it was true that a major portion of subsidies in India were spent on inventory management. In 2001, 'the 230 million rupees spent every day on managing stocks' accounted for two-thirds of the food subsidy bill (as against 18 per cent in 1998–9).[33] This may have been profitable for producers, but despite the term 'food subsidy', it in no way benefited consumers. In fact, the sale of stocks would have been in the latter's interest (Krishnaji 1990). Only 5 per cent of the 'food subsidy' reached consumers living below the poverty line (Shankar 2004).

The FCI also benefits from credit granted at a relatively low interest rate,[34] as well as subsidized railway freight charges with a priority for the movement of goods. Were it not so, it would be even less competitive than private trade. A number of critics point out the rampant corruption at all managerial levels, its bloated bureaucracy, and its overly powerful trade unions. Very rarely do observers like Acharya (2002) attribute cost-effective management to the FCI. In any case, assessment is not an easy task, if we take into account the maintenance costs of the railway network and, above all, the external effects (externalities) of public sector origin enjoyed by FCI's competitors. The private sector benefits from roads maintained by the government, from commercial infrastructures built by public investment, etc., and there is no lack of reasons to spring to the defence of the FCI. For example, the distribution system in some states is totally bankrupt, which impedes lifting stocks from the FCI even though it is ready to provide more to the states. The FCI 'has to buy whatever is offered at MSPs which it does not fix; and deliver allocated supplies to states, again at prices which it does not control. Moreover, these prices are pan-national and pan-seasonal, so demand is largest from most distant locations and in periods involving longest storage' (High Level Committee 2002, §2.24). Perhaps what was also not taken sufficiently into account was that the price rise was partly due to the extension of the PDS all over India. The average FCI supply distance is approximately 1,500 km. And the FCI has to supply ever-increasing quantities over ever-increasing distances, but at the same price. In 1971, less than 12 million tonnes were distributed through 242,000 FPS. In 2003–4, nearly 23 million tonnes were sold through nearly 476,000 FPS.

The problem is that while the overall subsidy has increased, the same holds true for the subsidy per quintal.

> So long as cheap imported wheat constituted the bulk of the quantity distributed through the public distribution system, the overall subsidy burden was very small. However, with the world market prices of wheat rising sharply after 1971, the burden of subsidy began to increase at a rapid rate. In addition to this, by the middle of the seventies the distribution of rice was also subsidised. (Tyagi 1990: 131)

At the beginning of this century, global wheat market prices were at a low ebb, but since India no longer imported wheat, this has brought no relief. On the contrary, it has impeded exports.

(f) One possible solution, it is said, would be *to reduce input subsidies* to alleviate the national budget. This would also have the advantage of reducing certain wastage and pernicious effects, such as the over-utilization of irrigation water, power and fertilizer in some regions. It has been often stated that the rise in input subsidies compounded by the decline of government investment in agriculture had increased the gap between irrigated regions (which use too many inputs) and other regions (which do not irrigate). At present, only central fertilizer subsidies have been considerably reduced, and some of the states have imposed a steep hike of duties on power supply. The problem is that contrary to the food subsidy, agricultural water and power subsidies are borne by the state governments rather than the centre, which in no way lessens the centre's financial burden. The centre often fills in the holes in the state budgets, eventually. Further, any hike in input prices would imperil small farmers. Finally, farmers unions would protest, insisting upon the withdrawal of certain measures or at least an raising of the procurement price as compensation. And tough luck if the latter demand offers small farmers no benefits—to the contrary, since they buy from the market and do not sell their produce.

> Let us cut out the nonsense and call a spade a spade: the government is of the rich, by the rich, for the rich. Food grain stocks are not supposed to be released either free or at low prices to the hungry and the needy. The purpose of stock-building is to provide the fullest insurance to rich peasants. As for the poor, they are expected to fend for themselves; they should not be greedy

and hanker after a portion of the huge stockpile of grains. (A.M., 'Calcutta Diary', *Economic and Political Weekly*, 22 June 2002: 2383)

On the whole, given the inefficiency of the PDS, quite a few observers did not hesitate to condemn a policy only meant to support agricultural prices through procurement, 'with the poor providing only an excuse for the huge subsidies and physical losses in food grains' (Rao and Deshpande 2002: 3678). The total cost of the food system has increased faster than has the procurement price, which means that the state kept spending more without satisfying the farmers. The vicious circle was then closed—since PDS prices were the same as in the open market, and sometimes higher, for the same quality, sales fell, inventory increased, and this consequently raised the financial burden. The crisis was aggravated by an increased selection of beneficiaries, which in turn led to piling up of stocks by reducing sales.

To these criticisms of a rather economic nature was added social censure about malnutrition, which meant that the PDS was criticized both by the 'left' and the 'right', for doing too much and for too little. Everybody unanimously denounced the surplus stock position at the beginning of this century, until the stock shrank in 2004. The discord revolved around its utilization.

The Solutions Implemented, or how to Dispose of Stocks

In 2006 the issue was no longer to dispose of stocks, but to refill them through imports. This sudden change had not been due to bad harvests, but the liberalization of wholesale markets through the State Agricultural Produce Marketing (Development and Regulation) Act, 2003. This central 'model act' encouraged or forced the states to dismantle the monopoly of regulated markets and let Cargill, ITC, and other big companies directly buy from farmers. Procurement dropped to 9 million tonnes, depleting the stocks, and even leading to imports.

Liberalization, no doubt, is changing the deal. It is to be expected, however, that in times of low global prices public procurement becomes again the main outlet for farmers, at the risk of inflating government stocks. India would be back to the situation of 2001. Let us examine the solutions implemented for disposing stocks at that time.

(a) *Resale in the Open Market*

Accounting and financial approaches favoured 'open market sales', since sometimes subsidies could then be avoided. From the late 1970s, the government had begun to sell wheat from old stocks to flour mills, at subsidized rates, especially in predominantly rice consuming regions, in order to popularize its consumption. This system was later abandoned in 1986, and replaced by direct sales through the FCI in the open market, again at subsidized rates but with no target population in mind. The first open market sales took place in 1985. They increased in frequency for wheat, but rarely for rice.

However, this resale gave rise to numerous problems. The first issue raised was that of socio-economic justice. As in the case of exports, the rich wholesalers and traders were the ones who benefited from a system designed above all to feed the poor, and often through subsidies. Spatial justice too came under fire. The FCI's sale prices were lower in the north, due to lower transportation costs (Map 3.18). Thus, spatial equalization was reduced proportionately.

On the other hand, these sales, especially when they were subsidized at the initial stages, provoked a slump in prices in some local markets to the detriment of surplus farmer's interests. Finally, private buyers stopped buying on the open market, preferring to wait and purchase food grain at cheaper rates from the state, rather than directly from farmers at the MSP. However, when market rates were low, they were the first to resell to the state at the support price, using farmers as the figurehead (High Level Committee 2002). Such practices only contributed to the rising inventory in FCI warehouses.

(b) *The Rise in Distribution in the Name of the 'Right to Food'*

The social approach was in favour of offloading stocks directly for the benefit of the poorest of the poor in the name of the 'right to food'. Warehouses maintenance budgets would be reduced and empty stomachs filled. Even in the United States, weren't food stamps launched since the 1930s, following the Keynesian remedy of shoring up demand while reducing agricultural overproduction? Such a deadlock brought another actor into the game: the judiciary.

In 2001, a severe drought in Rajasthan followed by starvation deaths highlighted political weakness at two levels: the NDA

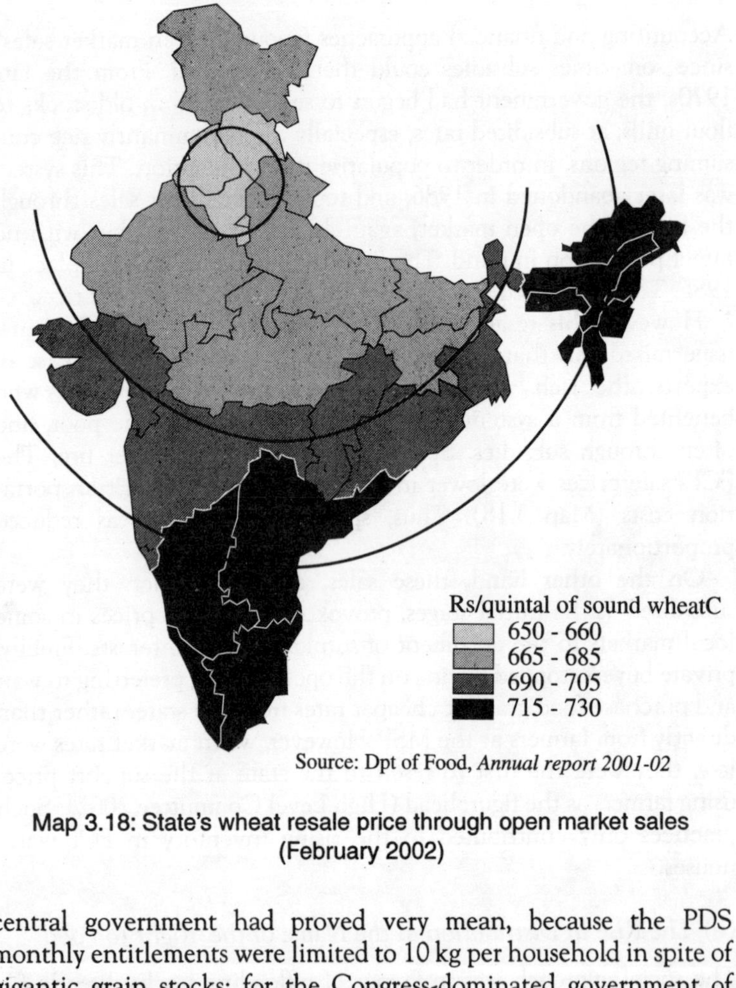

Map 3.18: State's wheat resale price through open market sales (February 2002)

central government had proved very mean, because the PDS monthly entitlements were limited to 10 kg per household in spite of gigantic grain stocks; for the Congress-dominated government of Rajasthan, it proved its apathy with a policy of 'labour ceiling' (relief work employment was restricted to 5 per cent of the drought-affected population) and the denial of starvation deaths. Since both the state and central governments turned inactive, one way to solve this dead end was to approach the judiciary. A powerful opinion wave carried journalists, lawyers, researchers, and activists to form the *Akal Sangharsh Samiti* (ASS—Network to Fight Drought and Famine) (Khera 2006). The People's Union for Civil Liberties, an

NGO member of ASS, used a tool that has become part of the judicial system in the late 1970s: it lodged a Public Interest Litigation (PIL) in the Supreme Court against the Civil Supplies Ministry, the FCI, and six state governments, citing Article 21 of the Constitution that guarantees the right to life.

In November 2001 the Supreme Court passed its interim order: all states should reopen closed ration shops; existing nutrition relief programmes should be legally accessible to all citizens; Antyodaya and Integrated Child Development Schemes should be effectively implemented; the state and union governments should ensure transparency in these programmes and give wide publicity to them; and finally, it was the responsibility of all state governments to provide free midday meals to school children A year later, taking cognizance of the apathy of some state governments in this matter, the Supreme Court warned them that central transfers would be withheld if they failed to implement the programme (Gaiha 2003).

Hence, the Supreme Court had defined a new right, not present as such in the Constitution despite its prolixity: the right to food (Drèze 2004; *Social Action* 2004).[35] Every Indian citizen, henceforth had the right of access to the national food grain stock if he or she had a genuine need. Far from being a fossil inherited from the era of shortages, in a way, the PDS became one of the pillars of Indian democracy. Thus, a new player had entered the food supply system, the judiciary. Commissioners were appointed by the Supreme Court to monitor the implementation of its orders in the various states. Their annual reports clearly highlight the 'continuing large scale failures by several governments to comply with various directions of the Supreme Court' (Saxena and Mander 2005). The judiciary's presence was increasingly felt in the daily life of Indians, especially since through PIL any citizen can seize the court of any matter concerning public interest. The Right to Information Act, passed in most of the states, is one more important judicial tool that should give some public control on administration and representatives' accountability. Active NGOs such as Ration Kruti Samiti in Maharashtra are working at every level, from the urban ward to the state and the centre (Jenkins and Goetz forthcoming), meeting every power (from the judicial to the political, not to speak of the power of people through public hearing—*jan sunvai*). Clearly, civil society is understanding that no solution can be found or implemented without involving new actors and making use of all the tools that the Indian democracy has put at its disposal. Judges are compensating for the failure of a number of elected representatives; in spite of active parliamentary Standing Committees on Food,[36] the Supreme Court is taking a part of the place of the Lok Sabha—is a judicial democracy supplanting India's representative democracy?

Supreme Court's orders are not always implemented by states nor other actors. One can wonder what is the power of an ordinary citizen if even the apex court lacks power to be heard. Nevertheless, a lot of change was accomplished in the first years of this century, to a large extent thanks to the growing awareness of people of their rights. Hence other distribution systems would also develop side by side, but in no way could this hide the truth that on an average, 30 per cent of stocks were either sold in the open market or exported (Figure 3.11).

(c) *Increasing 'Food for Work' and Free Midday Meal Schemes*

For a long time, government cereal stocks were utilized for purposes other than distribution through the PDS as such. But in the recent past, such practices have seen a considerable rise due to the huge stocks. In this respect, the following may be cited:

- Cereals distributed since 1985 in tribal zones at lower than PDS price under the *Integrated Tribal Development Programme.*
- Other structural uses, such as army rations, student hostels, and other institutions have received stocks.

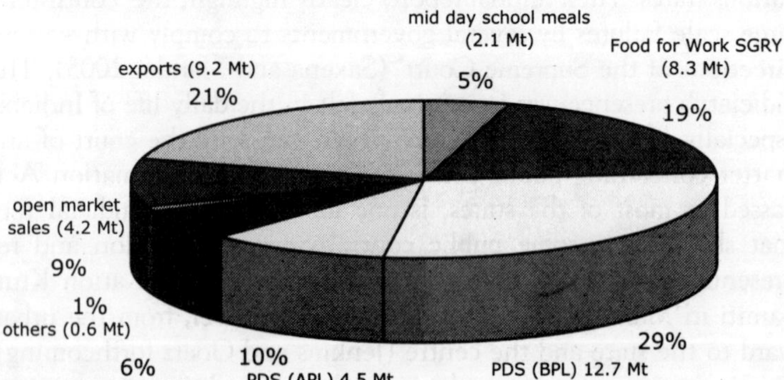

Figure 3.11: Utilization of government cereal stocks (triennial average 2001–2 to 2003–4)

- Need-based distribution has occurred in times of crisis (2,000 tonnes as earthquake relief in Gujarat in 2001). After the 2002–3 drought, the Andhra Pradesh government made 10 kg rice available for free to 1.6 million families for six months. And it promised 1,500 truckloads of hay to areas under severe fodder shortage. The centre seized the opportunity to dispose off 7 million tonnes of cereals.
- The World Food Programme supports a number of projects involved with food grain (Food for Work, Integrated Child Development Services, etc.).[37] The FCI supplies cereals locally, with the WFP taking the responsibility of refilling its stocks.

Two such programmes were recently in the news: food for work, and free midday meals in schools.

A reincarnation of the public works launched during the colonial period, the Food for Work programme was introduced in 1977 with three main aims: to give employment to the poor, create development infrastructure, and, unofficially, dispose of excess accumulated wheat stocks by ensuring a certain turnover.[38] (Even today, wheat constitutes three-quarters of the food grain distributed.) In fact, salaries are paid partly in kind, at a higher subsidy than PDS rates. During the 1987 drought, 6.6 million people were employed every day on public works sites, and we can only agree with Drèze and Sen (1989) that this programme was a major tool for avoiding a famine. According to these authors, it played an even more important role in revenue generation than in PDS distribution, which rather contributes to stabilizing prices. In 1995–6, the programme rose to 1.2 billion work days, but the momentum slackened gradually, and in 2001–2, a lack of funds brought it down to 523 million work days for 1.3 million tonnes of cereals distributed. If we add the tonnages distributed free during natural calamities, some of the years showed impressive figures (up to 11.5 tonnes in 2003–4), although they were lower than the quantity distributed through the PDS (22 million tones for the same year). On an average, 19 per cent of the stocks went to the SGRY (the current name for the Food for Work programme) in 2001–4 (Figure 3.11).

The programme received an impetus after the Congress-led coalition came to power at the centre in 2004. In 2005, a National Rural Employment Guarantee Scheme that envisages 100 days of guaranteed employment for at least one person from every poor family has been passed. It amounts to generating 5 billion workdays during difficult years. The programme is meant to be ubiquitous, for it shall progressively encompass the whole nation. It is also meant to improve the food ration, provide work to the unemployed, improve rural infrastructure, utilize food stocks—and all this, without inflationary pressures, thanks to limited cash payments.

In theory, this Food for Work programme would offer nothing but advantages (Drèze and Sen, 1989; Mahendra Dev 2004). Its utility can be contested in already advanced cases of undernourishment, when it becomes impossible for people who are already too weak to work. 'It is primarily preventive rather than curative as an anti-famine strategy' (Drèze and Sen 1989: 115). On the flip side, the food grains are sometimes hijacked (fraudulent employers using bulldozers instead of workers), the work undertaken fails to match needs, or is badly maintained, or falls into the hands of vested interests.

Drèze (2001) identified three reasons for government apathy during times of crisis (inclement weather, food shortages). First, short-sightedness or even disdain is evinced by urban politicians (both in the state capitals and in Delhi), sitting far away from the disaster-affected rural areas; secondly, budgetary constraints make state governments hesitate to launch further relief measures, while at the same time it is too great a temptation to seize food grains meant by the FCI to be sold at BPL rates and resell them covertly in the open market and thus fill state coffers (or certain private pockets). Finally, there are structural constraints, since the more food grains distributed through the PDS, the more prices will fall, which in turn makes it necessary to raise agricultural support prices and increase budgetary allocations. That is why Drèze recommends the following solution: more Food for Work schemes, lower support prices.

Drèze also strongly believes in midday meal schemes. 'Invented' with the help of CARE by the Tamil Nadu government in 1957, this scheme was extended to all parts of the country in 1995, but the centre provided to the state government free uncooked food products only, which was not enough of an incentive for poorer and more disorganized states. The free midday meal scheme was made mandatory only after a 2001 Supreme Court judgement. Initial results seemed promising. About 2004, the scheme provided a meal to 120 million children, and was the largest school feeding programme in the world despite the fact that it is yet to be actually implemented in some states. Drèze and Goyal (2003) found that there was a 15 per cent increase in student enrolment in the states of Chhattisgarh, Karnataka, and Rajasthan, more so in respect to girl child enrolments, and improved nutritional levels amongst the poorest students. Caste and class prejudices could also be reduced thanks to this kind of commensalism. Some observers also pointed out that fertility rates too would fall since children could no longer be sent to labour and that better nourishment would reduce child mortality rates.[39]

But on the flip side, numerous cases of food poisoning were also reported, which raised questions about the bad quality of the food served. Manpower and space shortages sometimes resulted in kitchens disturbing classrooms. Though the mixing of castes did show some progress, it was still far from being accepted universally, as many parents refused to let their children eat alongside 'untouchables', more so when cooks from these castes were recruited. But such problems can in no way belittle the relevance of this scheme, which was very cost-effective, considering its reach (less than 0.5 per cent of the GDP when all the country's schools are covered), improving nutrition, schooling as well as sociability—a scheme that will truly ensure food security.

Last, *Antyodaya Anna Yojana* (Food Programme for the Rising of the Last) is the most recent of the anti-poverty schemes, created within the PDS in 2001. 15 per cent of the poorest BPL households (i.e. 10 million families) were entitled to 5 kg of food grains at a special price.[40] It was officially decided that a quarter of BPL families would be covered under this scheme in 2003–4, and the quantity entitlement was increased to 35 kg from 2002. This third tier of the PDS was induced by a World Bank initiative aimed at separating the 'moderately' poor from the 'very poor'. However, it may be felt that this additional selection is a filtering operation that is as impracticable to implement as that of BPL families.

(d) *Growing Criticism of Beneficiary Selection*

The logic behind 'targeting' PDS beneficiaries needs to be reviewed. The authorities wish to eliminate non-needy families in order to concentrate subsidies for the poor, and kill two birds with one stone —bring down the budgetary allocation and at the same time design a more 'social' policy. The price elasticity of poor-household expenditures is high—in fact, they are the first victims of any increase in PDS prices. Thus, it was necessary to spare them as far possible, by sacrificing households that were above the poverty line. After all, even in Roman times, the famous system of *annona*—wheat imports organized by the Roman State for free distribution—was meant most of the time for poor Roman citizens, and the eligible people—*plebs frumentaria*—was registered in regularly updated lists (Garnsey, 1989).

The growing legion of detractors of the targeting procedure in India had many criticisms to make. For instance, the reduction of distribution flows goes against one of the main objectives of India's food policy—price stabilization. Inventory management costs increase when the selection is narrowed down too much and reduces the customer base. This has led to an increase in misappropriation and frauds, given the price differential. Since APL families tended to buy more from the open market, prices rose, making things more difficult for the poor. Above all, this led to social injustice, for some non-poor families too were included in the list (inclusion errors) or destitute families had slipped through the net (exclusion errors) (Swaminathan 2000). A study conducted in Gujarat in 2001 showed that 25 to 35 per cent of rich households managed to include themselves in the BPL list, whereas 10 to 15 per cent of the poorest were left out (Hirway 2003).

An inquiry in a poor Andhra Pradesh village (Swaminathan 2000) revealed that 63 per cent of BPL card-holding families were 'non-poor' (monthly income above Rs. 182 per head), whereas 60 per cent of the 'poor' did not have a card! In the same state, most households did not receive new cards between 1983 and 2003 despite the rise in the number of family members. According to an ORG-MARG poll, 18 per cent of BPL households did not possess a ration card.

In real terms, the TPDS functions as a revenue transfer from the central budget to the state budget, since some of the states made the decision to subsidize more households than the centre had provided for. In those years of high inventory, New Delhi did not balk at supplying more than the allotted food grain stock to provide for the 'poor', but refused to do so at BPL prices. It then fell on the states to fund the sale of 'APL rice' at 'BPL prices'. It was understandable that states tried to haggle over the price, as their budgets provisions were very limited.

At first, they resorted to delaying tactics (in 2000, only 18 of the 32 states and Union Territories had actually completed their BPL household census, and in 2005 only 23). Then, they argued that the number of poor families was higher than Planning Commission estimates. It was true that according to the Commission, people living below poverty line (37 per cent of the rural population and 32 per cent of the urban population in 1993–4) abruptly plummeted to 26 per cent of the total population in 1999–2000.[41] Andhra Pradesh insisted that it had 30 per cent BPL families, and not 22 per cent as claimed by the centre. It argued that the Commission erred in taking the deflationary effects of Andhra Pradesh's own rice subsidy programme into account in its estimate—in some way, it was making the state pay twice for its social policy. In 2005, four States (Tamil Nadu, Andhra Pradesh, Gujarat and Karnataka) had issued 15.4 million additional BPL cards and had allocated resources from their own budget to distribute rations to these households (Saxena and Mander 2005).

'If these poverty estimates remained in the ivory tower of academia it would not matter: but now targeted food distribution is being directly linked to poverty estimates, so their failure to capture ground reality becomes very dangerous' (Patnaik 2004: 27). The shortcomings of the selection criteria have to be acknowledged. The poverty line corresponds to the ability to buy 2400 calories of ration in rural areas and 2100 calories in urban areas (plus some non-food basic needs), which amounted respectively to about Rs. 370 and 560 per month per head in 2006. Even if adjustments are made at state level to take cognizance of regional differences in the cost of living, this comes to a ridiculous level.[42] Next, the poverty line is compared with the household income, a figure that is open to even more debate. Official criteria applied in 1997 by the Ministry of Rural Development added external signs of wealth—for example, if a woman owned more than three saris or if a man owned a bicycle, that could summarily exclude them from the list of BPL households (Hirway 2003). The income level of agricultural workers is always calculated on the basis of the legal minimum wage, which is never put into practice, and on the basis of a very optimistic estimate of the number of workdays per year. It should also be borne in mind that 90 per cent of India's working population is employed in the informal sector, where by definition incomes are not easy to precisely assess. Inhabitants of 'unnotified slums' (slums that are not officially recognized) cannot presumably benefit from the PDS, whereas their nutritional state would generally justify their inclusion on a priority basis. In rural Andhra Pradesh, whereas monthly income supposedly determines access to BPL cards, in practice, the real criterion is the size of landholding. This penalizes owners of vast but barren holdings, of which there are many in non-irrigated regions. On the other hand, in irrigated regions, quite a large number of relatively well-to-do families are classified under the poor category, despite owning high yielding tracts (Krishnaji and Krishnan 2000).

All said and done, many 'non-poor' families suffer from malnutrition if not from under-nourishment. According to the NSSO, in 1999–2000, no less then 80 per cent of rural households spent 60 per cent of their budget on food, as did 40 per cent of urban dwellers. (It should be borne in mind that the selection criteria designed in the United States for eligibility for food stamps is that one-third of the family budget should be spent on food. Under those terms, 90 per cent of the Indian population would become eligible for the TDPS.)[43] Is it worth a costly and inefficient targeting process? Food insecurity is compounded by the fact that India's inadequate administrative machinery is unable to succeed in this task, even if the selection procedure were justifiable.

The High Level Committee (2002) opined that on the whole, the 'targeting' of the PDS was way off target. The PDS ought to continue to reduce regional imbalances and stabilize prices and not seek to cover the poorest households as special cases. Its role is more geographic and economic than directly social in nature. It would be more practical to offer uniform prices for the whole population, at the same time distributing additional food coupons or other benefits to households needing special treatment, within or without the PDS.

Spatial Equality not Totally Discarded

Along with the liberalization policy, the 1990s witnessed the decline of the main tools for fighting against regional inequalities, which shall be dealt with in detail in Chapter Four. Planning funds were reduced, the public sector was shrinking, and centre to state fund transfers were curbed for fear of a huge budget deficit. From a political viewpoint, whereas the 'internal federalism of Congress was another means by which demands by regions and groups could be bartered' (Khilnani 1999: 103), this was no longer the case since the growth of non-Congress regional parties. Of all the mechanisms set up during the first decades of Independence, only a few survived, and the food system was one of them. Despite it all, since its economic cost could still be born given its political importance, since international institutions had accepted its continuation as such, there was nothing astonishing in the fact that it remained important in terms of spatial policies, with ever-huge food grain flows being transported over great distances.

The reticence shown by the state to trim its own wings can be seen in the changes made in the Essential Commodities Act. It may be recalled that this Act—passed during a period of shortages in 1955—allows state governments, within the legislative framework provided by the centre, to keep a close watch over 'the production, supply and distribution of, and trade and commerce, in certain commodities', especially food grain, apart from fodder and seed cakes, sugar, cotton, jute or onions. Malfunctioning and corruption led to a manifold increase in criticism against it (Mooij 1999a). But it was only in 2002 that an order was passed, laying down that 'any dealer may freely buy, stock, sell, transport, distribute, dispose, acquire, use or consume any quantity of wheat, paddy/rice, coarse grains, sugar, edible oilseeds and edible oils and shall not require a permit or license therefore'.[44] According to the Finance Minister, the lifting of controls ought to lead to a 'country-wide integrated market of agricultural products'.[45]

Was this the end of controls? Not at all! State governments still have to implement the order through their legislatures. And, these governments tend to create 'distortions'—always seeking more funds, they impose heavy duties on commercial transactions, which deter private traders and thus increase the FCI's obligation to buy more. Further, it is quite believable that governments will remain faithful to a lucrative system. Its abrogation passed on paper does not mean that it ceases to exist in practice. Finally, the order itself provides the arms to fight against itself: 'Nothing contained in this Order shall affect the operations of the Public Distribution System (Control) Order, 2001, issued by the Central Government and orders of the State Governments issued in pursuance thereof.' The PDS retains its priority, which means that controls continue to prevail in most cases. And while the same order reduced the number of essential commodities to seventeen—exit electrical irons, switches, cement, and synthetic textiles—it nonetheless continued to cover agricultural products.

The maintenance of the enormous food distribution machinery was left in the hands of the FCI—Indian Railways combine for transporting food grain from one end of the country to the other, although, in the name of market integration and private sector efficiency, more space for other players would have been expected.

(a) *Railway Logistics, Above All*

Three months after launching relief operations for drought affected farmers [in summer of 2003], some southern and central livestock farmers in France are still awaiting the arrival of the promised hay. Transporting fodder collected from the cereal farming districts of the north remains the main concern of this sector. In many regions and districts, the FNSEA and the Confederation Paysanne [farmers' unions] condemned the sluggish implementation of this measure. 'The army sent just a few pathetic convoys and the French Railways parsimoniously allocated a few rafts—that too at exorbitant rates,' criticised the union (...). Some 122,000 tonnes of hay were transported to deficit districts, where it was offered at a 'reasonable' price according to the FNSEA, in order to fight against speculation by certain traders. Around 125,000 tonnes were expected to be transported in the following weeks. The remaining 125,000 tonnes still have no takers for transportation. The imminent rainy season gives rise to the fear that they may rot in the fields before being lifted. The tarpaulins do not offer enough protection against humidity (...). [The FNSEA] wants 'additional rafts', but above all, it wants the transportation of these stocks to be given priority over other goods. (G. Dupont, in the French daily *Le Monde*, 24 october 2003)

The PDS rice and wheat purchase maps (Maps 3.19 and 3.20) revealed two more-or-less nested western and eastern crescents, which signified two highly segmented markets. That is another challenge to be met by the FCI's logistics department. Does the map of FCI transports reflect the same geographical divide? Yes in the case of wheat. Map 3.9 shows essential inputs from Punjab and to a lesser extent from Haryana, from where distribution to the western crescent began. From April to December, the Northern Railways network provides twenty trains a day for transportation. The distances covered are indeed huge. For example, it takes 6 to 7 days

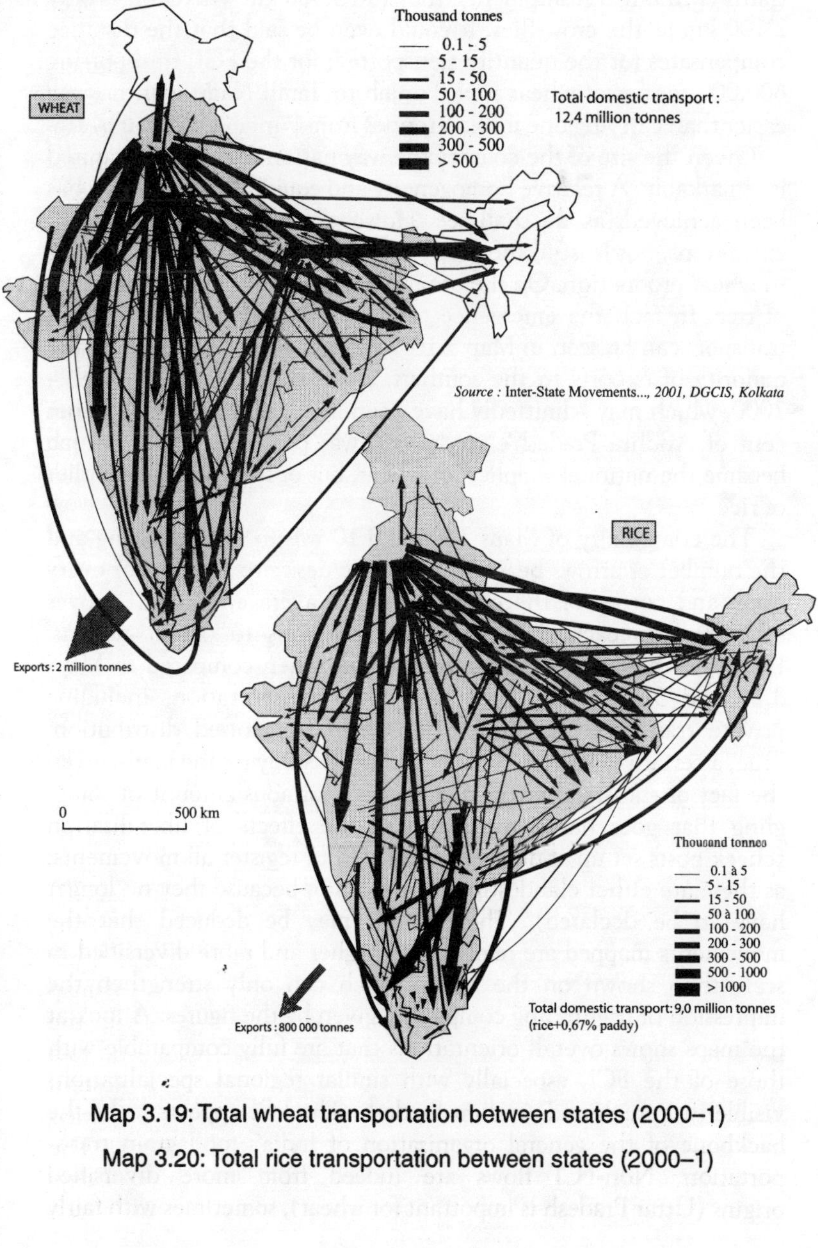

Map 3.19: Total wheat transportation between states (2000–1)

Map 3.20: Total rice transportation between states (2000–1)

to cover the distance between Punjab and Kerala through direct trains (without transhipment): they run 3,500 km whereas it is only 2,100 km as the crow flies. It could even be said that the distance compensates for the quantity transported: for the FCI, transporting 600,000 tonnes of wheat from Punjab to Tamil Nadu is in no way easier than carrying one million tonnes from Punjab to Maharashtra.

Given the size of the country the way national space is organized is remarkable. A relative homogeneity and equitable distribution has been achieved, as we shall see. However, there are a number of exceptions, not least in the food system, due to Punjab's pivotal role in wheat production. On the other hand, it is not so bad in the case of rice. In fact, the emergence of a second southern pole for rice transport can be seen in Map 3.10—Andhra Pradesh takes over the majority of exports to the southern states from Punjab. In 1999–2000, which may admittedly have been an exceptional year, 52 per cent of Andhra Pradesh's production was procured. Thus, Punjab became the national supplier for wheat, but only a regional supplier of rice.

The complexity of Maps 3.9 and 3.10 was in itself amazing and the number of arrows bear witness to the desire to provide for every nook and corner of the country. On an average, the FCI moves 400,000 bags each day from surplus regions to deficit regions. However, these maps seem rather simple when compared to Maps 3.19 and 3.20, which show the *total* transportation, including private transportation in addition to FCI-organized distribution. True, a certain margin should be read while studying the maps, given the fact of statistical errors due to the enormous amount of smuggling that goes hand in hand with the effects of liberalization (check posts set up at different points fail to register all movements, as these are either clandestine operations or because they no longer have to be declared). Therefore, it may be deduced that the movements mapped are really much higher and more diversified in scale than shown on the maps, which can only strengthen the impression of frightening complexity given by the figures. A look at the maps shows overall orientations that are fully comparable with those of the FCI, especially with similar regional specializations visible in Punjab and Andhra Pradesh. The FCI appears to be the backbone of the general organization of India's food grain transportation. Non-FCI flows are indeed from more diversified origins (Uttar Pradesh is important for wheat), sometimes with fairly different destinations (West Bengal is important for rice), but they only give flesh to a skeleton that has already been created by the FCI.[46]

Let us end with a final comparison with the situation that prevailed in 1960–1, before the Green Revolution (Maps 2.5 and 2.6). That situation involved a radically different framework, since it was directed from the coasts to the hinterland, with imports constituting the main flows and Punjab capable of supplying Delhi alone at the time. To take a leaf out of Marc Côte's remarks on Algeria, we could speak about an 'inverted space'. This was especially the case with wheat, the only cereal distributed in large quantities through the PDS at that time. Already, enormous distances were being covered to ensure distribution, although the tonnages involved were paltry in comparison. Although the graphic scales are slightly different, what can clearly be seen is how the flows grew as consumption rose. The spatial relationships with regard to wheat and rice flows are almost the reverse. In fact, in the 1960s, wheat movements were both quantitatively higher and geographically more diversified than in the case of rice (wheat flows took place between almost all the states). Abundant wheat imports originated at all coastal ports, whereas rice supplies largely came from domestic production, already dominated by Andhra Pradesh and to a lesser extent Punjab and present-day Chhattisgarh. In 2000–1, rice flows almost caught up with the quantities of wheat transported (9.0 million tonnes as against 12.4 tonnes of wheat), and the spider's web they spun was extremely dense, as they did not suffer as much from the polarization of their origin as wheat flows. (However, they were also affected by the north-south direction of most flows.)

Central food grain allotments are organized on a monthly basis through 'monthly movement plans', depending on the requirements of different states, the inventory status, and local procurement, as well as storage capacities and rail transport. Monthly movements are more than two million tonnes now. The cardinal principle is always to store three months buffer stock in every state. Warehouses in Kashmir have to be full by December, as the winter snows would block movement. There is also the problem of overcoming difficulties in regions affected by heavy monsoons. Apart from the state-level monthly plans, 'daily movement plans' are also drawn up to provide for district-level movements and storage. When the local level is reached and trucks replace trains to move food grains to taluk/tehsil warehouses over distances of less than 300 km, the FCI passes the baton on to its miniature clones—the State Civil Supplies Corporations, responsible for real distribution as well as procurement.[47]

As a corollary, there are legal 'breaks of load' when the central government hands over the responsibility to state governments. Central storage depots at major hubs and important railway stations store a substantial part of the tonnage. The central government's responsibility ends once the stock is delivered to the secondary depots, often found at train/truck transit points. After that, transportation becomes a part of 'distribution' and thus a state responsibility. Mountain states (north-east, Himachal Pradesh and Uttrakhand) are placed under a special category for which the FCI reimburses transportation costs from the 'central depots'. However, Acharya (1983) observed that less densely-populated regions like Rajasthan and Madhya Pradesh deserved similar privileges but have been denied them.

The Indian Railways is considered a colossus with 1.5 million employees and 108,000 km tracks—Atlas holding up almost the entire public food distribution system. Nearly the entire FCI food stock is transported by rail (98 per cent in 2000–1). 27 per cent of India's rail traffic involves food grain flows. Albeit better than the road network in most African countries, half of India's roads are still untarred and compare unfavourably with the Chinese network in quality, especially as regards the main highways. Hence, trucks are used only at either end of the network, at local procurement and distribution levels. Trains are more viable for distances above 300 km. (Private traders pay the same freight charges as the public sector does, but 90 per cent of the cereals traded by the private sector are moved by truck due to shorter distances and the FCI's priority status in train movements.) Coastal shipping is marginal due to the heavily congested ports and transhipment problems (truck-train-ship-train-truck . . .).[48]

Only one-fifth of the railway network is electrified and less than three-fourths has broad gauge. There are two bottlenecks in the national network: Balharsham, south of Nagpur, the country's geographical mid-point, a junction between the South Eastern, South Central and Central Railways; and Assam, where the double track rail network ends at Guwahati and where monsoons, extremists as well as shortages of trucks and warehouses make grain movement a difficult proposition. The problem is less of raft availability, and more of slow unloading operations which affect the upstream network and have repercussions on food grain originating regions.

The Indian Railways is supposed to transport three types of flows on a priority basis. Priority A is for the army, and priority B involves food grain and other movements at the behest of the state. (Priority C concerns other essential commodities such as cement and fertilizer.) The company would happily escape these requisitions since the freight charges fixed by the government are quite low.[49] The priority categories involve high costs, efficiency is at a low level for such movements, and offloading from trains becomes more and more difficult. The difficulties states face in receiving all the food grain allocated by the centre also have to be borne in mind. Either due to financial crises or because they possess abundant stocks in the absence of consumer buying, states sometimes do not know what to do with the food grain and end up shutting down depots and bringing wagons to a standstill. Other sectors than railways too experience the same problems: a system meant to overcome shortages is unable to handle abundance.

But the rail network is choked during times of shortage too, when the previous year has recorded a low harvest or when consumer buying through the PDS has increased. For instance, in 1996, the FCI estimated a shortage of three trains to supply the south each month (on an average, seven trains out of twenty originating in the north-west left for the south). The situation eased a bit during the following years, thanks to good monsoons, but also two other reasons —(i) infrastructure investments, thanks to which today diversions are necessary in case of strikes rather than overflowing warehouses, and (ii) Andhra Pradesh's rising role, which made supply decentralization possible. In 1996–7, the FCI moved 23.6 million tonnes; in 2000–1, only 16.2 million. That year, during peak periods, there was only one train that left for the south from Punjab–Haryana, as against seven from Andhra Pradesh—it had been the other way around fifteen years ago. Orissa and Madhya Pradesh undertake their own procurement and in certain years, Assam too is a surplus state (due to smuggling from Burma).

However, on the whole, the average distance covered by rail by a sack of grain was 1,400 km in 1980–90 (Chopra 1988). Today, it has reached 1500 km and at times even more (1665 km in 1995–6).

For during deficient harvesting seasons, it was (previously) necessary to move food grains from the port of import, and (now), from Punjab. During good seasons it is necessary to transport procured food grains and move them to exporting ports. Therefore, peculiar circuits could not be avoided, like sacks of grains sent from Punjab to Bangalore for the PDS, but which were later moved to Vishakhapatnam Port due to lack of takers, to be exported in the end.[50] (Detractors often suggested that since the FCI is not subsidized for intra-state rail movements, it purposely plans long hauls across state boundaries.)

On the whole, it is not conceivable to expect 'good years' for the railways. Problems are aplenty, whether there is deficit or surplus food grain production. Hence, the Indian Railways are a replica of the apparatus that enables it to function: a precariously balanced system, perpetually undergoing the shocks created by an over-ambitious policy or unsuitable tools.

(b) *Market Integration*

> While in one bazar, famine prices of four rupees per maund might be ruling, in another, not thirty miles off, the price would be but about rupee one and a half for the same quantity, yet no flow from the full to the exhausted market could take place, because roads were not in existence and means of carriage unknown. (Baird Smith, *Report on the North Western Provinces Famine of 1860-61*, quoted by Drèze 1995: 78)

Like many other commercial institutions in emerging countries, the FCI is caught between the devil and the deep blue sea. In fact, some experts opine that markets are sufficiently integrated to do away with the FCI, or at least downsize it substantially. This is a notion that is worthy of a debate.

When markets are integrated, it translates into a similar change in prices—this means the 'co-integration' of price series. Two markets are said to be spatially integrated if import costs in one are equal to export costs in the other, in addition to transportation and marketing costs. If this is not the case, it indicates infrastructure deficiencies, as much as the barriers raised between different political units. Indeed, that is the position taken by macro-economists. Harriss-White (1996) emphasized that the Indian situation (and it may be said, that of most countries of the South) was different and did not lend itself to such conclusions. A market was far from a neutral place where transactions were finalized in a straightforward manner. 'Derived markets' nest within, drawing sustenance from the former: an information market on price fluctuations, a by-products market, etc. To this should be added 'rental markets', so necessary for the proper functioning of transactions, such as transportation, storage of products or recruitment of labour. Indeed, there are a number of internal markets within the main market whose operations are based on 'power structures and relations and institutional idiosyncracies' (ibid.: 38). All these structures are closely 'interlocked not simply by their flows but also by the structure of their control', with the result that prices are determined by socio-economic relations (debts, patron–client relationships, relatives, etc.), as much as by the simple supply and demand relationship. So their specificity in terms of controls and powers makes comparison between the various cereal markets difficult, even if they are close by. Kaplan (1988), working on France in the eighteenth century, similarly differentiated between 'the market' as a principle (liberal economy model) and 'the market' as a place (where this principle could hardly be applied).

However, we must add that it is not just because both markets are 'integrated' that at the end of the network small farmers do not have to sell their produce at low rates to traders to whom they owe money, immediately after the monsoons; nor that poor consumers have necessarily the means to purchase food grains at relatively stable but higher prices. Market integration by itself does not render a food policy superfluous, as the latter strives for more justice for small farmers and poor consumers. But it is true that such integration, were it achieved, would constitute a reason to modify the objectives and modalities of a food policy.

Therefore, it is interesting to study whether there are any strong parallels in the changes in respective prices, which could be indices for at least partial market integration. In an article that did not follow Harris-White's perspective but came down harshly on different statistical integration computations, Ghosh (2000) concluded that rice markets were already relatively integrated in India, both at the intra-state and inter-state levels. Hence, government intervention was no longer necessary.[51] Conversely, restrictions still imposed from time to time on food grain movements by some state governments could only lead to price instability and regional disparities. While defending the FCI's policies, Acharya (2001) estimated that integration had taken great strides forward during the 1990s—but only for wheat and rice. Already in 1971, Lele had pleaded for total trade liberalization, citing the efficiency of the private sector and the fully acceptable market integration—and may it be said, two years before the government nationalized wheat trade.

Yet, to say the least, these findings need to be qualified. States in which the calorie intake is the lowest, especially in the peninsular south, are the states where cereal production per head is also the lowest (Maps 1.3 and 3.3). These are relatively rich states in most cases, with a far more diversified food bowl due to cultural reasons as well. However, we may still wonder whether this situation does not betray the inadequacies of inter-state trade, since cereals are 30 to 70 per cent cheaper in Uttar Pradesh than in southern India—a price difference that poor southerners can only compensate by reducing their consumption.

High price fluctuations are seen both at national and regional levels, which goes to prove that the goal of integration into a single market with its stabilizing effects—where surplus areas would compensate deficit areas—has not been achieved. To be more accurate, if we can find a high level of integration between urban markets, an integration between urban and rural markets, let alone amongst rural markets, is far from evident. Movement restriction by the government is one factor preventing integration, but the major reasons are, no doubt, the generally poor state of infrastructure (transportation, marketing chains, information, etc.). The most striking cases can be found in the north-eastern quadrant: Assam, Bihar, Orissa and Uttar Pradesh—where farmers are often selling their produce at lower than the minimum legal support price. In this scarcely-developed area, the support price system is a failure. That being the case, it seems that regional agriculture has become the victim of its own success. In the 1980s, these states enjoyed a 4 per cent cereal production growth rate, which was more than in Punjab–Haryana. Conversely, in the 1990s, the rate fell below that of Punjab. The state found it difficult to support prices in order to compensate for a poor road and trade infrastructure (High Level Committee 2002).

It is not possible to keep government procurement centres throughout the country open all year round, waiting for clients. The finances of the FCI and corresponding state agencies do not provide for that. One could even think that compliance with the ceiling price could be ensured in an indirect manner—not through government purchases, but private trade, because of an improved transport infrastructure and the cheaper cost of information and marketing (bear in mind the spread of computers and the Internet in certain rural areas), and easier access to regulated markets. Is not state intervention itself, with all its controls and restrictions at state border posts, one of the reasons for the low market integration? Would not freed private trade manage to smooth out price fluctuations and availability? However, doubts still persist. Even the critics like Tyagi (1990) are hesitant about private players, especially due to the credit costs involved for traders.[52] Private trade could play a positive role by reducing regional price disparities through its distribution. But it cannot work if transport costs are higher than this differential.[53] Market integration would remain a mirage without an efficient transport system. In 1999–2000, rural areas accounted for 75 per cent of cereal consumption, often in landlocked regions with a low purchasing power. These are not *a priori* very attractive markets for the private sector, even less so for big companies wanting to sell branded and packaged products. More reason to continue with the FCI system if ever its network covered these zones appropriately!

In the medium term, a solution may be found via competition between the food system's different players. The system could be liberalized while continuing with the government infrastructure, private players and the administration emulating each other, to the benefit of farmers as well as consumers. The end of the pseudo-monopoly of market committees (*mandi*) in grain wholesale trade, in 2003, has clearly opened a new track. In the meanwhile, 'the case for public presence in physical grain trade lies in that existing markets are imperfect as regards both competition and integration, that farmers cannot be assured MSP without presence of public agencies, and that, although inefficient, FCI is able to distribute at margins lower than charged with private trade' (High Level Committee 2002: § 2.37).

(c) *New Powers Devolved to the States: Decentralizing the System*

During the 1990s laws and constitutional amendments were passed for promoting decentralization, in favour of the states and more in favour of the local bodies. Added to the official efforts of liberalization and withdrawal of the central government, it is not surprising that this process concerned also the food system.

Practices long disparaged by New Delhi started being promoted, even at the cost of diluting spatial equality.

1. Decline of National Solidarity in Procurement

(a) The decline of national solidarity in procurement with states desirous of withholding their own stock is no longer reprimanded. Gujarat, Jammu & Kashmir, and Tamil Nadu did not permit central procurement within their states in 2003. But the FCI was not necessarily upset about it. Since 1997–8, the official policy had been 'decentralized procurement'. The state governments were supposed to take the responsibility of procurement in return for a pre-determined central subsidy. The Tamil Nadu strategy became a model for the entire nation. In fact, since 1977, the Tamil Nadu Civil Supplies Corporation had undertaken the task of building buffer stocks meant for Tamil Nadu alone. The deal was that if there were surplus food grains after feeding its population, Madras would transfer them to the centre.[54] Such practices were encouraged from that time onwards. The general goal was for the central government to restrict itself to building national buffer stocks and supplying states whenever the need arose. The FCI budget would be reduced, and since every state had deficit areas neighbouring surplus areas, such decentralization would improve logistical efficiency as stock movement distances would be shorter. Henceforth, rupees rather than food grains were supposed to circulate between the centre and the states.

But for long very few states accepted the system. It was more tempting to let the FCI undertake deliveries during surplus periods. Decentralized procurement appeared sometimes advantageous only when shortages prevailed. Secondly, the logistics involved in food grain movements were necessarily very complicated, and the State Food and Civil Supplies Corporations were incapable of undertaking these operations without FCI help. Further, Punjab stated that it could not ensure procurement by itself and felt even less capable of selling its huge harvests. Andhra Pradesh was fully in agreement. These two states were governed by parties supporting the fragile NDA government at the centre, which was obliged to listen.

Kerala too did not feel up to ensuring its rice supplies (the PDS accounts for half of its consumption). The High Level Committee (2002) added that federal subsidies were often delayed and in insufficient quantities, and that banks kept a stricter control over credit granted to states than the FCI. And then there were critics like the social activist, Vandana Shiva, who feared that India would 'end up replacing FCI's monopoly with that of Cargill' or some other MNCs.[55] Tamil Nadu, Uttar Pradesh, Uttarakhand, Gujarat, Chhattisgarh, Orissa, Madhya Pradesh, and West Bengal were subscribing to this system in 2003–4, for officially 24 per cent of total procurement (*Annual Report 2004*, Department of Food).

From a strictly geographical point of view, we are left to wonder whether it is possible to overcome spatial inequalities when decentralization is complete. States structurally deficient in food grain, like those with surpluses, would remain so if decentralized procurement was extended throughout India. India would become the victim of what Raffestin (1980: 189) calls the 'myopia of regionalism', which is no better than the 'presbyopia' of centralized states.

(b) Over-subsidization practices by some states no longer creates a risk of reducing supplies to other regions in the country. Henceforth, these appear to be means used by the centre to offload a part of its budgetary burden on to the states. For long, many states had been pursuing a relatively autonomous policy *vis-à-vis* New Delhi. Some like Kerala had developed a PDS circuit of such proportions that a major part of the central network was directed towards supplying them. Well before the Targeted PDS was created, other states had adopted a differential price policy in favour of the poorest sections. Once the TDPS was established, the central government identified the percentage of below poverty line (BPL) households in each state, and proportionately allocated quantities to be sold at subsidized prices. But it was always possible for the states to take these measures further, in two ways: by identifying a larger number of BPL households—for electoral purposes, but also for reasons of social justice if New Delhi had been particularly miserly; and by offering these poorest households a 'more subsidized' price than those fixed by the centre. The states can also take over supplies to FPSs without burdening their management with the costs involved for transport from the regional depot to the shop ('doorstep delivery').

2. Resorting to Alternative Systems

Two alternatives to the PDS may be distinguished, systems similar to the FCI, or real substitutes for the PDS.

Some systems are similar to or actually scaled-down models of the FCI, such as the Maveli shops system in Kerala. In fact, since 1980, this state supplemented FCI distributions with the help of a parallel circuit, by importing its own supplies and selling rice at a cheaper rate than the PDS (Mooij 1999a). In certain cases, these systems are mere extensions of the FCI, such as the Rice Credit Line scheme in Andhra Pradesh. The latter was established by an NGO close to the authorities, which permitted self-help groups (often consisting of poor women) to sell rice that they had bought on credit from the FCI in the local market. The food-supply efficiency of such a scheme makes for an interesting study, given that this could be a substitute to the PDS in remote areas not covered by the latter. This is also a micro-credit-based development programme, since these women can also then set up other business activities with the profits made in this manner. Obviously, this scheme does not escape the criticisms levelled at the PDS as regards rice or wheat supply to areas that neither cultivated nor consumed these cereals earlier. Other NGOs then adopt other strategies.

As regards real substitutes counteracting the pernicious effects of the PDS, in 1994, another NGO from Andhra Pradesh, the Deccan Development Society, launched a scheme for reclaiming waste land by sowing coarse cereals and pulses in the scarcely irrigated Medak district. There too, the objectives were manifold: biodiversity concerns—to sustain varieties or even species that may disappear; nutritional concerns (sorghum and peas had better nutritional value than white rice); food grain distribution concerns for the benefit of poor consumers, identified in a 'participative manner' rather than by the administration; employment generation at village level through the development of farming activities, thereby reducing migration; greater empowerment of women, the main protagonists in this scheme; and due consideration of livestock needs, which then got plenty of fodder (Srinivas and Thaha 2004). The initial results were promising, even though they were at the mercy of the vagaries of monsoons or opposition from a section of the local administration. Such a scheme was much more rooted in the local agro-food context than the Rice Credit Line experiment, which had only tried to help the neediest by giving them the food and income they lacked, even if it endangered 'traditional' rainfed farming in the long run. Here the reasoning was purely regional, emphasizing local development in its strongest sense, and denouncing the national logic promoted by the PDS.

This scheme was totally in sync with the widespread opinion that questions the advisability of a general network if it harms local interests. It looks as if the time of decentralization had come. In India as elsewhere, decentralization is encouraged in all sectors and by all political sides. In many NGO discourses and, of late, even among senior government officials, it is supposed to go hand in hand with participative action, and users and local population have to affirm their needs and desires. They would be taken into account; in many cases, they would even be asked to participate in the design and implementation of schemes (Chaturvedi 1997). And so much the better if this 'good governance' costs the government less. The food system is undergoing the same paradigm shift as irrigation and urban public services. Henceforth, to decentralized procurement is supposed to correspond a PDS system managed by village panchayats in rural areas. In fact, since 1993, the Constitution had cited this sector as the council's responsibility. It is the panchayat that has to identify the BPL families; local 'vigilance committees' are to see to the proper functioning of distribution. There are always limitations to decentralization, the world over; giving more power to the local population inevitably means giving more to the elite, in some cases without the oppressed enjoying greater autonomy. The fact remains that a part of the solution undoubtedly lies there itself: local criteria for the selection of beneficiaries, better dovetailing with the Food for Work Programme at the local level, occasional coarse cereal procurement—all sorts of initiatives taken at the local or micro-regional levels that could help the PDS function better or help find alternatives to it (Krishnaji and Krishnan ed. 2000).

At the same time, the management of distribution at state level has to be strengthened. Instead of a situation where the states have no option other than to buy more or less food grain allocated by the FCI, they must have the latitude to create their own systems based on their agro-nutrition preferences and internal disparities. 'For instance, a state could subsidize coarse cereals, use food stamps in urban areas, allow universal access in backward areas, and temporarily increase the subsidy rate in regions adversaly affected by floods, drought and other natural disasters' (Ramaswami 2002: 1134). Instead, the present reforms tend towards releasing the centre of certain responsibilities by transferring them to the states, without providing the latter any additional financial powers—another permanent feature of decentralization processes the world over. Ending subsidies for families above the poverty line is a case in point. In the past, New Delhi used what was yet to be known as the principle of subsidiarity, to demand that states take part in this task, but at the same time tried to give them as little autonomy as possible: a decentralization of means, but not of goals. The states now enjoy greater autonomy, but are very well aware how dear that freedom may cost them. A parallel can be drawn between the fable about *The Wolf and the Dog* and the situation where the poorest of states would prefer to remain leashed to the central government, but fed by it.

3. A Typology of the States

On the whole, a fairly unambiguous classification of states emerges, based on their food grain surplus or deficiency and on their relationship with the FCI. The first class is made of lower Ganges plain states (Orissa, Bengal, and Bihar). We have already mentioned the limited price support in these regions. We can see how difficult the FCI's task is in these poor states. The problem is not so much one of bringing grain into these regions, for grain is generally available here at relatively low prices, but one of maintaining prices without going against consumer wishes. The future of these regions depends on efficient distribution of the procured food grain. As for the rest, these states have less of a problem with regard to cereal availability than with their inhabitants' purchasing power, although the high agricultural growth in the 1980s proved later to be disappointing.

This is much less the case in Gujarat and Rajasthan, the peninsular south, the Himalaya and the islands, where availability is the issue. The semi-arid conditions in the peninsula, difficult conditions in the mountains, and diversification of crop systems in the south beyond Kerala, point to a growing deficit in wheat and rice, especially if millets are progressively excluded from the diet, with the adoption of the pan-Indian model based on the 'noble' cereals.

A stark contrast is presented by a third group of state consisting of Punjab, Haryana, and western Uttar Pradesh, where procurement prices are in general implemented because of the overall development levels and cooperation between the FCI and local authorities. This explains why despite certain allegations (especially against paddy procurement), for long the income earned by farmers was enough to keep them loyal to the rice-wheat rotation, something highly disputed on ecological and economic grounds. In fact, the paddy cultivation area even increased by 30 per cent in Punjab between 1990–1 and 1999–2000. There is a veritable vicious circle here, given that excess local production forces the FCI to intervene in an efficient manner and the centre to fix higher prices, which further promotes production levels. In the short term, one should listen less to farmer lobbies, and in the long term, eastern India has to account for a greater share of procurement—only then could the FCI afford to scale down its presence in the north-west in order to buttress the diversification of cropping systems.[56] Otherwise, the odds are that this diversification will take place by itself, but it will be far from painless. It is already clear that while wheat yields are still going up, rice productivity is stagnating in Punjab–Haryana. When input prices rise, the debt overload of farmers due to mechanization and 'artificialization' of cropping systems drive many of them to suicide.

Finally, there is another medium type of state, major suppliers in terms of procurement, that yet show a shortfall. Andhra Pradesh is one such state, and, to a lesser extent, Tamil Nadu. These are states that are a priori the most easily satisfied by the decentralized procurement system, given that government purchases and PDS allocations are almost at the same level, and thus the system could be left to function in a closed circuit within the boundaries of the state.

What About the Future?

Hence, the more trade is free, lively, extended, the more the people are promptly, efficiently and abundantly supplied; prices are more uniform, they come closer to the average and usual price, to which salaries necessarily adjust. Supplies through the care of the Government cannot be as successful. Its attention divided between too many issues, it cannot be as active as Traders who are occupied only with their commerce. The Government knows later, it knows less precisely the needs and resources. The Agents it employs, having no interest in saving, purchase more dearly, transport at higher cost, store with less caution; much grain is lost and spoiled. If they are not clever enough, or dishonest, these Agents can excessively swell the expense of their operations. They can allow themselves some culpable acts without the Government's knowledge. (...) Furthermore, when the Government takes care of the food supply of the people by trading grain, it has to trade alone; because he cannot sell at a loss, no Trader can be foolhardy enough to compete with it. Hence the Administration alone is in charge of filling the shortfall of the harvests. (Turgot, *Decree of the Council of the King* [of France] dated 13 September 1774)

Changes in the public food system are largely dependent on how it is assessed. We have already seen that while there were a number of criticisms levelled against it, these concerned very different, and at times even contradictory, aspects. Everyone agrees that the PDS has to be reformed, but for different reasons and often offering conflicting alternatives. The ultra-liberals want to dismantle the system without substituting it, whereas those who believe in a powerful welfare state desire to strengthen the PDS by making it universal once again. Padilla (1996: 211) proposed four criteria to assess food policies, which could be applied to the Indian system of intervention.

(1) 'The economic efficiency of food supply intervention'. The budgetary cost for India's agriculture and food policy, though enormous in absolute value, appears to be entirely acceptable given the country's agricultural character and nutritional problems. After all, is 1 per cent of the GDP such a huge amount if the system helps to sustain agricultural growth while assisting consumption? We should remember that in the United States, domestic food aid (food stamps) constitutes the first budgetary item in the Ministry of Agriculture (38.5 per cent of the budget in 2003, i.e. 43 billion dollars) (Devienne et al. 2005). Except for critics belonging to the liberal line of thinking, the amounts spent do not necessarily pose any problems. We could concur with Mooij (1999: 250) who concluded, on remarking that food subsidies account for less than a quarter of the federal military expenditure, that the issue is 'not how to reduce the subsidy burden, but how to make food policy more effective in reaching the most underprivileged classes'.

(2) 'The efficiency of public funding allocations and revenue distribution.' A cost-efficiency analysis gives mediocre results. The urban poor save less than 3 per cent of their total consumption expenditure, and the rural poor less than 6 per cent (NSSO 1999–2000). The state spends six to seven rupees to distribute one rupee

to the poor through the PDS (Ramaswami 2002; Mahendra Dev et al. 2003). An India that enjoys a high economic growth and a satisfactory balance of payments, as it does presently, can afford to allocate large funds for a modicum of relief to the poorest of its citizens, while expecting that either in the medium or long term, the economic boom will create highly satisfactory additional revenue. But we should also remember that the benefits of agricultural price support are reaped above all by (big) farmers with surplus production, while discriminating against city-dwellers and a large majority of the rural masses. Therefore, it is necessary to keep cereal prices down, even if that means maintaining certain input subsidies for the poorest of farmers and promoting a diversified cropping system.

(3) 'The repercussions on agricultural efficiency.' This criterion gives the most negative assessment. While price support helps many Punjab or Kaveri delta farmers to survive, farmers who are for the most part in a precarious situation, it reinforces continuous rice or wheat–rice single rotation cropping system, with appalling ecological consequences. A portion of the funds allocated to support these two cereals could be diverted to the production of other crops, in order to modernize a system that is out of sync with present-day priorities.

(4) The last criterion is the 'ability to induce sustainable food and nutritional improvement.' No considerable improvement in calorie intake took place, and furthermore, it is not sustainable because it depends on the quantum of subsidy. Nutritional improvement is even more unlikely given the mediocre nutritional content of rice and wheat. However, we should not forget that the PDS distributes one-third of the country's sugar and oil consumption.

When all is said and done, none of the four criteria are assessed as entirely satisfactory, although only one of them throws up an entirely negative finding. Therefore, the reforms to be introduced are numerous, even though the system does not have to be condemned as the whole. The upheavals experienced in the span of a few years—from a situation of shortages, imports, and the coercive acquisition of cereals, to a situation of general self-sufficiency, exports, and purchase through support prices—were not complemented by suitable changes either in the infrastructure or in the institutional apparatus, or even in the decision-makers' logic and strategies. Thus, the problem is twofold: a problem of infrastructure, but also one of *infostructure* or 'means of information and control within a much shorter time scale' (Dupuy 1994: 147).

The reforms envisaged, some of which have already been implemented, pertain to both procurement and distribution. As for distribution, there are a number of voices raised in favour of a return to a universal PDS. There are too many errors creeping up in beneficiary selection, and what the latter gained *vis-à-vis* the old system was negligible. Moreover, opting for such a course of action could in no way be considered a retrograde step. India now has a middle class that scoffs at the PDS product quality and, save during exceptionally bad years, prefers to buy in the open market for a price that is barely higher. Indeed, given the quality of products, the system by itself engineers an automatic selection process, attracting only the most needy. The issue is complicated because in most states the PDS also distributes sugar and oil, both of good quality. Thus, two distinct circuits should be established, while continuing with the selection process for non-cereal products. In that case, however, would the game be worth it?

Another solution would be a complete overhaul of the system and a changeover to food stamps. This would mean a simple transfer of credit instead of the physical transfer of food grain (Drèze and Sen 1989). Beneficiaries would be given stamps that could be exchanged for a fixed quantity of food grain, which they could purchase from any retail merchant; the latter would then exchange stamps for money from the government. This is a system chosen by the United States—the only OECD country where government food aid is in effect. From 1979 onwards, Sri Lanka too followed suit. Even if a counterfeit food stamp racket is probable, the diversion of food grain from the public distribution system would come to an end (Suryanarayana 1995b) and government expenditure would be considerably reduced with almost no transportation of food grain. However, there are three obstacles. Food stamp values would have to be determined in kind rather than in rupee terms to lessen negative inflationary effects. Above all, the system would imply that subsidized products are physically available. Thus, the management of such a system seems to be difficult in remote rural areas, whereas it would be very successful in high agricultural productivity zones and in urban areas, which are generally well stocked. Finally, switching over to food stamps would mean a radical change in the food policy. 'As with PDS targeting, a food stamps scheme also narrows down the objective of food policy to only one. Food stamps are meant to increase food security of the poorest people, not to stabilize prices or to support farmers incomes' (Mooij 1999: 248); and all would be over for the ambitious spatial equalization policy. 'If food stamps are created, what shall become our procurement? It is a chain!' a central Civil Supplies Ministry official once confided in me in 2004.[57]

In the case of procurement too, the suggestions cover the entire range—from cosmetic reforms to radical ones. Most experts suggested that the *system* as a whole ought to be dismantled, which meant that it should no longer be a single unified system. Since price support, procurement, and distribution are intrinsically linked at the time, their dissociation would turn them into three distinct tasks, independent of each other.

Thus, Sharma (1997) opined that during the tender process, the FCI should strike a deal with private traders for the delivery of a specific quantity of stocks to designated areas, which would then reduce the need for onerous public storage. Tenders could be called for on a quarterly basis, based only upon PDS needs and not taking farmers' requirements into account. In 2001, the report by the Prime Minister's Economic Advisory Council was in agreement with this line of thinking. It would lead to the establishment of large cereal trading companies, provided they were permitted to buy directly from the farmers without having to pass through middlemen or pay taxes on their turnover. The Food Minister himself accused public offices of 'waiting with gunny bags and procuring every tonne of grain arriving in the market', of constituting a 'contradiction'.[58] The purchase and sale of food grain 'should be left to the private trade'. The FCI should confine itself to building a 10-million-tonne buffer stock: it would in a way transform its contractor status to that of a subcontractor. The procurement and public distribution activities would be completely delinked, since the private sector would undertake food grain purchases and the government would intervene only at a later stage, to prevent a slump in prices. A warehouse receipt system would help farmers get credit against the hypothecation of their stocks.

We can see that the kind of action to be developed in this case would be at a more local level. The idea is to extend the Deccan Development Society's experiment and more systematically develop community food grain banks (Swaminathan 2001) run by self-help groups—somewhat similar to African village associations. Food grain, and perhaps later cereals other than wheat and rice, could be bought locally, if possible to prevent post-monsoon sales at low rates. And wherever possible, we can easily imagine collaborations with the public FCI system as well as with the Food for Work programmes.[59] The upstream consequences of such a trade policy would be the revitalization of coarse cereals, oilseeds and pulses production, neglected thus far, within the framework of an ecologically, economically, and socially sustainable 'evergreen revolution' (Swaminathan 1996; Griffon 2006).

On the other hand, and probably influenced by agricultural policy reforms in the United States and Europe, the Agriculture Ministry is taking a closer look at a system of direct compensation for farmers in case they have to sell their produce at a price that is lower than the support price. Such compensation would be paid through agricultural insurance, theoretically throughout the country. This would then lead to a complete dissociation between procurement in the strict sense of the word and price support. However, the High Level Committee on Food Grains Policy had two reservations: the cost of such a system, and the fear that the WTO would consider such grants as unacceptable under the 'green box' of measures tolerated under free trade (High Level Committee 2002).

The High Level Committee found very little expert support for the complete dismantling of the procurement system. With the passage of time, the notion of 'decoupling' support *vis-à-vis* production will of course become increasingly important as more and more countries adopt it, although, as the High Level Committee emphasized, 'this is a formulation from developed countries where production is surplus and the priority in farm support is to preserve the size of farming population. There is a contradiction in applying this to developing economies where the priority is to increase production while reducing the workforce share in agriculture' (High Level Committee 2002: §1.8).

Indeed, it is not possible to escape from fixing a ceiling on government stocks, beyond which the State would have to use all possible means, and in particular, programmes such as the Food for Work scheme, in order to dispose of food grain and improve rural infrastructure. The support price has to be contained in order to encourage crops other than wheat and rice. Most certainly, the situation of many cereal farmers remains precarious. But low yields are to be overcome through structural policies rather than price policies; by more abundant and better-managed irrigation, by laying roads and building trading hubs, by easier credit availability, rather than a consistent rise in procurement prices.

On the other hand, alternatives to public channels have to be promoted. Since 2000 there has been a rethink on the legislation that had since 1942 and especially since 1955 prohibited futures trading (Ahuja 2006). However, two problems are raised in this context: a social problem, given that the poorest farmers cannot afford to wait and are forced to sell their food grains at the support price, which is lower than the price richer farmers get later; and a politico-economic problem, which says a lot about the mindset of the political class and senior officials—encouraging farmers to partially take charge of warehousing would mean giving up any ambitions of 'scientific storage'. The authorities find it difficult to envisage a situation in which they would no longer be able to forecast the national availability situation. Indeed, they continue to believe that accurate assessment is necessary (and possible!) in order to act upon prices or to undertake planning.

In 2007, futures trading on cereals was eventually banned. It was the result of the current inflation in food prices. According to some experts, futures had aggravated price increase through excessive purchases of grain. This prohibition proves that liberalization, despite being a clear long-term trend, is far from going smoothly. Steps contributing to the dismantling of the public food machinery can always be brought into question and eventually cancelled.

This shall probably be not the case of the liberalization of direct purchase to farmers. We have seen that after 2003 the states allowed private companies to compete with regulated markets for buying from farmers. Even before this date (that is, somewhat illegally), in 2000, ITC, an Indian agrobusiness conglomerate, launched 'e-choupals'[60] (Annamalai and Rao 2003). In some villages a computer connected to the Internet provides free information regarding the prices of the day on the global market and on the nearest regulated market, and the price offered by ITC, including transportation cost. In this way farmers and agro-industrialists should benefit from the end of monopolies and middlemen. True, e-choupals are working more for soyabean, and shrimps, and less for wheat and rice. Commercial crops not in the public procurement circuit are the main targets of the project. Similarly, Madhya Pradesh was the first equipped state, while the north-west that is a more crucial region for cereal procurement is still neglected by e-choupals. In 2005, however, according to the ITC website, about 3.5 million farmers were reached by e-choupal services—that is, about 3 per cent of farmers. Jointly with contract farming that is developing in Punjab-Haryana, e-choupals show the progressive entrance of private companies into the world of farms. Small and marginal farmers will probably be side-lined by these new actors. Their farm size is often considered as non profitable for the companies. In the case of e-choupals, the local village hierarchy of gender, caste, and class cannot but prevent equal access for all to this service. Nevertheless, if the government does not forget its responsibility to check that transactions and contract rules are not excessively in favour of the corporate to the disadvantage of the farmers, the entry of the private sector could represent a useful alternative to the current flaws of public procurement and a new source of capital for agriculture and rural infrastructure.

In this matter, the ambit of the paradigm cannot be under-emphasized: the concept of food security, and even of food sovereignty, has found a new meaning. It is no longer based on cereal self-sufficiency, with a public procurement based on Indian food grains for building national stocks. With the liberalization of wholesale markets and the entry of international corporate players into the purchase of Indian crops, the food system gets globalized. 'There is a necessity to integrate farm production with national and international markets to enable farmers to undertake market driven production plan and adoption of modern marketing practices', the Act says. With this 'integration' into globalization, so to say, procurement shall be accomplished by (foreign or Indian) multinational companies. Storage shall be done at the global level, physically in various far-off countries or virtually by the game of futures trading or international markets. As for redistributions, possible imports shall enable them. In some years, imports, not national stocks, shall feed India.

Harsh criticism can be heard. As Vandana Shiva (2006) put it, 'the corporate hijack of India's wheat will push more children to hunger, and even starvation, and more farmers to suicide. It will also lead to a massive wheat swap—with global corporations exporting Indian wheat subsidized by India's tax payer and importing US and Australian wheat subsidized by US and Australian taxpayers and making super profits both ways, while wheat producers and the poor suffer. . . . India's food sovereignty is being given up to hand over India's food system to global agribusiness.' To this, Sharad Pawar, the Union Food and Agriculture Minister, replied that imports from Australia were cheaper than the added costs of procurement from Punjab farmers, storage and transport to south India.[61] Who is right? Perhaps both. Such a policy can bring excellent results (ration grain of better quality, more sustainable cropping systems in Punjab, etc.) as well as sad outcomes such as those predicted by Shiva. All depends on how this policy is implemented. The Indian government must follow a narrow path between maintaining an old-fashioned and unmanageable public food system and giving up any political control on behalf of free trade.

India's public food system has been discussed in these pages in its entire spatial dimension. Indeed, this had been done at the risk of pushing economic, social, and political perspectives to the second rung, because analysts often passed over it in silence, but also because this spatial dimension corresponded to a line of thinking that played a significant role in building the existing network. According to our thesis, this is one of the reasons why such a structure has survived the structural changes Indian agriculture went through over half a century. Why is it that in spite of all the criticisms coming from all schools of thought and all sections of the Indian population, the public food system was maintained against all the odds? The answer comes to some extent from a spatial perspective of the Indian territory. In the following pages I shall argue that the PDS has been continued not only for good reasons (agricultural price support, subsidized food supply), and for bad ones (vested interests and corruption), but also because it represents a perception of national space that remains extremely meaningful.

Indeed, since 1947, the republic has sought to turn the ideology of national space into a reality. The following chapter is dedicated to this ideology—apparently far removed from food supply issues, yet so close to them.

NOTES

1. This sector, which was at times under truly repressive protection by the authorities, received its raw material almost exclusively from the state. It was only in 1971–2 that it was allowed to buy from the open market for the first time. In return, even during times of scarcity, the state was

supposed to provide a certain quantity of wheat so that the mills did not remain completely idle.

2. This is also true of about 7,000 primary marketing cooperatives, federated from the district level to the Union, but which are for the most part para-public organizations.
3. Except in 2000–1.
4. The growth rates for the per capita agricultural output were negative for these three states during the 1981–91 and 1991–7 periods, despite their having the lowest per capita output of the 17 major states (Chand 2001).
5. Punjab State Cooperative Supply & Marketing Federation Ltd.—a 'cooperative' that also distributes inputs.
6. Haryana State Cooperative Supply and Marketing Federation.
7. Quantities purchased by the state increased 15-fold while per capita rice production only rose by 37 per cent.
8. *The Hindu Business Line*, 17 May 2001.
9. Notably because production costs are calculated by estimating the value of family work (costs called C_2 in the Indian administrative jargon) (Landes and Gulati, 2004).
10. Sai Bhaskar Reddy, personal discussion.
11. In the 1990s, FCI engaged in several interventions for sorghum, maize, and pearl millet (*bajra*). But losses were heavy during storage, and the bulk of procurement had to be sold as fodder material. The purchase record had been achieved in 1973–4 with 393,000 tonnes (including 42 per cent for just Maharashtra), i.e. 7 per cent of total grain procurement. In 1973 as in 1974, two bad years, Madhya Pradesh bought a lot of sorghum and maize from the western regions of the state, where the harvest was satisfactory, for resale it in the east where the harvests (particularly rice harvests) were disastrous (Acharya 1983). Indeed, these were the types of transfers that the 'decentralized procurement' policy currently wishes to encourage for wheat and rice. We would then achieve the situation close to the one Chopra had dreamed of (1988: 253), with regard to these grains 'as the poor man's cereal, meant to fill up all nooks and corners of the country as a shock absorber—to compensate, as it were, for the failures and shortcomings of the public distribution system in a big country like India'. As for Acharya (1983), he saw a solution in the local use of these cereals during the Food for Work programmes.
12. Parboiling paddy helps limit broken rice, but also spreads nutritive ingredients into the grain' inside, which will protect them a bit during polishing.
13. *Frontline*, 12 March 2004, p. 6.

14. I have never come across any reference to cereals being fed to animals, as was recounted in the case of the highly subsidized systems of the USSR and Egypt.
15. In India as many other countries, the PDS could be compared to housing construction programmes that fail to increase the purchasing power of applicants, or training programmes for the unemployed that are carried out in the absence of employment generation: all these schemes are considering only one part of the problems tackled with.
16. Regarding targeting in food programmes, cf. Timmer et al., 1986. It was the short-lived United Front government that engaged in this targeting though it was a priori unpopular, 'probably assuming that there was still a long time to go till the next elections (which proved to be a mistake)' (Mooij 1999: 58).
17. A standard 5-member household consumes 55 kg of cereals per month, if an individual consumes 330 g a day, as per the Indian Council of Medical Research. Thus, PDS quotas meet 64 per cent of the household needs. But the 35 kg also have to be effectively distributed.
18. In the 1970s, rice procurement was mainly on the states' account (Acharya 1983). They first met the needs of their own population with the grains procured, and only any surpluses that remained were delivered to federal stocks. As for wheat procurement, it was the centre's responsibility.
19. For a discussion and bibliography on the subject, cf. Landy (1999); Suryanarayana (1995c); and Howes and Jha (1994).
20. . . . and 23 per cent of sugar, with 55 per cent of edible oils (Department of Food, Annual Report 2000–1).
21. *Frontline*, 16 July 2004.
22. For poor households, the final selling price cannot legally be higher than half-a-rupee above the price defined by the central government (http://fcamin.nic.in/fcamin/ctzn_det.htm#Entitlement). In some states such as Andhra Pradesh, food grains are transported to the FPS to restrict possibilities of fraud by managers. This only succeeds in facilitating fraud by officials, and the fixed mark-up for the manager is still reduced.
23. Personal interview on 24.1.2005.
24. In 2005, during my stay in Hyderabad, rice coupons were out of print and the card holders were requested to photocopy them !
25. Speech by the Minister of Food, Shanta Kumar, *Hindu Business Line*, 3 September 2001.
26. 'The Government of ____ will issue special cards to BPL families and promises to issue 10 kg. of Rice/Wheat per month per family at the Fair Price Shop (FPS) listed in the card'. Or 'The Government of ____

would like to reiterate its commitment to the PDS with its focus on the poor' (http://fcamin.nic.in/ctzn_ind.htm).

27. Acharya (2001) does not see this as populism, given that it is rare for the government to deviate from the CACP's recommendations by more than 5 per cent.
28. For rice, the problem is aggravated by the fact that two minimum prices are defined according to whether it is of Common or Grade A quality. The second quality has a higher MSP than the first, even though, being cultivated mostly in the most developed regions, it actually has a lower cost of production. This is all the more questionable as the demand for common rice tends to exceed PDS supplies, unlike quality rice. The High Level Committee on Grain Policy (2002) therefore suggested that a single MSP be fixed.
29. J. Ghosh, 'The Missing Grain', *Frontline*, 24 October 2003, pp. 120–1.
30. 'Animals in other countries get a better quality of wheat than humans here', lamented the officials of the Karnataka Roller Flour Mills Association, furious about the fact that the FCI was selling mills more expensive and lower-quality wheat that that being exported (*Hindu Business Line*, 29 March 2001).
31. It stood at 0.83 per cent of central government expenditure in 2004–5.
32. Tyagi 1990: 129.
33. *The Hindu Business Line*, 1 February 2001. The official food subsidy amount was Rs. 176.1 billion in 2001–2, of which Rs. 120 billion were devoted exclusively to storage. The latter amount was higher than the entire central budget (Plan and non-Plan expenditure) for agriculture and rural development (*Hindu Business Line*, 28 May 2001). An exceptional year? At Rs. 62 billion in 2002–3, the storage costs still accounted for 26 per cent of the total 'food subsidy', i.e. almost as much as the subsidy for low-income BPL households, Antyodaya, midday meals in schools, etc., which stood at Rs. 75 billion. In 2006 7 food subsidy reached Rs. 242 billion.
34. However, in 2002, the rate was 11.65 per cent, which was quite high as compared to the low risks banks ran—though about one point less than rates normally were in India (High Level Committee, 2002).
35. Cf. also the excellent site of the *Right to Food Campaign*: www.righttofood.org.
36. See their annual report on http://164.100.24.208/ls/CommitteeR/Food/listofreports14.html.
37. *Cf.* http://www.wfp.org/index.asp?section=5.
38. The various programmes then created on the basis of this model, such as the National Rural Employment Programme, were brought together under the same umbrella in 1999, in the Jawahar Gram Samridhi

Yojana (Jawaharlal [Nehru] Rural Prosperity Programme—JGSY). In 2001, it was merged with the Employment Assurance Scheme, to become the Sampoorna Grameen Rozgar Yojana (SGRY or Composite Rural Employment Scheme).

39. Others deemed that the meal scheme for school children constituted the delegation by the families to the state of a part of their duties regarding children's bringing up, which could, on the contrary, be construed as encouragement for fertility.
40. In 2001 (and still in 2003), the prices stood at Rs. 2 per kilo of wheat and Rs. 3 per kilo of rice, as against BPL prices of Rs. 4.15 and Rs. 5.65 respectively.
41. When BPL households were being registered as of 1997, 'in Pune district, the number of poor families fell from 59,340 to 34,000 in the matter of a year, while in Yeravada district, the number fell from 12,000 to 261. The commonly used international poverty indicator is $1 per day. The new APL line stands at a quarter of this (Rs. 300 per month) (Motiram et al., 2004: 10).
42. U. Patnaik added that poverty line calculations are doubly biased—on the one hand, they correspond to the purchasing price of quantities consumed in 1973–4 to achieve an intake of 2,400 calories, and the figures have never been properly re-assessed since. On the other hand, the poverty line is far too dependent on price fluctuations. On the whole, it only allows for the purchase of 1800 kcal. It would be better to base calculations on actual consumption. Then, the figure we would get, for instance for rural Andhra Pradesh, would be 76 per cent of the population consuming less than 2210 calories per day in 1999–2000—as compared with the official figures for rural households in the same state: 11 per cent (in *Frontline*, 2 July 2004). For an excellent estimate of poverty rates in India, cf. Deaton and Drèze 2002.
43. Madhura Swaminathan, in a special issue of *Frontline*, 31 October 1997 devoted to the TPDS.
44. http://fcamin.nic.in/ecorder.htm.
45. Yashwant Sinha, according to *The Economic Times*, 28 February 2002.
46. The differences noted between the four maps may lead us to believe that wheat procurement does not work very well in Uttar Pradesh, as is the case with the PDS in West Bengal. However, it must be pointed out that these maps unfortunately refer to somewhat different time periods. And let us also recall the doubts raised concerning available statistics (for instance, Himachal Pradesh is curiously absent in the rice transportation map).
47. The four maps on FCI transports, however, show fairly large transfers by it inside states, particularly inside those with enormous regional

disparities, such as Uttar Pradesh and Andhra Pradesh (west to east for the first, but in the reverse direction in the second, given the location of irrigated areas).

48. It is negligible (about 100,000 tonnes), except for the Kakinada–Kollam link.
49. 0.41 Re/tonne/km in 2001 for grains, as against 0.83 for cement and 1.28 for petroleum products (meeting, Ministry of Railways, 30 March 2001).
50. *The Hindu Business Line*, 29 March 2001.
51. However, it may be noted that only fifteen markets could be taken into account for this study, in four neighbouring states (Bihar, Orissa, Uttar Pradesh, and Bengal) over the 1984–97 period.
52. By estimating interest costs at 22 per cent, Tyagi believed that private traders would not get involved in marketing operations without being assured revenue (defined as the difference between deficit and surplus years) of at least 35 per cent. As for international trade, he observed that it could not be effective unless world prices are at very different levels and moving in directions contrary to those prevailing in India.
53. Drèze and Sen (1989: 92) recall that often non-professional traders such as the rural poor, who transport bags on their heads, are involved in this trade.
54. In 2002–3, the centre paid Rs. 9 per kg of rice procured by the state of Tamil Nadu. Everyone got something out of the deal—the FCI (because the rice transported from Punjab to Tamil Nadu brought it Rs. 13 per kg), and the government of Tamil Nadu (which managed to get both recognition and funding for its policy of keeping its own stocks).
55. *The Hindu Business Line*, 29 May 2001.
56. There is talk of projects to reduce the areas under wheat and rice by one million hectares by providing direct help to farmers. However, the Punjab and Haryana governments demand federal funding to do so (High Level Committee, 2002).
57. Personal interview, 24th August 2004, New Delhi.
58. *Hindu Business Line*, 26 January 2001.
59. Cf. Rao and Deshpande (2002). Madhya Pradesh has already institutionalized a food grains bank programme called *Anna Kosh* (M.S. Swaminathan in *The Hindu*, 10 November 2001).
60. *Choupal* means a village place in Hindi.
61. http://www.ibnlive.com/printpage.php?id=12245&section_id=4

CHAPTER 4

A National Territory to be Covered with a Grid

> [In the traditional Indian village] the functions of each group or caste were related to the functions of other castes, and the idea was that if each group functioned successfully within its own framework, then society as a whole worked harmoniously. Over and above this, a strong and fairly successful attempt was made to create a common national bond which would hold all these groups together—the sense of a common culture, common traditions, common heroes and saints, and a common land to the four corners of which people went on pilgrimage.
>
> J. Nehru, *The Discovery of India,* 1985 : 248

'Territory', also often called 'place', is a trendy notion in social sciences, perhaps because of its manifold meanings (Dupont and Landy: 2005). It can mean an area appropriated and managed by a proprietor, or a legal rule, or administration, at any level from an individual housing site to a country. On the other hand, it can mean an area that entails feelings of belongingness, a sentimental attachment, linked to an identity. Among all the accepted meanings of 'territory', there are many that tally with each other. This is especially so in the case of the (mental) notion of a territory as a representation and the (politico-economic) notion of a territory as an object of planning. Could the second notion exist without the first? Could a territory be developed, without being imagined? These are the links that we would like to shed light on in India's case, through the spatial ideology that underlay regional planning and a part of the food policy.

The national territory was not born overnight after the fight for Independence. It was not a presupposed a priori notion. It was the result of a mental, political, and economic process: the fragmented and unequal colonial space, in itself to some degree integrated by the rail network and money circulation, but increasingly fragmented by social and spatial differentiations, slowly began to take shape as a nascent nation (Goswami 2004).

A key element for a mostly rural country at the time of Independence was the role that the villages could play in nation-building. 'The village can no longer be a self-contained economic unit (though it may often be intimately connected with a collective or co-operative farm), but it can very well be a governmental and electoral unit, each such unit functioning as a self-governing community within the larger political framework' (Nehru 1985 [1946]: 523). Nehru's aim was to achieve a sort of vertical integration, the village units forming the cogs of the great democracy wheel. To say the least, it would be appropriate to qualify the thinking according to which, for Nehru, 'the individual should be the nation's fundamental unit' (Jaffrelot 1998: 274). Thus, during the first half of the 1950s, the Planning Commission continued to insist upon the need for 'cooperative village management' (Dandekar 1994: 50). The fact that Nehru, a denigrator of *zamindars* and other landlords, granted such a political role to village society would be surprising, were it not for the need for village panchayats to be truly representative, in order to prevent the continuation of the present or past vices of rural society.

This was a very Gandhian thought. The Mahatma did not unduly idealize the village, which, he admitted, was dirty, unhygienic, hardly educated and practised untouchability much more than the city. But he stressed the solidarity, community spirit, and simplicity that were its basic hallmarks, at least before colonization—possibly underestimating the great caste and class divides. From then on, the Gandhian ideal village tended to be more of a monad than a molecule, open to the outside world only for bare essentials, thus less integrated to the nation than the Nehruvian village. Further, such autonomy went hand in hand with a production and consumption decentralization fairly incompatible with the grand design of a developed nation, according to Nehru's productivist and modern thinking. Thus, the inclination towards Gandhian mosaic was increasingly disputed after Independence, to be substituted by a more vertical and all-encompassing structure. Gandhi's *swaraj* was meant to lead to local autonomy, despite the risk of fragmentation and even balkanization. Nehru's planning had integration as its goal.

Admittedly, the difference in these two lines of thinking did not have a politico-spatial basis, since neither Nehru nor Gandhi considered the coexistence of a strong national sentiment and largely inward-looking village entities as necessarily contradictory. Differences arose because Nehru believed in modern day progress, but Gandhi did not. For Nehru, India's development lay in building dams and steel mills, not only through agriculture and rural industries. Yet, it was not possible to set up a steel industry in every village (China's Great Leap Forward was to provide proof by contradiction), and economic growth imposes serious limitations to local autonomy. It was also not possible to agree with Gandhi's denunciation of the railways, deemed guilty of shattering rural self-sufficiency and enhancing inequalities. The unavoidable spatial concentration of certain large facilities meant major road and transport corridors and a minimum geographic specialization to generate regional complementarities. Indeed, India had to be taken as an economic whole, and therefore as a political whole too—for in case of disagreements, it would be the decision taken at the highest level that would prevail. And it also had to be considered as a spatial whole—flows as intense as possible were to move across India, so that its entire territory would be well integrated. Thus, while for Gandhi, India was the sum of its villages (while towns were incidental), for Nehru, the whole was more than the sum of its parts.

Gandhi was assassinated as early as 1948, Nehru remained in power till his death in 1964. Thus, Nehru's ideas prevailed, giving rise to an aggressive planning and development policy. The PDS network was one of the outcomes.[1]

PLANNING THE TERRITORY OF THE NATION

> In a country with over 75 per cent illiterates, how will the concept of planning reach ordinary folk? Only when they see a road or bridge or tank being built, or an industry located in their village or in a nearby village, will planning become concrete to them. Without such visible evidence, their sentiments will not be touched and their enthusiasm cannot be roused. And popular enthusiasm is indispensable to democratic planning. . . . It is obvious that in the allocation of national resources a major part should be set apart for achieving an economic breakthrough. This should form the economic core of the plan. But the rest should be spent in such a way that there is a balanced regional development, and that specially backward areas are given priority in development. (M.N. Srinivas, 1962 : 14)

We must always realise the importance of the Centre, which blends all the different states and provinces and areas together. (Nehru's speech at a public meeting in Madras, *The Hindu*, 3 October 1953)

For long Indians were obsessed with the concern for 'national integration' even though, until the 1980s this idea was perhaps sometimes just political jargon and platitudes. After the rise of religious extremists, the concern for national integration somewhat lost its sheen for many, as the Christians and especially Muslims found themselves uprooted by some from the nation's bosom. Yet the exclusion was of certain human groups, not territories. Indeed, the RSS, which would like most Muslims to leave India, would never accept giving up Kashmir. In fact, this greatly differs from the extreme reasonings of racist South Africa, when the rejection of Black Africans through the apartheid system was coupled with the rejection of territories. In theory, the Bantustan states were independent (Gervais-Lambony et al. 2005). In India, there is this constant concern for the unity of the country, a unity under the perpetual threat of the 'foreign hand' (usual euphemism to designate Pakistan) or fifth column (in other words Muslims), imagined or real enemies. In fact, 'India's body' (Assayag 2001) is under permanent threat of dismemberment.

For a long time, national integration was sought through an aggressive economic development policy. Independent India, like many developing countries with a planned economy, decided to take in hand both the industrial policy and the regional planning policy, but the former was given priority. We have already seen how the PDS was initially a means to contain urban salaries. The latter, as is the case with any other regional planning policy in the world, can be assessed on the basis of two yardsticks. The first concerns the mode of planning—is it top-down, centralized planning, or a more participative type of decision-making? The second concerns content: did territorial planning lead to spatial concentration (as was often the case in the third world), or did it cause dispersion and scattering (as the attempt made by the French DATAR—Delegation for territorial planning and regional action, today renamed DIACT)? It is evident that both the answers are interlinked, given that concentration politics rarely admits participative measures. However, the PDS demonstrated that distribution and concentration concerns could coexist. And each time, it is appropriate to differentiate between discourse and reality.

The Discourse

(a) *Centralized or Participative Planning?*

The India inherited from the British Empire was not a homogeneous entity. The 562 princely states constituted almost half the territory and a quarter of the population. The special status accorded to border states preordained that the young federation consisted of three types of states—called A, B and C. The first rulers of independent India were aware of the great diversity of interest groups in the country. Its cultural heterogeneity, the size of the territory, and the desire to scale down regional inequalities (products of colonization characterized by the importance given to port cities), the diversity of political status accorded to spatial entities, the risks of secession, the illiteracy of the majority of the population, not to mention factors with a more directly economic bearing such as scant savings and scarce capital—all these compelled, if not authoritarian planning at least a directed economy (Byres 1998). It is symptomatic that the Constitution of India begins with a list of the spatial entities forming the Union in its Article 1—the patchwork had to be tailored to create a strong fabric. But in order to do so, you needed a particularly strong thread, at the risk of being crude and making holes in the fabric. 'Thus we arrive at the inevitable and ineluctable conclusion that, whether Pakistan comes or not, a number of important and basic functions of the state must be exercised on an all-India basis if India is to survive as a free state and progress' (Nehru 1985 [1946]: 533).

In choosing between local priorities and national interests, the 1950 Constitution was no more apt than the 1935 Government of India Act which had already drawn up three lists to separate central government powers from those of provincial governments—with a list of sectors reserved for the centre, a list of those reserved for the provinces, and a third list defining powers shared by both. This threefold division of responsibilities was adopted by the Indian Constitution, which was even more ambiguous here because in practice, the central government retained the bulk of powers, particularly with the help of Article 356, by virtue of which the Union Government could take over the powers officially granted to the states in the event of a political crisis. During the heyday of planning until the 1980s, the Planning Commission had very little to do with the states, despite the fact that its decisions affected them directly. The only interface was the National Development Council, which brought all state chief ministers, the prime minister, and Planning Commission members together. However, it essentially accepted the central decisions without discussing them a lot (Sharma 1987).

(b) *Spatial Concentration or Dispersion?*

It would be appropriate to channel private or government investments where they were required, and this was possible under state control. 'In our circumstances, I am quite certain that with an unplanned "free enterprise" approach, we cannot make any progress at all,' asserted Nehru.[2] 'If there is any progress, it will be lop-sided. We can put up factories here and there, but it will result only in riches here and greater poverty there.' In fact, even the 'Bombay plan' developed by private industrialists such as Tata and Birla in 1944–5, encouraged stringent government control and planning, with a politico-spatial concern for economic backwardness of princely states.

Admittedly, the resolution that set up the Planning Commission in 1950 stressed its resource management role and 'the needs of the nation', more than the needs of the population and the requirements of regional planning. The First Five-Year Plan (1951–5) too did not make any reference to territorial planning. The Second Plan (1956–60) did mention the necessity of 'balanced regional development', but history would see it as releasing enormous funds for investing in heavy industry in the name of 'self-relied development'. This would result in strong spatial concentration with territorial planning aiming at the maximization of production. This was the era of a specifically urban PDS, supplied by imports from the United States. Furthermore, the spatial perspective is completely absent in the 1967–8 Annual Plan.

The Fourth and Fifth Plans were marked by the progressive spread of the Green Revolution. They launched schemes based on 'area development' and 'target groups', chiefly through the construction of industrial zones, sometimes located in poorer areas. Small industries found favour for socio-economic reasons (they seemed more labour-intensive and less capital consuming), and for spatial reasons too, for they were considered best suited to be set up in 'backward' areas. At the other end, the central government undertook to establish new public-sector enterprises in non-industrialized regions, insofar as raw material proximity would permit, and to steer private industries there through licensing. A railway freight price-equalizing policy reduced the comparative advantage of coal and steel producing regions and—in theory—established a single price system across the country for cement and iron. After 1969, the 'Gadgil formula' broke down central aid into 70 per cent loan and 30 per cent grants (Vithal and Sastry 2002). But special category states enjoyed 90 per cent grants and 10 per cent loans. Currently, there are 11 Himalayan states in this category (Jammu & Kashmir, Himachal Pradesh, Assam, Manipur, Meghalaya, Sikkim, Tripura, Mizoram, Nagaland, Arunachal Pradesh and Uttarakhand). The year 1969 also marked the beginning of a policy of financial incentives (subsidies and tax exemptions) for activities in underdeveloped regions. This was discontinued because of its limited effectiveness, and from the Sixth and especially the Seventh Plan (1985–90) onwards, it was wisely decided to lay the emphasis on developing the infrastructure and 'growth centres' in these regions. These growth centres were launched in 1988 and in 2002 there were 68 such centres. For the most part, they were located in relatively under-industrialized states. These were industrial zones that enjoyed a favourable tax system, but their dynamism was not equal to official expectations (Sridhar 2003). In any case, the government's dilemma was understandable. Bombay might be rich, but it could not be stripped to clothe Madhya Pradesh or Orissa. India needed growth. That the number of Special Export Zones has been rising since the 2000 Act cannot preclude that the Mumbai SEEPZ zone, created in 1973–4, makes 60 per cent of their total turnover. The spatial equity policy could not be pushed too far: concerns regarding efficiency and, therefore, spatial concentration, remained the reality.

The Reality

We may recall the much-awaited trickle-down effect during the Green Revolution. It was hoped that the policy of concentration on which it was based would spontaneously go hand in hand with a certain social as well as spatial diffusion. The territorial planning efforts of the past would not have been in vain. However, not only did the trickle-down effect take place very slowly, and without covering every part of the country, but even the equity policy that preceded and succeeded it did not meet with the expected success.

Reality almost never reflected the prevailing discourse. The results first: what was valid for agriculture was even more so generally speaking. Inter-regional differences had accentuated (Sathyamurthy ed. 1995). In 1970–1, Punjab, the richest state, enjoyed a per capita net domestic product that was 39 per cent above the national average. In 1998–2001, it was higher by 47 per cent (Shetty 2003). There is no doubt that the current economic liberalization has created a more differentiated growth between regions. Indeed, it is Maharashtra which has been receiving the most foreign direct investment since 1991.

One of the first decisions taken in 1991 was to put an end to industrial licences, save for strategic sectors. The sectors that were in the domain of the public sector thus far were now opened up to the private sector. The location of industries was no longer controlled, except in the case of eco-sensitive zones, and save in the case of a polluting industry. Henceforth, the coastal states accounted for 45 per cent of national investments, despite the relative decline of Kerala and the agglomeration of Mumbai (whose saturation benefited its neighbouring districts).

Admittedly, several regional development schemes remain—Tribal Development Programme, Hill Area Development Programme, Desert Development Programme, etc. The north-east Himalaya still enjoy subsidies for industrial transport and investment. As we have seen, special treatment was meted out to this region even in the case of subsidized food distribution. Domestic aircraft carriers are compelled to assign at least 10 per cent of their capacity to non profitable routes. But the equalization of railway freight charges was done away with in the case of steel (though it continued for coal). Subsidies for investments in 'backward' areas were reduced after 1988. The centre still bears a huge burden with regard to regional action, since 45 per cent of state plans are funded by it. But it increasingly fell to the states to conduct their own development policy, obviously on a reduced scale, and this often meant favouring the setting up of companies in the already-developed regions and big cities. This was the case with the industrial 'growth centres' that were soon to become the responsibility of the states themselves (choice of location, management, and funding), rather than the centre (Sridhar 2003). So is it with the new Special Export Zones that need only permission from the authorities in Delhi. As we have seen, this is also the case with 'decentralized procurement', which impels states to build a major part of their food grain stock on their own, with the centre only intervening financially.

We shall not deal with one debated issue—that of determining whether imperfect territorial planning was not in reality a consequence of upper-class domination (Bardhan 1984), an 'intertwining of state and class with planning' (Byres 1998). Deshpande (1998) believed that the 'development' policy had accelerated and not slowed down spatial and social differences. The middle class, the bulwark of the government at the time of Independence, broke up into sub-groups, and inter-regional rivalries to obtain central subsidies were on the increase. We shall confine ourselves to pointing out that in reality, the spatial perspective was (and is) hardly evident in planning. It was practically non-existent in the literature of that period, much less than in Gaullist France of the same era, for instance, which was characterized by the fear of the 'French desert' versus Paris domination. Thus, very few maps were used and, even today, maps are a rare commodity in India (even among geographers!). 'National planning's basic plotting surface was not maps but national income accounts' (Lewis 1995: 211). This only translated the formidable lack of coordination as regards the location of facilities, whether in the Planning Commission, in the ministries concerned, or between them. We have already seen how difficult it was for the Ministries of Agriculture, Finance, and Food to cooperate in the field of food.

It must also be noted that 'town and country planning'—the English expression that usually translates the French *aménagement du territoire*—is rarely used in India. There is a Town and Country Planning Organization, but its main job is local-level urban planning. Indians speak more easily of 'regional planning', although a certain 'centralism' underlies this expression. Indeed, 'planning' has to be planned and can therefore only be conceived at higher decision-making echelons. Moreover, the term 'regional' corresponded to a scale of action undertaken not for itself (the aim was not to develop the region *per se*), but to the place the region occupied within the Indian Union. During that period, the region had to place national interest above self-interest. Let us not forget the recriminations expressed by the states with regard to the central food policy. Regional planning had a productivist purpose and if a steel plant was set up in Bhilai, it was less to develop Chhattisgarh than to raise the national steel output. It then becomes clear that planning objectives were more often presented in economic terms, or even social terms, rather than spatial terms. Space was merely an objective in the background.

The first consequence of this line of thinking was that the individual, the village, the neighbourhood, the micro-scale, individual interests, and group interests, all had to draw back before the higher interests of the nation and the macro-level (Heuzé 2004). The 1952 National Forest Policy claimed that 'village communities in the neighborhood of a forest will naturally make greater use of its products for the satisfaction of their domestic and agricultural needs. Such use, however, should in no event be permitted at the cost of national interests. The accident of village being situated close to a forest does not prejudice the right of the country as a whole to receive the benefits of a national asset.'[3] Similarly, it was 'the interest of the general public'—though this notion had never been fully explained—that gave justification to the 1955 Essential Commodities Act, which allowed the central government to infringe upon state prerogatives and especially those of the private sector for food grain. This meant that there were two types of 'spaces', corresponding to two radically opposed—and generally incompatible—perceptions. One was a space in the abstract—that of the planner concerned with national development; the other was a subjective space—which had an identity of its own and belonged to the inhabitants. 'Space' *versus* 'place', *terra nullius* from a legal point of view versus *locus,* such are the conflicts tragically experienced by the victims of large development projects, such as the tribal populations who were chased away from their homesteads by dams, much more easily since they rarely owned any title of ownership to their property. 'The concept of abstract space enables developers to maintain a highly objectified and external relation to the landscape, which becomes emptied of people, history, entitlements, myth and magic' (Whitehead 2003: 4229).[4] Indeed, we cannot accuse Nehru of lacking historical sensitivity; the fact remains that the deviations of the driven planning of his era (and later too) abounded in human drama and uprooting.

The second consequence was that administrative planning proliferated at the cost of local democracy, but it was all done in the name of national growth—not to give a leg up to backward regions, nor to divert private or public capital from already rich areas or groups.

Anyway planning would not have been able to curb the strong growth trend. We should remember that planning was just indicative and not imperative within the framework of a mixed economy. Hence India found itself facing a doubly painful situation, with the state machinery resembling an all-powerful Leviathan, without wanting to, or being able to, prevent disparities from growing (or, at least, continuing at the same level).

Corruption and the capture of administrative power by private interests only partly explain the paradox. The complexity of planning had to be understood at least at two levels, centre and state (Chakravarty 1994). The economic sectors also have to be assessed by the yardstick of their spatial potential: what could planning deal with? To put it simply, three sectors—infrastructure, agriculture, and industry. Infrastructure meant railway lines and networks; agriculture meant horizontal development 'in belts'; but industry, could only be conceived spatially as more or less large 'points', not belts—at least where heavy and semi-heavy industries were concerned. Whereas the First Five Year Plan laid emphasis on the first two sectors, the Second Plan stressed industry, in particular heavy industry. The plans that followed contained a more or less balanced approach, but there was always resistance to favouring infrastructural and agricultural networks at the expense of industry. Thus the industrial concentration points remained so many isolates on the Indian development map.

As for the rest, the partial failure of these policies should undoubtedly be seen as typical of all development and planning. Except for absolute control over the economy, as in communist countries, the leading trends set in motion by private players cannot be offset by the administration, although they can be modified marginally.

In a cross-nation comparison, Evans (1995) defined two types of states: 'predatory' and 'developmental'. 'Predatory states extract at the expense of the society, undercutting development even in the narrow sense of capital accumulation. Developmental states not only have presided over industrial transformation but can be plausibly argued to have played a role in making it happen' (ibid.: 12). It is difficult to fit India into either of these types and Evans qualified it as an 'intermediary' type, unintentionally admitting that his typology was too narrow. But he went a bit further by defining the four possible 'roles' of a developmental state. 'The first two, "custodian" and "demiurge", represent variations on the conventional roles of regulator and producer. The second pair, which I call "midwifery" and "husbandry", focus more on the relation between state agencies and private entrepreneurial groups' (ibid.: 13); then the aim was to establish new enterprises or, more generally, to encourage entrepreneurial groups to develop themselves.

A spatial perspective might help us understand what 'role' the Indian state played. In fact, if we assume that each of these roles contributes to fashioning a particular type of national space, we could suppose that the characterization of the Indian space would allow us to classify the types of action undertaken by the government. Accordingly, the national territory ought to reveal the type of state to which it owes most of its shape. A 'predatory' state would create deep regional imbalances, benefiting the capital in particular, producing an urban network suffering from 'macrocephaly' (the capital city being its 'big head'). A 'developmental' state, on the other hand, would foster territorial balances. In particular, the 'custodian' state would seek a better distribution of development throughout its territory. Indubitably, in that case the ideal spatial form is defined by Christaller's hexagons in south Germany—regularly and hierarchically 'nested' areas of influence covering the entire space. In case of striking imbalances, the state could don the role of 'demiurge' and create growth centres that were more or less integrated with the rest of the territory. This may face the risk of building veritable 'cathedrals in the desert'. The 'husbandry' and 'midwifery' roles too could ideally lead to a harmonious distribution of development all over the national territory. The difference from the custodian and even more from demiurge states would lie in a more dispersed form of development, as most of it would have been undertaken by the private sector. Small cities, small enterprises, Indonesian-style *desakota* structures linking towns and villages in a dense activity and population network, would be the result.

Where is India placed in such a typology? No urban macrocephaly is visible. Mumbai has 6 per cent of the Indian urban population. Regional imbalances are relatively low, given the country's size. Most certainly, the ancient past is at least as responsible for this situation as the policies implemented since 1947. We can nonetheless believe that the Indian state is more 'developmental' than 'predatory', as Evans too concurred, and its role has been mainly that of a 'custodian', despite certain aspects of the 'demiurge' state (cf. Orissa's industrial townships) or 'midwifery' (protection of small scale industries, land reforms).

In the writings on the subject, the Indian food policy was never studied from the regional planning perspective, and even Bhadouria's (1986) excellent work only dealt with the impact of a strictly agricultural policy. Nevertheless, the public food system also illustrates the 'developmental' character of the Indian state, and even its 'demiurge' role with respect to the magnitude of the mechanism put in place between producers and consumers. If, despite all this, what comes to mind are the system's many malfunctions and pernicious effects, as well as numerous frauds and diversions often condoned by the authorities, then the adjective 'predatory' might at times seem more appropriate. There is another limitation to Evans' typology: the terms 'predatory' and 'developmental' are perfectly reconcilable. Assessments vary at first according to the *scale*. At a sufficiently general level, the administration could seem to play a more positive role, despite the fact that a field study would show up all the malfunctions and corrupt practices. So it would be a developmental state at the national level, but a predatory at the local level. The reality is even more complicated: both institutions and individuals can simultaneously achieve both the objectives of socio-economic development and enrichment through bribes and misappropriation of funds. For example, it is *baksheesh* that facilitates the smooth operation of procurement, whilst consumers have to make additional payments in appreciation of the administration's efficiency. 'In short, the Indian state is not only rent seeking, but also developmental' (Mooij 1999: 240).

GANDHI'S REVENGE? THE REBIRTH OF 'LOCALISM'

It is important not to oversimplify the divergence between the spatial ideas of Nehru and Gandhi. During Nehru's lifetime, many policies had indeed a Gandhian flavour. The Community Development Programme, launched in 1952 on the occasion of Gandhi's birthday, had as targets agricultural production, the creation of infrastructure for and by the entire community (by promoting cooperatives), and greater village and individual self-sufficiency under a new ethic. The programme as such had a mixed outcome, but the development infrastructure created then survives till today, and its role in pursuing the Green Revolution was far from negligible. The 'development block' was established at more or less the *tehsil* level. At the village level, village level workers, called *gram sevaks*, spread the message of agricultural extension, the development of small-scale village industries, and health and housing.

Confronted with the programme's weakness and local democracy's shortcomings, a huge decentralization plan under the name of *Panchayat Raj* was launched in 1957. It provided for the election by direct suffrage of a local council (*gram panchayat*), replicated by other bodies at the block and district levels, thereby supposedly giving a voice to the rural masses. In this matter too, there was a fairly mixed success; there were scarcely any states that held regular elections to these bodies. Later, once a new decentralization wave accompanied liberalization and concerns about state withdrawal, it became necessary to amend the Constitution in 1992–3, with the panchayats officially becoming the third tier of government (their equivalent in cities is supposed to be ward committees), thereby providing consistency to these local 'self-governments'—although this is still not the case everywhere. From now, development policies crafted by the central and state governments must be in tune with actions taken by local communities—i.e. two poles at either end of the ladder striving towards the same goal. The inherent risk was that the Union states might find themselves sandwiched between the central and local governments, falling victim to the 'hour-glass' model , 'with the states at the narrow waist, the union power-wise broad at the top, and sub-state institutions function-wise broad at the bottom' (N. Mukarji 1999: 76). In fact, many state governments passed legislations to grant very limited powers to local bodies, or did not transfer the promised funds. There was also the issue of the rules of the game as played by politicians. With alliances between political parties becoming indispensable for the capture of power at the centre, the state's importance was not likely to diminish. That has already been seen in Andhra Pradesh's strategies. Mere vassals at one time, without many privileges during the 'Congress system' that prevailed before 1967, the Chief Ministers began increasingly to gain weight in central decisions, either because their loyalty was suspect and they had to be kept in good humour, or because institutional changes gave them greater room for manoeuvre. The states began to follow their own path, irrespective of their political hues. This was the case especially after liberalization in the 1990s.

Along with these 'general' political decentralization measures, it must also be noted that there are other forms of more 'sectoral' decentralization—intended, at least on paper, to foster more participative management and relieve the state of some of its prerogatives. Other aims include those of developing Joint Forest Management for forests and the Participatory Irrigation Management for irrigation, for instance. However, the initiatives are ambiguous each time, given that they are supposed to support the 'rightist' view favourable to state withdrawal (and international donors), as much as the 'leftist' view, upholding people's participation. From a purely spatial point of view, it is a question of 'un-integrating', creating new local power places, and adding local knots to the too smooth rope of national integration tying New Delhi to the rest of the territory. One of the risks is that it gives free reign to centrifugal movements based on identity, which could imperil the Indian Union.

A FOLIATED TERRITORY AND MULTIFOLD IDENTITY

It is a truism of anthropology that a person can have different identities according to the context, without these identities necessarily being at loggerheads. These identities can be increasingly inclusive or nested (Gujarati, Indian), or may partially overlap (Hindu, male, Indian)—all Hindus in the world are not Indian. Even in the latter case, the disparity in the referents does not necessarily denote conflict or rupture, much less treason. Such identities do get spatially transcribed into a 'territory', taken in the sense of an appropriated space (Gervais-Lambony et al., 2005). In fact, identity projected onto a space creates a territory, which conversely plays a role in fashioning this identity. How then do we reconcile the plurality of territories, which is a corollary of the plurality of identities? How to maintain a unique national territory with so many identities?

'France is a person', wrote Michelet, an historian, in his *Tableau de la France* (1833). This expression was taken up by Vidal de la Blache the geographer (1845–1918), and by many other scholars (Lefort 1992). 'Marianne' is a national emblem of France, a woman typically symbolizing the civic virtues of the Republic. At the first glance, this secular symbol appears quite removed from the deification of India which began in the same period, in the form of *Bharat Mata*, Mother India. The two beautiful women have the same love for the nation in their eyes. Above all, for Vidal, it was a means of taking Renan further, who opposed the notion of an identity based on natural borders or 'race' and argued that Alsace had to belong to the French territory if Alsatians were *feeling* French in spite of their Germanic language. 'Geographically, France appeared as a person because its national identity was dependent on people's free will' (Paule Petitier, in Robic, 2000: 132). Indeed, this is an idea very akin to that of secular India, created out of the adherence of individuals and groups, going beyond their ethnicity and religion, 'an elective conception of nationhood' (Robic 2000: 9) that distinguished France from Germany as it did India from Pakistan (the latter's Muslim identity reminiscent of the German *Volksgeist*).

National integration involved both the people and the territory: a pluralistic nation with a pluralistic territory. Independent India had to overcome this obstacle: initially, identities revolved around caste, village, region, and language, and were based much more on the local scale than that of India as a whole. I noted how little farmers in Karnataka—who were passionate about their state's politics—knew about what went on at the national level. 'The usual social space of the poorer people in the rural areas even today does not extend beyond fifteen-twenty miles from their home. . . . India, it is obvious, will not be built in a day,' wrote the sociologist Srinivas in 1962 (13). Language too reflected this reality: in Tamil (Daniel 1984), *nadu* signifies 'country' in every sense of the word, from India to the micro-region. Thus, *Tamil Nadu* denotes 'land of Tamils', and reflects the intermediary scale of the provincial state. Only the term *desham* exclusively denotes India, but it is of Sanskrit origin, and the fact that it is borrowed proves that the notion was superimposed later on to what has been an extremely regional identity till then. On the one hand, there was a concept associated with an identity, experienced every day and rooted in the soil; on the other hand, a political, abstract and finally fairly remote concept.

Independent India's challenge was to strengthen the *desham*. The idea was not to develop a national identity at the cost of a *nadu* identity, but at least develop it alongside, without necessarily provoking rivalry. In fact, 'since the 18th century at least, local patriotic feelings have constituted a learning programme for developing the sense of belonging to a supralocal level. And, after the second half of the 19th century, the growth of regional patriotism has merged with nation building' (Assayag 2001: 205).

Going further, '*tecam* [*desham*] and *kiramam* [revenue village] are terms whose meaning is relatively context free, universal, and fixed, whereas *natu* and *ur* [village settlement] are person-centric terms that derive their meaning from the contextually shifting spatial orientation of the person' (Daniel 1984: 70). However, Hinduism is a religion with highly individualistic values and rituals—there is no common *dharma* valid for all castes and communities; no single form of worship that is celebrated by everyone. 'It is, therefore, not at all odd for the Tamil to readily accept a very person-centric, idiosyncratic, and shifting definition of space. Space, like time and *dharma*, is meaningful only in its relationship to particular places and at particular times' (ibid.: 72).

This was seen as a trump card by the builders of the new India, as there was no need to fight a given identity and territory to replace it with others, and there was no need to prohibit the use of the mother tongue in school and substitute it with a national language, as was done in some regions of France at the end of the nineteenth century. They just needed to *add* or to strengthen one element of the range of identities that was already in place : that of the nation, endowed with its territory.

HINDU NATIONALIST TERRITORY

Failed Secularization of the Holy Land

Nehru tells us (1985 [1946]: 59) how, so as to make himself understood by the common man and rural folk during political meetings, he used to invoke *Bharat Mata*—a notion popularized by a nationalist poet, Bankim Chandra Chatterji (1838–94). Bharata was the name of a mythical king in the epic *Mahabharata*, after whom the country was named. To convey the idea of nationalism optimally, Nehru did not hesitate to use a Hindu idiom. This idiom was rooted in the holy texts, and in a concept of India seen as a maternal, female figure, which can be found in the contemporary discourse of Hindu nationalist movements (Assayag 2001).

So Hinduism was clearly used to further nationalism. The

distance between 'nation' and 'community' is never too great—there is no better way to weld a *Gesellschaft* than through the shared sentiment of *Gemeinschaft* (Deshpande 1998). Nurtured by the cliché of kaleidoscopic-India, the nationalists of the early twentieth century were compelled to draw from the orientalist vision of age-old syncretism. Admittedly, India had never experienced political unity, but according to orientalists the nation already pre-existed as a cultural identity founded on religion (Pouchepadass 2003). Thus, the fundamental perception of a national territory had to pass through religion. Appearing in the First Article of the Constitution, the specifically Hindu name of *Bharat* (India) was officially retained as Independent India's new patronymic ('India, that is Bharat, shall be a Union of States'). However, this was a dangerous game to play, for the appeal to sentimental nationalism partly built upon Hindu values, practices, and myths could fertilize the seeds of communalism that had already been sown by the Hindu Mahasabha or the National Volunteers Association (RSS: Rashtriya Swayamsevak Sangh)—the party of which Gandhi's assassin had been a member.

It was well and truly through Hinduism that the 'common national bond' unifying India appeared as a 'land to the four corners of which people went on pilgrimage' (Nehru 1985 [1946]: 251). In order to establish that the 'concept of the unity of India is essentially a religious one,' Srinivas (1962: 105) too recalled that even pilgrims from Rameshwaram in the south were supposed to take a pot of sea water and empty it into the Ganga. Many an Indian believes in the existence of a secret tunnel linking the northern Ganga to the Kaveri in the south. A large section of Nehru's politics consisted of furthering and transforming this patriotic-religious sentiment, by turning it into a secular one, with the intention of avoiding other bloody partitions and integrating the non-Hindu population into the new India. For Nehru, an atheist, it was important for a new religion devoted to Mankind to slowly supplant other faiths: dams and steel plants were 'modern India's temples', he emphasized on many occasions (Brosius 2001). The new nation-worship was not very dissimilar to the one established by the French Third Republic: the same 'sacred secularism (*laïcité*)' (Raffestin 1985: 104), the same faith in progress and modernity, the same worship of fatherland and democracy—with, in addition, the marvel of seeing an unified and independent nation at last. India is one of the few democratic countries, along with France, to celebrate its National Day with a military parade to demonstrate the country's might. In Indian schools, 26 January, Republic Day, is an occasion to hoist the colours —children standing at attention, teachers hoisting the tricolour in the presence of portraits of Gandhi and other founding fathers. Sometimes, a map of India is also drawn in flower petals below the flagpole.

The fact that the flowers may be saffron carnations—the colour of Hinduism, and that the map of India could be a symbol of Mother India demonstrates the flawed secularism of the Nehruvian era. On the one hand, the French term 'laïcite' is an incorrect translation of 'secularism' : secularism does not postulate a more or less watertight separation of religion and the State like in France, but the State's neutral stand in religious matters—a neutrality that could be entirely well-meaning and by and large quite full of holes as far as religious influences were concerned. The most important thing was that the State should be perceived as being above any kind of religious identity. On the other hand, we should take into account the deeply religious population of India, both in its belief as well as in its practices, coupled with the growth of Hindu political movements since the 1980s.

These movements are generally referred to as 'Hindu nationalist'. This does not mean that they are followers of Nehruvian nationhood, nor even Gandhi's integrating nationhood, which welcomed all religions and all communities in the name of secularism. In fact, they believe in a nation based on a religious criterion—India should be a Hindu nation. She can indeed welcome other religions, provided that Muslims, Sikhs and Christians accept an acculturation that would enable them to blend into 'Hinduness' or *Hindutva*. This is 'ethnic nationalism' as opposed to Nehru's and Gandhi's 'universal nationalism' (Jaffrelot 1998). Nevertheless—and this is a crucial point for the PDS' geographical approach—these two types of nationalisms are not contradictory in their approach to space. Though not very far from Gandhian thought with regard to the aspect of local 'community' or the concern for decentralization, Hindu nationalists are close to Nehru, owing to their concept of an all encompassing and integrated national territory. The fact that the latter two perceptions of the territory, coming to power one after the other in independent India,[5] were complementary and not divergent could not help but have strong implications in the spatial structure of a network as important and widespread as the food distribution system.

Indeed, the latter was to be one of the pillars of the integration of the national territory.

Hinduism—A Geographical Religion

The fact that Indian territory occupies an important place in Hindu nationalist thoughts and demands is not surprising. Hinduism is most certainly a geographical religion. We shall see that the notions of circulation and integration, so significant in the public food system, also occupy an important place.

At the regional level, there is no hill or river without a presiding deity, which does not give birth to a local legend that is in itself more or less easily interwoven into a pan-Indian epic or a Purana. No sacred place is isolated, each is 'part of a complex fabric of reference and signification that constitutes a cumulative landscape' (Eck 1998: 168). Thus such places also played the vital role of 'knitting together into one religious society the numerous heterogeneous groups in India, and giving them all the sense that their country is sacred. Patriotism is invested with a religious quality' (Srinivas 1962: 106). Sacred geography also exists at the national level (Map 4.1) – holy places are visited by pilgrims of every origin, from the most famous Saivite *lingas* (symbol representing Lord Shiva) to the most venerated *sangams* (confluences of holy rivers), and to the more recently in vogue Tirupati temple. On the whole, it engendered 'a radically localized worldview'; 'Hindu mythology is profusely linked to India's geography—its mountains, rivers, forests, shores, villages, and cities. It "takes place", so to speak, in thousands of shrines and in the culturally-created mental "map" of Bharata' (Eck 1998: 187, 169).

Thus, the role of the geographical territory is essential for affirming Hinduness. Anyone who crossed the seas—*kala pani* or black waters—and left the subcontinent, lost his purity, and one's 'polluted' state was likely to excommunicate him from the Hindu community. Such conceptions were carried to their heights by V.D. Savarkar, founder of the 'Great Hindu Association' (*Hindu Mahasabha*) and author of the famous *Hindutva* (1923), a booklet written during the many years the British had kept him in prison. This short text, written in a rather disjointed and hallucinatory style and crammed with Sanskrit quotations, placed Indian territory at the forefront of Hindu identity. A Hindu was 'a person who regards

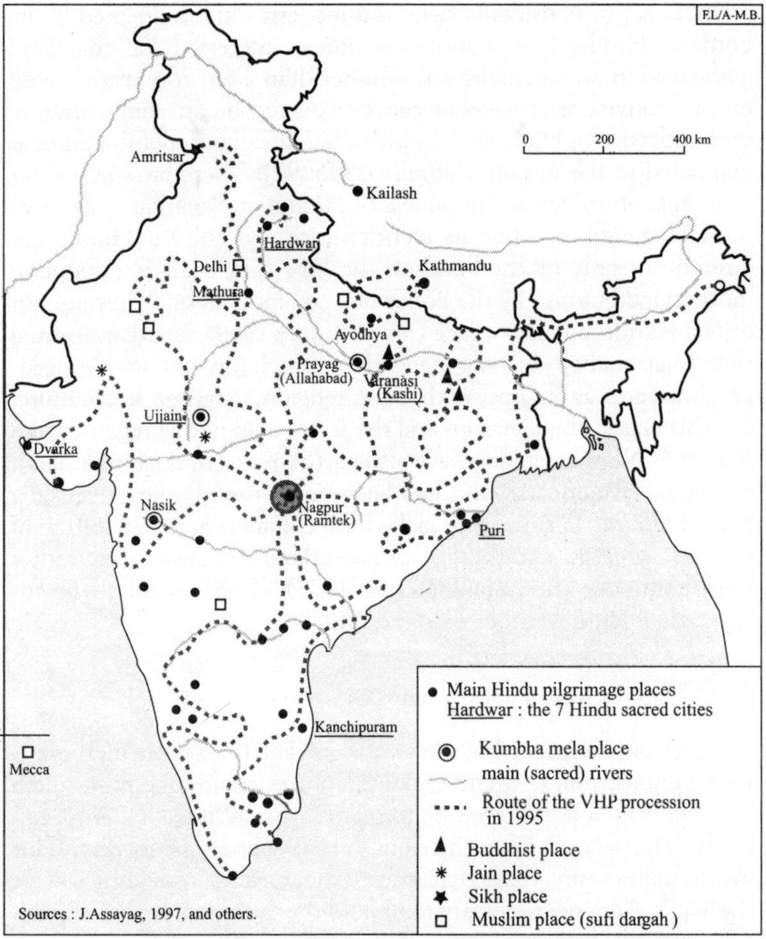

Map 4.1: Hindu pilgrimages and nationalist processions

this land of BHARATVARSHA, from the Indus to the Seas as his Father-Land as well as his Holy-Land that is the cradle land of his religion' (Savarkar 1969).

India is not considered here as a modern state delineated by its borders. Hindu Nationalists are more interested in the land 'perceived in an organicist way—rather than a territory in the sense of an anonymous space that can be covered by an administrative grid. Indeed, this choice ties in with their devaluation of the State as compared to the nation' (Jaffrelot 1996: 90). Therefore space is far from enough to define Hinduness or *Hindutva*. Savarkar added two more elements to define its identity: race and culture. Hindus are 'united not only by the bonds of the love they bear to a common motherland but also by the bonds of a common blood. They are not only a Nation but also a race (jati)'. In July 1939, Savarkar asserted that 'Nationality did not depend so much on a common geographical area as on unity of thought, religion, language, and culture. For this reason the Germans and the Jews could not be regarded as a nation.'[6] Neither could the Muslims (despite Hindu forefathers), nor could 'Americans' who had been naturalized Indians ever be a part of *Hindutva*, since they lacked the common Sanskrit culture of Hindus. *Volksgeist* rather than Fatherland, genius-nation rather than contract-nation (Finkielkraut 1987)—India ought to be inhabited by Hindus rather than citizens.

The Chequering of Hindu Territory

An area can be marked out in two ways. The first, static method, is to have fixed points where Hindu identities could take root, much like the principle followed by former Christian 'missions' in pagan lands. The second, more dynamic one is spatial chequering. This means maintaining flows that irrigate the territory, providing it with the sap and energy necessary to uphold the faith and further expand a power or ideology. Pilgrimages and processions belong to this category.

Temples belong to the first type of positioning and so also do *shakhas*, local branches established by Hindu nationalists. The RSS, a party created in 1925, adhered the most to structuring the country's social, political and physical space in this manner (Jaffrelot 1993). Its approximately two million members gather in 50,000 *shakhas*, as claimed by the RSS today, where regular paramilitary training is held, along with propaganda sessions, as close as possible to village and neighbourhood people.

The second type of marking is done in a more fluid manner, by meticulously organizing pilgrimages and processions. These processions are held at local level and progress through the town or village with as spirited a display of faith as possible—sometimes passing by a mosque while hurling insulting slogans against Islam or even throwing pork trotters inside Muslim compounds. At the national level, huge processions with particularly symbolic routes were organized from 1983 onwards (Assayag 1998 and 2001). One example was the procession organized by the Vishwa Hindu Parishad (VHP) in 1983 that was symptomatically called the 'sacrifice for unity' (*ekatmata yagna*). Apart from 47 small, regional five-day processions, three big processions (*yatras*) criss-crossed every part India for two months, from Hardwar and Kathmandu in the north to Kanyakumari and Rameshwaram in the south, and from Gangasagar in the east to Somnath in the west. 'Significantly, the three processions crossed in the middle of the country, in Nagpur, which is not a pilgrimage centre but the headquarters of the RSS. This meeting in Nagpur was duly compared with the *triveni*, the confluence of the three holy rivers (*sangam*) in Prayag (Allahabad), one of India's most sacred spots' (van der Veer 1994: 124). India's unity was represented by a picture of Bharat Mata, hoisted on trucks clad as 'traditional' chariots, which also carried two jars—a huge one containing the sacred water of the Ganga and another smaller one filled with local river water. Alongside Indian flags, the country's maps drawn or pasted on walls, chariots, and in propaganda video films bore testimony to the religious importance of the land (Brosius 2001).

Other huge processions modelled on this followed suit, but most of them were prevented from taking place by controlling forces, as the authorities feared that their itinerary could cause riots. It should be said that these organizations often chalked out extremely ambitious programmes, like the one the VHP launched in 1995—its 'pilgrimage for unanimity', when only some of the processions were able to converge in Nagpur, or rather in the neighbouring town of Ramtek, more or less at India's geographical centre. Map 4.1 shows the kind of capillary flows that the Hindu movements were aiming at, weaving a particularly fine and ubiquitous web. It was definitely a pioneering front—not in the shape of a linear frontier, but a space that identified itself with the entire nation, a space for an everlasting mission aimed at re-conquering the land through this 'patriotic pilgrimage' (*deshbhakti ki teerth yatra*).

Officially the objectives of such processions are not political. However, when they roll out during the pre-electoral period, they indisputably come out in support of the BJP, a political party born out of Hindu nationalist movements. Above all, they stoke the communal fire by selecting a particularly sensitive political place like Somnath (whose ancient Hindu temple was razed to the ground by Mahmud Ghazni in the eleventh century) as their starting or ending point, and particularly Ayodhya, in Uttar Pradesh, Rama's birthplace, where an unused mosque was destroyed by Hindus in 1992. The riots that followed led to 1200 deaths within a few days across the country. A temple was supposed to be built at the site, but though the statues and pillars have already been sculpted, nothing had been erected there so far.

The construction of the temple pointed to another method of integrating the Hindu space—movement not by pilgrims nor militants, but products. In 1989, bricks made all over the country and even beyond it, thanks to donations by the Hindu diaspora, converged in Ayodhya to help build the temple. Each brick was inscribed with its geographical indicator, a testimony to the importance of the origin and the strong feeling provoked by donating a *Ram shila* (brick for Rama). Indubitably, if these dispatches were to be mapped, we would have an excellent spatial image of *Hindutva*, whose dissemination would have sent Savarkar's expansionist dreams into raptures, although north India would probably be over-represented.

The Ayodhya bricks, like the processions meeting in Nagpur, depicted a converging movement, which, to all intents and purposes, took on an essential geometrical shape—that of a wheel. The *chakra* or the Wheel of Law, Vishnu's weapon, and Gandhi's spinning wheel—are all symbolized by the wheel. The wheel is also present in the Indian national flag. It does not simply represent a round shape, cycle, or regeneration. It symbolizes radiating energy —increasing influence. There is a centripetal radiation, as could be seen in the processions or bricks that all converge on a central place, but also a centrifugal radiation, set in motion from a given centre. One example is the VHP's plan in 2002 (which it finally gave up) to exploit the Godhra tragedy. What happened was that in Godhra railway station in Gujarat, fifty-nine Hindu militants perished in a fire that had, perhaps, been set deliberately (about 2000 Muslims died in the ensuing reprisal). The VHP then announced that it would transport the ashes of the victims to all corners of India and scatter them in 750 different locations. Another 'centrifugal' plan was to build a temple at Pokhran, India's atom bomb testing site and source of national pride, then gather radioactive sand and take it in a procession across the country. Commemorating Pokhran meant killing two birds with a single stone for these Hindu movements—by playing upon the patriotic fervour, they could touch the religious nerve of Hindus at the same time. A sacred union, against the common enemy, Pakistan, was sacred for Indian Muslims too. It was doubly so, both in the religious and patriotic sense, for the Hindus.

FROM DIAMOND-SHAPE TO CROSS

'The BJP did not propose a return to a traditional Hindu polity, it had no Gandhian picture of a stateless India composed of village republics. . . . The Hindu nationalist aspiration to redefine Indianness always presumed the availability of a strong state as the instrument to forge an identity' (Khilnani 1999: 188, 190). But Hindu nationalist movements concurred with Gandhian philosophy in their misgivings about the state. This was an extension of an old Brahmin tradition of defying temporal power and denigrating it to reinforce the priest's authority. As the RSS ideologue, D. Upadhyaya, said in 1965, 'In our socio-political set-up, the king and the state were never considered supreme. . . . The mightiest of the king did not ever disturb the Panchayats. . . . Thus the State was concerned only with some aspects of life of the Society.'[7] Going back to the utopia of the united villages of yore, Hindu nationalists joined the Gandhians in a discourse advocating decentralization. They claimed that this would help establish local autonomy and consensus decision-making.

The entire ambiguity of the stand taken by Hindu nationalists emerged. On one hand, their conception of territory went totally against Nehruvian ideas, as they rejected centralized planning. It then merged with the Gandhian discourse, 'while laying the emphasis on decentralization, the primacy of social coherence inspired by the varna system and the strong devaluation of state authority over the society and religious matters' (Jaffrelot 1998:

286), while at the same time expressing its attachment to *swadeshi*, the autonomy of the national economy. But on the other hand, the Hindu nationalist concept of territory was closer to Nehruvian thought in its all-encompassing aspect, given the desire to chequer the territory in order to cover it entirely. When the nationalist BJP came to power after four decades of Congress rule, they could not help but continue with their concern for spatial integration and pursue plans in continuity with its earlier post-Independence history. It is easy to see that the food supply system survived the political change in 1998, because (beside many other reasons) it was deemed to be an integrating tool by both parties.

Across all these different approaches to Indian territory, it was the same concern for integrity and integration that emerged—in a nation yet to come out of the trauma of the Partition in 1947 (Gupta 2000). One indicator of this fact was the great obsession with the map, not as a tool (we have seen how unimportant geography is in India), but as a symbol. It was a colonial inheritance from two points of view.[8] The British began their triangulation operations in India even before they set similar work in motion in the United Kingdom. Indeed, their population census went hand in hand with a territorial census. On the other hand, the Freedom Movement, and now Hindu nationalists viewed the map as a symbol of the nation (Assayag 2001; Brosius 2001). Anderson (1991) stressed that many maps functioned as 'logo maps', mark of 'imaginary communities' or, to be more precise, of the establishment of nation-states. 'It is an icon, revered with piety', says Foucher (1988: 71) of the map.

Such a statement is paradoxical if we recall that the present Indian culture ignores the use of maps in daily life. Can national maps be 'logos' when so few Indians can read maps of their region, of their city? Is there not a contradiction? The answer was found by Ramaswamy (2006) in her study of temples dedicated to Bharat Mata. The Varanasi temple, inaugurated by Gandhi in 1936, hides a relief map of India in marble in its middle section, which 'uses a water inflow system to reproduce the sea level and flooding in country during the monsoons' (Claveyrolas 2003).[9] But this amazing temple attracts few pilgrims or Hindu visitors. Till 2002, there was no picture of Bharat Mata in the temple: India was represented in a geographical, not anthropomorphic manner, and the absence of any painting or statue of the goddess made the temple unattractive. To some extent, this proves the defeat of the nationalists. 'Indian nationalism [had] "solved" the problem of getting Indians to die for an abstract territorial space named "India" by inserting the image of Bharat Mata into the empty social space of the map of India' (Ramaswamy 2006: 176). But nationalism lost out. The absence of goddess picture in the temple could not attract all the castes and the religions of India. As a result, even Hindus hardly visit the temple. 'It is not so much Bharat Mata who needs the map to prop up her identity, but the map that needs the familiar image of the goddess to legitimize its claim to (cartographically) represent "India" ' (ibid.: 175). The paradox is explained. The goddess is worshipped, not the map.

Beyond this ambiguity, it seems as if the common feature of the space venerated by Hindus and the space administered by officialdom is that both can be reduced to the four cardinal points—four symbolic extremities that sum up the national territory. Amongst the seven sacred towns of Hinduism where one can attain deliverance (*moksha*), four are the most important for pilgrimages —the four that represent the cardinal points (Map 4.1): Badrinath in the north, Puri in the east, Rameshwaram in the south, and Dwarka in the west. Many travel agencies specializing in pilgrimages organize *char dham* tours (tours to the four divine abodes) in buses fitted with video players (Claveyrolas 2003; Jaffrelot 1996).[10] Even today, officials in Delhi spout readymade expressions to describe India as a whole: for instance 'from Kashmir to Kanyakumari, and from Kohima to Kutch'.[11] They simply repeat stock phrases already used by Nehru (1985 [1946]: 60). To raise 'common problems of the peasants from north to south and east to west', he told them of his 'journeying from the Khyber pass in the far north-west to *Kanya Kumari* or Cape Comorin in the distant south'. Savarkar mapped Hindu territory in a similar fashion, 'from Kashmir to the Cape [Comorin] and from Attock to Cuttack' (Savarkar 1969: 79 and *passim*). These are alliterations we come across again today to designate BJP's huge electoral processions, such as the one undertaken by L.K. Advani in March 2004, who set forth in a bus from Kanyakumari to end up in Amritsar, and wanted to begin the second west-east leg of the cross, 'from Porbander to Puri'.[12] The echoes of consonants and the resonance of syllables are like proof of the unity of India, the four corners of which are reflecting the multiform identity.

'Giving a name to space means creating a territory' (Gumuchian 1991: 103). These city names that are identified with cardinal points are 'ideological places' carrying the embryo of a nation, 'well known and famous points, the imagination of which sums up the idea of an entire country'.[13] There are somewhat similar to what Nora (1984) described as 'places of memory'. Here their emblematic quality does not stem as much from their character as from their conjunction—just as each segment of the *mandala* represents nothing when it is not placed within the general geometric shape symbolizing the universe or the divinity. These four cardinal points, dotted with emblematic places (Srinagar, a coveted Muslim town; Kanyakumari, a holy place at the tip of the peninsula where pilgrims throng to gaze at the point where their country ends), form an archetypal image that guides both the citizen's perception of the nation and the objectives of Indian-style development

Comparing this with the French instance throws more light on the matter. The dominant spatial schema in France's territorial identity is indubitably the Paris—'province' duo—the latter term, that means 'everything in France except Paris', does not exist in the same sense in almost any other language, so strong is its specificity in the French context. Not only territorial planning, but also a major chunk of the political discourse remain based on this opposition—either to curtail it or to indict it. In a certain sense, town and country planning in France consists of creating in reality the ideal geometrical models identified with France's territorial shape in the nineteenth century, namely the hexagon idealized by Levasseur (1875) or the octagonal harmony outlined by Reclus (1877): the matter is fighting against excessive concentration in Paris. In India the dominant imagination is not founded on such an antinomy but on the four points defining a national territory that has to be irrigated by all kinds of currents. They can be seen in major contemporary public works, like the Golden Quadrangle project aimed at building remarkably symmetrical highways chequering the country, which we shall describe briefly here.

Similar to the French ideal of hexagon is the Indian dream of moving, so to say, from the diamond-shape to the cross. The diamond-shape represents India's four metropolises, the *char dham* of the urban structure: Mumbai, Kolkata, Delhi, and Chennai, the last demographically so distant that the foursome has a tendency to become a threesome. The four points are roughly in the shape of a diamond from point to point (Map 4.2), covering much of the national territory, matching the relatively balanced urban Indian network (Landy 2002). But the term 'diamond' can be misleading, for the four points are not the four angles of a quadrilateral: here we have a geometrical figure that has no sides, since there are not yet well etched urban corridors or routes linking these four cities. It was to bridge this gap that a huge four-lane highway project was launched in 1998—the 6,000 km long 'Golden Quadrangle'. But even when this diamond is well and truly completed, there will be a huge void in the middle, at the heart of the under-urbanized Deccan. The peripheral territories will then have to be linked up. The central government thought about it. It decided that at the same time, it would also build a cross-shaped highway in the middle of the diamond (7,000 km), comprising two east-west and north-south corridors, in strict compliance with the geometrical shape.[14] It is not surprising that the official rhetoric took up what could be called *topoi* from two points of view—common 'places' embellished by the usual alliterations. Hence, it was asserted that the project would go from 'Kashmir/Srinagar to Kanyakumari, and from Silchar to Saurashtra'.[15]

Such voluntarism does not fail to remind one of the US objective of the 'integral chequering of the territory' (Bonnafous 1994: 327) through highways, conceived in the 1950s. The French experiment went in the opposite direction, where the original programme, launched in early 1960s, was based more firmly on the economic viability of the investments, which only resulted in the strengthening of the radiating structure's heavy axes converging on Paris, weighing down the hexagon. The Indian plan on the other hand considered the national territory as a whole, to be integrated as equitably as possible. It was not by chance that the plan to interlink the main rivers for the sake of a better sharing of water resources between the various basins recently returned to centre stage, during the previous Hindu nationalist government.[16]

To summarize, cartography can be regarded in three ways. The simplest is the topographical map used by the military, the administration and tourists. The most ideological is the icon-map used by Hindu nationalists. The one occupying the middle ground would be

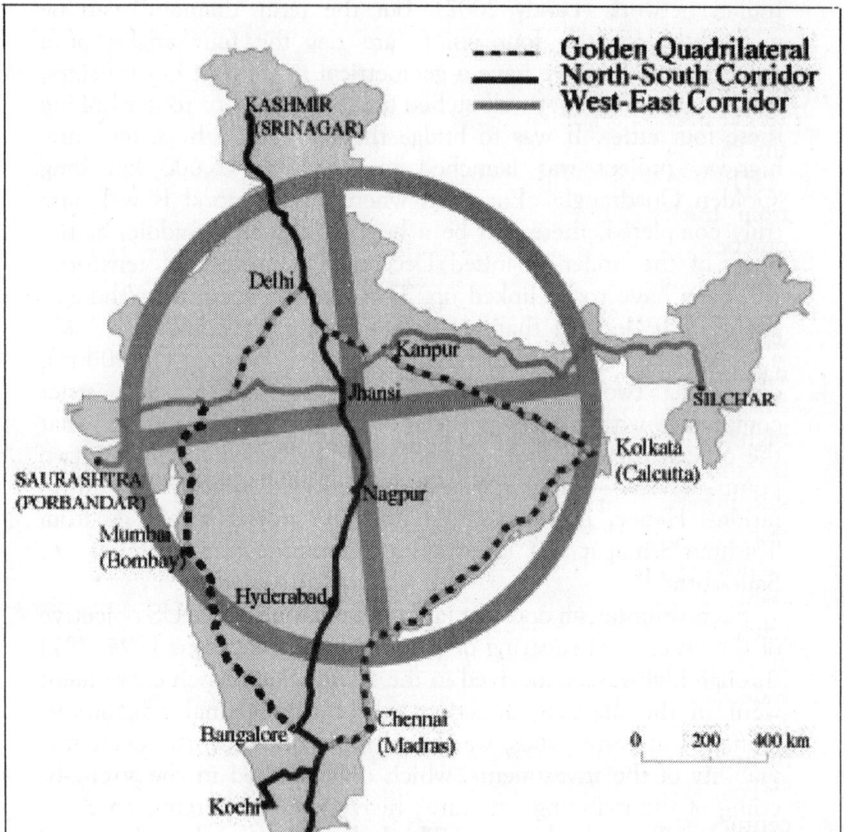

Map 4.2. The highway *chakra* (1999-2007)

our diamond-cross combination map, which is at the same time a programme, fundamentally political like the icon-map, and also a more prosaicly economic map of a highway development project.[17] This is undoubtedly the typical stamp of 'farsighted states'—which, according to Raffestin (1980), is what centralized States are: they think and see big. In their territorial control, they bestow greater importance on 'terminal points rather than intermediate points' (ibid.: 188). It is therefore no surprise that such a role was assigned to the cardinal points.

The Hindu nationalist spatial ideology was extremely different from the Nehruvian, but often translated into similar spatial practices. That is one of the premises of this work: the massive Hindu processions, highways project, and subsidized food grain circuits stem from the same concept of a space to be nurtured. The wheat exported by Punjab's farmers, who take pride in 'feeding the nation', are functionally akin to pilgrims travelling across India. To this end, we shall compare Maps 4.1 and 4.2 on processions and highway routes respectively, with Maps 3.9 and 3.10 on the transportation of FCI grains. Whether it is the movement of men in saffron or wheat bags is of no consequence: the same concern for territorial integration run through both. It is a 'paradigm of national identity', a 'symbolic representation of the territory that promotes a stable and relatively consensual union, which provides an active schema in which a multitude of practices and other representations at different levels can be constituted without contradictions'. Indeed, these words about Vidal de la Blanche's *Tableau de la Géographie de la France* (1903), written by Robic (2000: 8) seem to fit India's 'paradigm of national identity' perfectly.

Foucault (2004) had already pointed out that in eighteenth-century France, a new worry gnawed at the sovereign's mind: not only did he want to establish a territory by strengthening its frontiers, but by ensuring the *circulation* of people or goods to structure the national space and provide it with a real, deep-seated management system. Hindu pilgrims return home bringing along a small pot of water from the Ganga, or a little sand from Rameshwaram—that is how Hinduism's most holy places radiate across the entire territory. In 1999, the mortal remains of soldiers killed in the Kargil war against Pakistan were first brought to Delhi for a national funeral. They were then airlifted to the respective state capitals, where they were given a state funeral. It was only subsequently that they were handed over to their families.

Rather than truly homogenizing regional differences, the aim is to interlink the regions. Strict spatial equality is less important than enabling circulation. Linking the cardinal points to one another is more important than creating a homogeneous space between them. Hence, it is better to build a cross-shaped highway than to increase the density of the secondary road network. Indeed, the territory continues to be placed in the symbolic realm. So it is not surprising that the *chakra* can be seen on the highways project map, with the various highway branches symbolizing the spokes of the wheel.

Hindu nation/Indian nation—these opposing ideologies adopt the same approach to space. It is also true that some groups and individuals believe in a combination of these two spatial ideologies. From 1998 to 2004, the nationalist BJP was at the helm of affairs in India. Did not the food policy, in a sense, support the territorial control strategy of the Hindu nationalist party? That was probably one of the reasons (less important, true, than the pressure of the Supreme Court!) for continuing the oft-criticized system. The BJP government pursued the PDS restructuring process initiated in the 1990s, making it more restrictive and target-specific. But procurement continued to flourish and the total tonnage distributed remained quite considerable. And the Congress' return to power ensured the continuation of the subsidized food supply policy.

Admittedly, very few official documents concerning the food supply policy actually clearly mention this perception of space. On the FCI website, however, one can read: 'Regularly rice and wheat procured in the northern states is moved to far flung corners, Imphal in Manipur or Kanyakumari in Tamilnadu and to the higher reaches of the Himalayas in the North.' This site is also packed with eloquent photos (men carrying bags on their backs in Kashmir, bags being carried by goats, etc.) showing the efforts to cover the whole territory. But it is mainly in interviews, if the question is raised, that this perception is dealt with. The scarcity of testimonies does not, however, mean that our theory is false. What we have is just the paradox of so evident and shared a representation of the national space that it is not spontaneously referred to by anybody as an explanation for the choice to continue with the PDS. In fact, the customary observations made in this regard by interviewed people (justifiably) lay the emphasis on the divergent logics of the different states and on regional, group and individual egoism—in short, exactly the reverse of what 'national integration' ought to be. So there should be no confusion between the sphere of representations—where the will to integrate national space is more or less present, and the sphere of reality—where disintegration could predominate. Supporters of the PDS (a minority of experts and media) defend it on the basis of economic calculations and political or social arguments, but very rarely do they base their defence on regional planning or on 'positive externalities' (Bonnafous 1994) brought about by the structuring of the territory effected by the food supply system.

It remains to be seen to what extent the subsidized families are aware of their integration with a *national* network (or at least a state government network), of being catered to by a *public* service, in order to evaluate to what extent the system can play a positive role in strengthening citizenship and identity. Indeed, the fact that the PDS is linked to the national territory in this way means that nationality is in turn associated with the PDS. Scarcely any Indian state issues identity cards: it is the ration card, containing more information, which is used as documentary evidence for many administrative purposes. This is so because to obtain a PDS ration card, it is necessary to give an address, and the administration has to acknowledge the address as true. So granting this card corresponds *de facto* to a residence certificate. For those 14 per cent of the urban population living in slums in 2001,[18] possession of this card means the right to housing and the right to live in those cities: in short, citizenship.

In 2005, a youth from the old city in Hyderabad confirmed the following to me: 'We do not buy rice with this card. But it is useful for kerosene and nationality (*sic*).' This was a Muslim youth—he belonged to a religious minority that was dominant in numbers in the walled city but found itself in an insecure situation *vis-à-vis* the rest of the city or the state. Of a sample of thirty Muslims questioned in the Old City, 40 per cent used the card just for this purpose: 'to prove we are Indians', as against a mere 3 per cent of the thirty Hindus polled in the same area (Ruby 2005). In that year, Andhra Pradesh had announced that it was issuing a new card (laminated and bar coded), bearing the entire family's photograph, which could be used for the purposes of rations, identity, and voting, and as a residence certificate and a birth certificate for the whole household!

It remains to know to which extent all this is specific to India. We cannot draw a general comparative picture at the world level, but a quick look at neighbouring countries will be illuminating.

A COMPARISON OF FOOD POLICIES IN SOUTH ASIA

To now we lacked the space to make a comparative study. We have not referred to food supply systems basically meant to meet consumer needs, even if it is to the detriment of farmers due to heavy imports (Egypt). Many lessons could be drawn from subsidy systems more akin to India's, which strive to supply consumers above all from domestic production alone (Zambia used to do it, China still does), although the subsidized rations are mostly cornered by city dwellers and officials (Indonesia). We shall now restrict ourselves to South Asia (Islam and Thomas 1996), first because rarely do we find nations outside Asia trying out an integrated food policy, but above all given our theory: Hindu territoriality strengthened the perception of national space, and the whole in its turn influenced the gradual extension of the PDS to the four corners of India. Thus, we could well believe that countries that were a part of the British Empire when the embryo of the PDS was formed (1942), but whose population comprised of a non-Hindu majority, could not set up as developed a distribution system as in India. We could even add that these countries, formerly part of the British India, were forced to create a new rapport with their national space—at least Pakistan and Bangladesh, after 1947 and 1971 respectively. So the age of their national territoriality added to the absence of Hindu territoriality would (partly) explain the weakness of their public distribution system's spatial expansion.

Of course, there are so many other developmental factors for the decline of the PDS that our thesis cannot either be strictly confirmed or overruled. Hence, the following passages ought to be read more as suggestive, nothing more.

URBAN-BASED DISTRIBUTION SYSTEMS

In Pakistan, the statutory rationing system (that is a public monopoly on wheat supplies) was in effect in big cities until the 1960s (Alderman et al. 1988). In the 1970s–1980s 30 per cent of the total wheat flour consumption passed through government ration shops, subsidized at about 30 per cent. Monthly quotas went up to 7.5 kg per adult between 1976 and 1980, but in practice, they were much higher in the cities, at a cost that reached 8 per cent of budget expenditure in 1978–9. Sugar was also available in ration shops until 1983. The entire procurement and distribution process was organized at the federal level, and not unlike in India, the basics of the operation were left to the provincial governments. However, the distribution system was directed above all at the urban population, with government officials and armed forces personnel being the main beneficiaries. In 1986, 82 per cent of the 40,000 shops were concentrated in Sind and particularly Punjab (57 per cent), and only 5 per cent of rural Pakistani households declared that they purchased rationed wheat flour, as against 19 per cent of urbanites.

In Bangladesh, the Public Food Distribution System (PFDS) accounted for 13 per cent of the cereals consumed in 1990–1. In 1977, a public sales system in the market was added to sales through ration shops, which were more subsidized. Ration shop prices were just 45 per cent of open market prices in the 1970s, rising to 80 per cent in the 1980s. The same social and spatial disparities as in Pakistan prevailed there. In six major cities, there was discrimination in the colonial system in favour of government servants or the employees of the major companies (statutory rationing). The situation only started improving gradually in 1949, and it was only from the 1980s that the rural poor were able to be beneficiaries (*modified rationing*), which ended up benefiting 15 million cardholders (Dayal 1997). In the mid-1980s, 70 per cent of PFDS distribution was allotted to urbanites (but only 27 per cent of the poor city dwellers benefited from it).[19] There were large scale 'leakages' as in Pakistan, certainly higher than those in India, which reduced the importance of both these systems, until they were officially ended between 1991 and 1992, to be replaced by Food for Work type programmes.

In *Sri Lanka* the distribution system was quite a generous one but only for a short while (Edirisinghe 1987). Paddy, wheat and sugar continued to be subsidized after Independence in 1948. In fact, until 1973, every week every individual was entitled to purchase one (sometimes two) kilos of paddy, with at least one kilo thrown in for free.[20] An attempt to reduce subsidies in 1953 led to riots and caused the government to fall.

Working Towards Self-Sufficiency Through Procurement

Trying to achieve self-sufficiency revolved around wheat in Pakistan, rice in Bangladesh, but never really took off in Sri Lanka. The state was compelled to purchase a part of the produce, either to plough it back into the public distribution system or (more recently) to sustain market prices. Between 1986 and 1990 the *Pakistani* government procured almost 73 per cent of Punjab's surplus wheat and, despite liberalization, today wheat support prices continue to prevail in Pakistan. In 1982, procurement in Pakistan accounted for 31 per cent and 35 per cent respectively of wheat and rice production (the latter for export purposes[21]), without however being able to dispense with additional imports to supply ration shops. In *Bangladesh's* case, the figures were respectively 8 per cent and 3 per cent and purchases were made mostly through traders, with the result that farmers often drew very little benefit from the support price. In the latter case, food grain production rose from 8 to 18 million tonnes between 1962 and 1992, mainly due to agricultural support prices and fertilizer subsidies. In fact, there was a sixfold rise in the quantities marketed, and the increase in wheat consumption combined with imports effectively contained rice prices. In 2000–1, public distribution (1.9 million tonnes) accounted for 9 per cent of food grain consumption, against procurement and imports of 1.1 and 1.6 million tonnes respectively.[22]

In *Pakistan*, wheat imports remained corresponding for example 4 to 9 per cent of national availability in terms of a five-year average in the 1980s. In *Bangladesh*, the share of rice imports was smaller, since wheat imports—mostly supplied by international aid agencies—were meant to overcome cereal shortages. Assessing cereal needs was extremely difficult in both instances, due to the complex situation as well as a complicated bureaucracy. Above all, memories of the 1972–3 famine made Bangladesh, in particular, increase buffer stock imports, which in any case were seen as very lucrative by some officials and politicians. The *Sri Lankan* government wanted to curtail paddy production prices for a long time, in order to reduce the food grain subsidy amount. However, the main effect of the policy was a fall in rice production, leading to increased imports, especially wheat flour from the United States. The electoral victory of the UNP in 1977 sounded the death knell of the system, primarily due to financial constraints (food grain subsidies accounted for 6 per cent of the GDP and 17 per cent of the State budget).

LIBERALIZATION

In *Sri Lanka*, from 1978 onwards, direct rice distribution was restricted to the poorer half of the population,[23] and was subsequently abolished in 1979 to be replaced by food stamps, also distributed to half the population. This could be construed as generous given the official figures, according to which only 30 per cent of the population was categorized as 'poor' (Edirisinghe 1987; Drèze, Sen and Hussain 1995). As a *quid pro quo*, paddy prices were deregulated. Therefore food grain subsidies accounted for only 1 per cent of GDP and the food stamp system was instrumental in dismantling the dense but costly ration shop network. Other distributed articles remained under subsidy for everyone, in particular wheat flour. In fact, the subsidy on the latter was withdrawn only in 2002, falling victim to its costs, both in terms of the budget and imports, and also the competition it gave to domestic rice cultivators. In 1999, 1.7 million families or 8.5 million people (almost half the population) were allotted stamps worth 500 Sri Lankan rupees every month, though their value depreciated extensively due to inflation. Besides, 10 per cent of the poor received no food stamps, whereas 30 per cent of the rich did. The role of the *Samridhi* (prosperity) programme in distributing money and credit to the poorest third of the population since 1995 is yet to be evaluated.

In 1988–9, *Pakistan* gave up its monopoly over external trade in rice. In 1987, it had done away with the ration shops system for subsidising wheat flour because of its near total lack of efficiency and high cost. In fact, 80 per cent of the wheat given by the government to the mills disappeared from official channels. But for obvious social and political reasons, a new system was launched with wheat being sold directly to consumers, with reduced subsidy but at the same price in all provinces, without any quantitative restrictions, and benefiting a greater number of people than the previous system. Towards 1998, the State purchased a quarter of the country's wheat produce at the support price. Food grain subsidies came in two forms (Pasha et al. n.d.): the less important one was through the intermediary of the Baitul Maal corporation established in 1992, which was equivalent to a monthly grant of Rs. 200 to 240,000 households through the *Atta* (flour) Subsidy Scheme; the second was the wheat subsidy itself, defined by the difference between the procurement (or import) price and the price at which it was sold to the flour mills —i.e. 0.5 per cent of the GDP in 1997–8 (Rs. 11 billion, of which 7 billion were paid by the provinces).[24] Flour price regulation and mostly prohibited inter-provinces movement completed the arrangement, in favour of which riots broke out in a popular uprising in 1997. In 2001, Pakistan gave an undertaking to the IMF to remove wheat subsidies for mill owners and consumers over a two-year period. Indeed, such commitment was not the first. It is true that a large number of mill owners benefit by abusing the system, that farmers are discouraged by the relatively low market prices, that smuggling to neighbouring countries is common practice for the same reason, and that the removal of quotas and the selection of beneficiaries in no way prevent the rich from enjoying a windfall. In 2008, a revival of ration card occurred with the Bachat Card scheme that ultimately is supposed to reach the poorest quarter of the population.

In *Bangladesh*, domestic market rice price stagnation in the early 1990s helped the government, which wanted to liberalize the system and reduce costs, to gradually reduce distribution subsidies. 1991–3 was the period of dismantling the main public distribution circuits, reducing the rice procurement price, and liberalizing foreign trade. Apart from the army and the police who continue to benefit from subsidized rations, food for work or child/women's nutrition programmes are the present incarnations of a policy that claims to be in favour of the free market (Ahmed et al. 2000). Nevertheless, the government has to continue to make its presence felt, at least for electoral considerations. In 1998–9, a period of major flooding, 33 per cent of the 2.1 million tonnes of wheat and rice distributed by the PFDS were through the Food for Work programme. 22 per cent was allocated to the Vulnerable Group Feeding programme, which covered the entire poor population of the country that year (4 million ration cards with an entitlement of 16 kg of free food grains every month), whereas it normally only covers areas affected by nature's fury (del Ninno, Dorosh 2003). Although classically 'Indian-style' subsidized food grain sales reached only 12 per cent of the total population, Bangladesh certainly did not entirely give up its food policy. Between 1990 and 2000, total public distribution reached 1.9 million tonnes of wheat and (secondarily) rice per year.

On the whole, these public procurement and distribution systems are remarkable by their size in comparison with most food policies in other developing countries. However, they rarely reached the magnitude of the Indian citizen. Their share in national consumption may have been higher than India's, but that was more often on account of imports. More so, they catered to mostly urban populations. In this context, the spatial expansion and total coverage of the Indian PDS is unique. It is true that it came somewhat late and that, towards the end of 1980s, when the systems in other countries of the south had started undergoing reform and the liberalization (earlier than in India), the PDS was also suffering a strong 'urban bias'. It was because its system continued to develop and expand in the last two decades that, theoretically, the PDS managed to cover almost the entire territory of the Indian republic. This reinforces our theory of India's specificity: if successive governments did not reduce the enormous spatial coverage of the system, if the winds of liberalization vainly struggled to dismantle it, it was partly because of the existence of a concept of territorial integration and aggregation, developed in equal measure by Hindu nationalism and Nehruvian thought.[25]

NOTES

1. However, this did not mean that Nehru's ideas totally prevailed within the Congress or within the Government, nor that they had been 'set in stone' once and for all within the framework of a clear doctrine (Khilnani 1999).
2. A speech that initiated the debate on the Second Five-Year Plan in the Assembly, on 23 May 1956, in *Nehru* 1968: vol. 3, p. 98.
3. http://forest.ap.nic.in/forest % 20 Policy–1952.htm
4. Cf. also the ideas of M. Heidegger, H. Lefebvre and A. Berque, and the developments of these ideas by Gervais-Lambony (2003), as well as Hirsch and O'Hanlon (1995).
5. As for the Gandhian perception, it was only able to take concrete shape during the short period when a 'ruralist' coalition came to power in New Delhi (1977–80). In any case, these pages do not claim to be exhaustive

in this regard and are undoubtedly extremely simplistic given the diversity of perceptions within these three major groups, roughly defined here as Gandhian, Nehruvian, and Hindu Nationalist.

6. Quoted by R. Ravishankar, 'The Real Savarkar', *Frontline*, 2 August 2002, pp. 116–18.
7. www.bjp.org/history/chapter4.htm.
8. However, the fundamentally colonial and 'modern' nature of cartography has been criticised by Raj (2003).
9. It was a cartographic rendering of the 'Greater India' dear to Hindu nationalists, stretching from Afghanistan to Singapore, with no political borders shown, albeit with all the rivers and mountains. Upon its creation, the Benares temple was indubitably 'secular' in inspiration, and even today, visiting it is more like a visit to a museum than a temple. But the ambiguity is still patently visible, particularly since the first poster of Mother India was put up in 2002, and there is a tendency to 'Hinduize' the veneration of India's territory (Claveyrolas 2003b). The Bharat Mata temple in Hardwar, visited by much larger crowds, is clearly Hindu nationalist.
10. Shankaracharya, the eighth-century Hindu philosopher, established his four main monasteries in the *char dham*, 'the four corners of India', with the objective of 'national integration', according to some interpreters (quoted by Eck 1998: 181).
11. One example of publicity for the FCI published in *The Hindu*, 27 January 2004.
12. *Frontline*, 9 April 2004, p. 123.
13. P. Vidal de la Blanche, *Tableau de la géographie de la France* (Hachette, 1903), p. 10, quoted by Robic, 2001, p. 220.
14. The east-west branch undoubtedly deviates toward the north in order to correspond to the Gangetic valley, as a result of which the two axes cut each other far from the geometric centre of the country. But the north-south corridor is remarkable in its straight layout, cutting across some of India's least populated areas.
15. Cf. for instance, *The Hindu Business Line*, 26 October 1998.
16. 'This will increase the inter-dependency between the citizens of the country and will lead to National Integration', affirms the river-linking project's official site (http://riverlinks.nic.in).
17. Maps 3.9 and 3.10 on the FCI's transportation could belong to this third category, if India did not prefer to rely on tables of figures at the expense of mapping, and if maps were distributed by the state.
18. The proportion rose to as much as 23 per cent in million-plus cities.
19. http://www.unu.edu/unupress/food/8F043e/8F043E07.htm.

20. In 1973, the ration was limited to 500 g free and 1 (or 1.5) kg at a subsidy of about 30 per cent.
21. Compulsory procurement rice quotas continued to prevail in Punjab until 1986, when they were replaced by voluntary procurement (Islam and Thomas 2000: 71).
22. *Bangladesh Bureau of Statistics and Directorate of Food.* Theoretically, procurement is done directly from farmers, but a number of intermediaries nonetheless manage to slip in between the producers and the administration.
23. Targeting seems to have given rise to relatively little 'urban bias' and social injustice, given that 78 per cent of the poorest urban quintile and 83 per cent of the poorest rural quintile were beneficiaries (Sahn and Alderman 1996).
24. There was a short-lived food stamps programme between 1992 and 1994.
25. The universal and efficient nature of the system that prevailed in Sri Lanka for a short time was an exception, made possible by the country's small size, to which high literacy level and political awareness must be added. In fact, would it be possible to introduce a Buddhist perception of space that would be considerably like that of the Hindus? As for the rest, the fact that all these South Asian countries shared strong similarities, does not contradict the hypothesis of India's uniqueness, for a different reason—it is probable that sometimes the other countries emulated their large neighbour.

Conclusion

The preceding pages have retold the history of a public food system initially based on compulsory sales and imports, later graduating to agricultural support prices; from a restricted number of only urban beneficiaries in the beginning, to its spread to rural areas; from an import-dependent state to a self-sufficient cereal producing state, now almost depending on exports. A system that played its part in the success of the Green Revolution by guaranteeing outlets for farmers, which showed the way to an improvement in the calorie intake of the population, but seldom that of the nutritional situation, and at a high cost, with a low level of efficiency and significant pernicious effects in terms of its ecological consequences. It was a system that also contained obvious geographical and political dimensions that made the integration of the four corners of the republic possible within the same structure.

To describe this system in its day-to-day functioning, we have to go down to the state, district, village, and ward level—in other words, the 'field'. We have only given brief explanations at these scales. What you have read so far was more about the system as it was conceived and imagined. The description is appropriate with regard to the national territory perceived as a space through which integrating 'flows' had to be organized. The food system thus appears to be an intellectual schema projected on to the national space, with all the imperfections that such projections of the ideal over the material bring with them (Godelier 1984). Whether through the flow of goods, people or ideas, national integration emerged through a purifying Hindu missionary message as well as through the spread of agriculture and price equalization, through RSS *shakhas* or through PDS FPSs, through processions of militants converging upon Nagpur and Ayodhya or through trains distributing grain across the country, through itineraries that covered most temples and rivers or marketing networks determined to reach regions that were the farthest removed from the national food market.

One thing should be understood clearly: it is not because we have placed the integration of the national territory on centre stage that it should be considered as the only possible explanation for the development of India's food system. Indeed there are several other and more important factors, as we have seen. However, since it had been ignored too long, it deserved to be unearthed and analysed. But another criticism could be made: why has the concern for national integration been highlighted when the PDS did not correspond to it? Did the PDS not put Punjab at loggerheads with Kerala, the finance minister against the civil supplies minister, poor households against rich households, and farmers against consumers? Wasn't it a factor in the corruption and division of society as well as space? Indeed it was. But it is not because the PDS at times almost defeated the very purpose of its existence that we should say nothing about its *a priori* underlying concepts. The notions of national integration and circulation in all four corners of the country stem from the abstract realm of ideal schemas. Their application to the PDS structure, however, belong to the real world, and so cannot be compared to them.

Besides, we have sufficient proof that the PDS was reckoned to be not only necessary but also useful, that the state was deemed to be responsible for its good functioning, and that it was therefore a real public service. Hunger continues to prevail in India—it is the reality of certain severely underprivileged regions or groups and is also present in the political rhetoric, when the government is blamed for serious lapses in dealing with food crisis situations where droughts are merely catalysts, or when Maoist guerrillas of the People's War Group in Andhra Pradesh conduct what they call 'famine raids', ransacking rich landowners and merchants.

Discontinuing the system would not be a good idea. Nevertheless, a sweeping reform does indeed seem to be necessary. Given below is a summary of the main changes desirable:

- discontinuation of the physical distribution of rations in generally well-supplied rural areas and in cities, to be replaced by food stamps
- universal distribution for the rest of the country, which would remove the extremely defective selection of beneficiaries, and further the objective of national integration
- invitation of tenders by the FCI from private traders for supplies, which would confine public procurement to certain specific regions

- alternative food security support, similar to the Deccan Development Society: procurement and distribution should be dealt with in a decentralized manner as far as possible.

As a result, the 'system' would remain only partially a system. Specifically, production, consumption and buffer stocks would be dissociated. On the whole, however, the system would become more flexible, more efficient, and more just: a real food policy would still continue to operate.

In the beginning the PDS was oriented towards urban and industrial food supply. It later evolved into a productivist instrument of growth by setting up agricultural product outlets, and then a mode of social security proposing to feed the whole Indian population throughout the national country. It was given new objectives, without losing its former purpose. From a temporary system stemming from the post-Second World War situation, it turned deeply structural. Both the centre and the states were deemed to be responsible for feeding their citizens, primarily through PDS shops, which thereby contributed to reinforcing 'state legitimacy' (Mooij 1999a: 189). It is difficult to see how, in the short term, the system can be discontinued. Whether legitimately or otherwise, too many groups and individuals benefit from the system.

Bibliography

EPW: Economic and Political Weekly, Mumbai.

Acharya, K.C.S., 1983. *Food Security System of India*, New Delhi: Concept.

Acharya, S.S., 1997. 'Agricultural Price Policy and Development: Some Facts and Emerging Issues', *Indian Journal of Agricultural Economics*, 52, 1: 1–47.

———, 2001. 'Domestic Agricultural Marketing Policies, Incentives and Integration', in *Indian Agricultural Policy at the Crossroads*, ed. S.S. Acharya and D.P. Chaudhri, Delhi: Rawat, pp. 129–212.

———, 2002, 'Food Security and New International Agreement: Perspectives from India', in G.S. Bhalla et al. (eds.), *Agriculture and the World Trade Organisation: Indian and French Perspectives*, Paris: Ed. Maison des Sciences de l'Homme, pp. 151–78.

Acharya, S.S. and Chaudhri, D.P. (eds.), 2001. *Indian Agricultural Policy at the Crossroads*, Delhi: Rawat.

Ahluwalia, Deepak, 1993. 'Public Distribution of Food in India: Covering, Targeting and Leakages', *Food Policy*, 18, 1: 33–55.

Ahmed, Raisuddin et al. (dir.), 2000. *Out of the Shadow of the Famine: Evolving Food Markets and Food Policy in Bangladesh*, Baltimore: Johns Hopkins University Press.

Ahuja, Narender L., 2006, 'Commodity Derivatives Market in India', *International Research Journal of Finance and Economics*, 2: 153–62.

Alagh, Y.K., 1995. 'Poverty and Food Security: Toward a Policy System for Food Security', Bombay, *EPW*, 30 December: A.142–A.150.

Alary, Véronique and Hache, Emmanuel, 2001, 'Perception du risque financier en milieu rural: Etude comparée sur quatre États de l'Inde', *Revue Tiers Monde*, no. 'La liberalization économique en Inde: inflexion ou rupture', 165: 155–74.

Alderman, Harold, Ghaffar Chaudhry, M. and Garcia, Marito, 1988, *Household Food Security in Pakistan: The Ration Shop System*, Working Papers on Food Subsidies 4, Washington: IFPRI-PIDE.

Anderson, Benedict, 1991. *Imagined Communities: Reflections on the Origin and Spread of Nationalism*, London: Verso (2nd edn.).

Annamalai, Kuttayan and Rao, Sachin, 2003. *What Works: ITC's E-Choupal and Profitable Rural Transformation*, World Resources Institute,

University of Michigan (www.dgroups.org/groups/oneworld/OneWorldSA/docs/TICTEIV_pdf.pdf)

Anon. 2002. 'Madhya Pradesh: Undernutrition and Starvation Deaths', *EPW* 38, 18, 3 May: 1751–5.

Assayag, Jackie, 1983. 'Espaces, lieux, limites: La stratification sociale du village en Inde du Sud (Karnataka)', *Res.*, 5, pp. 85–104.

———, 1998. 'Ritual Action or Political Reaction? The Invention of Hindu Nationalist Processions in India during the 1980s', *South Asia Research*, 18, 2: 125–49.

———, 2001. *L'Inde, désir de nation*, Paris: Odile Jacob.

Asthana, M.D. and Medrano, Pedro (eds.), 2001. *Towards Hunger Free India: Agenda and Imperatives*, Delhi: Manohar–WFP.

Aubert, Claude, 1999, 'The Grain Trade Reforms in China: An Unfinished Story of State vs. Peasant Interest', mimeo.

Azoulay G. and Dillon, J.C., 1993. *La sécurité alimentaire en Afrique: Manuel d'analyse et d'élaboration des stratégies*, Paris: Karthala.

Banik, Dan, 1998. 'India's Freedom from Famine: The Case of Kalahandi', *Contemporary South Asia*, 7 (3): 265–81.

Bansil, P.C., 2000. 'Demand Foodgrains by 2020 A.D.', symposium *Agricultural Incentives and Sustainable Development*, CSH-IIC, 3–4 April 2000, Delhi.

Bardhan, Pranab, 1984 (2nd edn. 1998). *The Political Economy of Development in India*, Delhi: Oxford University Press.

Bayard, Jean-François (ed.), 1996. *La greffe de l'État*, Paris: Karthala.

Beuzit, Morgann, and Bougamont, Olivier, 2001, *Demain, l'Inde choisira-t-elle d'exporter son blé?*, master dissertation, ESA, Angers, 3 vols. mimeo.

Bhadouria, B.P.S., 1986, *Disparities and Development Policy: A Regional Perspective*, Delhi: Anmol Publ.

Bhalla, G.S. (ed.), 1994. *Economic Liberalisation and Indian Agriculture*, Delhi: Institute for Studies in Industrial Development.

Bhalla, G.S., Hazell, Peter and Kerr, John, 1999. *Prospects for India's Cereal Supply and Demand to 2020, Food, Agriculture and the Environment*, Discussion Paper 29, IFPRI.

Bhalla, G.S. and Hazell, Peter 2003. 'Rural Employment and Poverty', *EPW* 38, 33, 16 August: 3473–84.

Bhalla, G.S. and Singh, Gurmail, 2001. *Indian Agriculture: Four Decades of Development*, New Delhi: Sage.

Bhalla, G.S., Racine, Jean-Luc and Landy, Frédéric (eds.), 2002, *Agriculture and the World Trade Organisation: Indian and French Perspectives*, Paris: Ed. de la Maison des Sciences de l'Homme.

Bhalotra, Sonia, 2002. 'Welfare Implications of Fiscal Reforms: The Case of Food Subsidies in India', Discussion Paper 2002/32, WIDER, Helsinki.

Bharadwaj, Krishna, 1998. 'Agricultural Price Policy for Growth: The Emerging Contradictions', in T.J. Byres, *The State, Development Planning and Liberalization in India*, Delhi: Oxford University Press, pp. 198–253.

Bhatia, B.M., 1991. *Famines in India 1860-1990*, 3rd edn., Delhi: Konark.

Bonnafous, Alain, 1994. 'Réseaux de transports', in Auray, J.P., *Encyclopédie d'économie spatiale*, Economica, pp. 325–32.

Bourguinat, Nicolas, 1997. 'L'État et les violences frumentaires en France sous la Restauration et la Monarchie de Juillet', *Ruralia,* 1 (http://ruralia.revues.org/document2.html).

Bourguinat, Nicolas, 2001, 'Libre-commerce du blé et représentations de l'espace français: Les crises frumentaires au début du XIXe siècle', *Annales HSS*, January–February: 125–52.

Boussard, J.M., 2002. 'Market Dynamism, Trade and Comparative Advantage in Agriculture and Food Industries', in Bhalla, G.S. et al., eds., *Agriculture and the World Trade Organization: Indian and French Perspectives*, Paris : Ed. de la Maison des Sciences de l'Homme, pp. 241–60.

Brosius, Christiane, 2001. 'Remapping Space: The Sacred Cartography of Nationalist Pilgrimages in Hindutva Videos', symposium *The Politics of Authenticity: The Case of Modern and Contemporary Visual Arts in India,* Paris, 7–9 February.

Byres, T.J. (ed.), 1998. *The State, Development Planning and Liberalization in India*, Delhi: Oxford University Press.

Caro, Patrice, Dard, Olivier and Daumas, Jean-Claude (eds.), 2002. *La politique d'aménagement du territoire: Racines, logiques et résultats,* Presses Universitaires de Rennes.

Cassen, R.H., 2002. 'Well-Being in the 1990s: Towards a Balance Sheet', *EPW*, 37, 27, 6 July: 2789–94.

Chakravorty, S., 2000, 'How Does Structural Reform Affect Regional Development?', *Economic Geography*, 76, 4: 367–94.

Chakravarty, Sukhamoy, 1987, *Development Planning: The Indian Experience*, Delhi: Oxford University Press.

Chand, Ramesh, 2001. 'Regional and Sectoral Disparities in Economic Growth and Incomes in India', in Acharya and Chaudhri, ed., *Indian Agricultural Policy at the Crossroads*, Delhi: Rawat, 589–604.

———, 2003. 'Minimum Support Price in Agriculture: Changing Requirements', *EPW*, 38, 29, 19 July: 3027–8.

———, 2005. 'Whither India's Food Policy? From Food Security to Food Deprivation', *EPW*, 40, 11, 12 March: 1055–62.

Chandrasekhar, C.P., and Ghosh, Jayati, 2002, 'Food Economy in Disarray', *The Hindu Business Line*, 28 May.

Charvet, Jean-Paul, 1996, *Le blé*, Paris: Economica.

———, 2004. *L'alimentation dans le monde*, Paris : Larousse.

Chaturvedi, Pradeep (ed.), 1997. *Food Security and Panchayat Raj*, Delhi: Concept.

Chopra, R.N., 1988. *Food Policy in India: A Survey*, Delhi: Intellectual Publ. House.

Claveyrolas, Mathieu, 2003. 'Construire *le* territoire sacré hindou : l'exemple de Bénarès', presentation at symposium AJEI, 21 November, Poitiers.

Cobb, Richard, 1965. *Terreur et subsistances 1793-1795*, Paris: Clavreuil.

———, 1975. *La protestation populaire en France 1789-1820*, Paris: Calmann-Lévy.

Corbridge, Stuart, G. Williams, M. Srivastava, and R. Veron, 2003. 'Making Social Science Matter – I: How the Local Sate Works in Rural Bihar, Jharkhand and West Bengal', *EPW*, 38, 24, 14 June: 2377–89.

Courade, Georges, 1992. 'Le fait alimentaire, territoire à conquérir de la géographie', *Revue Tiers-Monde*, 33, 132, issue 'Le fait alimentaire': 743–62.

Crampton, J.W. and Eldene, S. (eds.), 2007. *Space Knowledge and Power: Foucault and Geography*, Aldershot: Ashgate.

Cummings, Ralph W., 1969. 'Buffer Stocks', *Seminar*, pp. 49–84.

Cummings, Ralph W. Jr., Shahidur, Rashid, and Gulati, Ashok, 2006. 'Grain Price Stabilization Experiences in Asia: What have we learned?', *Food Policy*, 31: 301–12.

Currey, Bruce, and Hugo, Graeme (eds.), 1984. *Famine as a Geographical Phenomenon*, Dordrecht: Reidel-Kluwer.

Currie, Bob, 2000. *The Politics of Hunger in India: A Study of Democracy, Governance and Kalahandi's Poverty*, London: Macmillan.

Dandekar, V.M., 1994, *The Indian Economy 1947-92*, vol. 1, *Agriculture*, Delhi: Sage.

Daniel, E. Valentine, 1984. *Fluid Signs: Being a Person the Tamil Way*, Berkeley: University of California Press.

Dantwala, M.L., 1969, 'Summary of Discussions at the Seminar on Foodgrains Buffer Stocks', in *Seminar*, 1969, pp. 1–11.

———, 1996. *Dilemmas of Growth: The Indian Experience* (ed. P. Visaria et al.), New Delhi: Sage.

Davis, Mike, 2001. *Late Victorian Holocausts: El Niño Famines and the Making of the Third World*, London-New York: Verso.

Dayal, Edison, 1997. *Food, Nutrition and Hunger in Bangladesh*, Avebury: Aldershot.

Deaton, Angus and Drèze, Jean, 2002. 'Poverty and Inequality in India. A Re-Examination', *EPW*, 37, 36, pp. 3729–48.

del Ninno, Carlo and Paul A. Dorosh, 2003. 'Impacts of In-Kind Transfers on Household Food Consumption: Evidence from Targeted Food Programmes in Bangladesh', *Journal of Development Studies*, 40, 1, pp. 48 78.

Deshpande, Satish, 1998. 'After Culture: Renewed Agendas for the Political Economy of India', *Cultural Dynamics*, 10, 2, pp. 147–69.

Devienne, Sophie, Gilles, Bazin, and Charvet, Jean-Paul, 2005. 'Politique agricole et agriculture aux États-Unis', *Annales de Géographie*, 641, January-February, pp. 3–26.

Dorin, Bruno, 1994. *L'économie oléifère de l'Union indienne. Evaluation d'une stratégie d'autonomie*, economics thesis, Université de Montpellier 1.

———, 1999, 'Food Policy and Nutritional Security: Unequal Access to Lipids in India', *EPW*, 26 June–2 July.

———, 2004. 'Globalization and Self-Sufficiency: A Tentative Revolution in Oilseeds', in Landy and Chaudhuri (eds.), *Globalization and Local Development in India: Examining the Spatial Dimension*, Delhi: Manohar, pp. 171–98.

Dorin, Bruno and Landy, Frédéric, 2009. *Agriculture and Food in India*, Delhi: Manohar–CSH.

Dorin, Bruno and Thomas, Jullien, 2004 (eds.). *Agricultural Incentives in India: Past Trends and Prospective Paths Towards Sustainable Develop-ment*, Delhi: Manohar–CSH, 2004.

Dorin, Bruno, 2005. 'Inde: le grand chasse-croisé alimentaire', *Démeter 2005*, Colin, pp. 43–75.

Drèze, Jean, 1995, 'Famine Prevention in India', in Drèze et al., pp. 69–177.

———, 2001. 'Starving the Poor', *The Hindu*, 26 February 2001.

———, 2004. 'Democracy and Right to Food', *EPW*, 39, 17, 24 April, pp. 1723–31.

Drèze, Jean and Goyal, Aparajita, 2003. 'Future of Mid-Day Meals', *EPW*, 38, 44, 1 November, pp. 4673–84.

Drèze, Jean and Sen, Amartya, 1989, *Hunger and Public Action*, Delhi: Oxford University Press.

———, 2002. *India: Development and Participation*, Delhi: Oxford University Press.

Drèze, Jean, Sen, Amartya and Hussein, Arthar, 1995 (eds.). *The Political Economy of Hunger*, Delhi: Oxford University Press.

Dumont, Louis, 1975. *La civilisation indienne et nous*, Paris: Armand Colin, 1975.

Dupont, Véronique and Landy, Frédéric, 2005. 'Segregation and Territory: What Do We Mean?', in Gervais-Lambony et al. (eds.), *Reconfiguring Identities and Building Territories in India and South Africa*, Delhi: Manohar–CSH, pp. 43–72.

Dupuy, Gabriel, 1994. 'Réseaux', in J.P. Auray, *Encyclopédie d'économie spatiale*, Paris: Economica, pp.145–52.

Durand-Dastes, François, 1982. 'Famine et sous-alimentation en Inde', *Tricontinental*, no. spécial Famines et pénuries, Maspéro, Paris, pp. 11–25.

Dutta, Bhaskar and Ramaswami, Bharat, 2001. 'Targeting and Efficiency in the Public Distribution System: Case of Andhra Pradesh and Maharashtra', *EPW*, 36, 18, 5 May, pp. 1524–32.

Eck, Diana L., 1998. 'The imagined landscape: Patterns in the construction of Hindu sacred geography', *Contributions to Indian Sociology*, Sage, 32, 2, pp. 165–88.

Edirisinghe, N., 1987. 'The Food Stamp Scheme in Sri Lanka: Costs, Benefits, and Options for Modifications'. Research Report 58, Washington: International Food Policy Research Institute.

Etienne, Gilbert, 2003. *Le développement à contre-courant*, Paris: Presses de Sciences Po.

Etienne, Gilbert, Aubert, Claude and Maurer, Jean-Luc, 1998. *Feeding Asia in the Next Century*, New Delhi: Macmillan India.

Evans, P., 1995. *Embedded Economy: States and Industrial Transformation Princeton*: Princeton University Press.

Finkielkraut, Alain, 1987. *La défaite de la pensée*, Paris: Folio-Gallimard.

Foucault, Michel, 2004. *Sécurité, territoire, population: Cours au Collège de France 1977-1978*, Paris: Gallimard-Seuil.

Foucher, Michel, 1988. *Fronts et frontières*, Paris: Seuil.

Frankel, Francine, 1978. *India's Political Economy: The Gradual Revolution*, Princeton: Princeton University. Press.

Frontline, 1997. *Special report on 'Weakening Welfare: The Public Distribution Mess'*, 31 October.

Gaiha, Raghav, 2003. 'Does the Right to Food Matter?', *EPW*, 38, 40, pp. 4269–76.

Garnsey, P., 1989. *Famine and Food Supply in the Graeco-Roman World*, Cambridge: Cambridge University Press.

George, P.S., 1985. *Some Aspects of Procurement and Distribution of Foodgrains in India*, Washington, IFPRI, Working Papers on Food Subsidies, 1.

———, 1996. 'Public Distribution System, Food Subsidy and Production Incentives', *EPW*, 28 September, pp. A.140–A.144.

Gervais-Lambony, Philippe, Landy, Frédéric and Oldfield, Sophie (eds.), 2005. *Reconfiguring Identities and Building Territories in India and South Africa*, Delhi: Manohar–CSH.

Ghosh, Madhusudan, 2000, 'Cointegration Tests and Spatial Integration of Rice Markets in India', *Indian Journal of Agricultural Economics*, 55, 4, October, pp. 616–26.

Ghosh, J. 2003. 'The Missing Grain', *Frontline*, 24 October: 120–1.

Gilbert, Anne, 1986. 'L'idéologie spatiale : conceptualisation, mise en forme et portée pour la géographie', *L'espace géographique*, 1, pp. 57–66.

Godelier, Maurice, 1984. *L'idéel et le matériel*, Paris: Le Livre de Poche-Arthème Fayard.

Goswami, Manu, 2004. *Producing India: From Colonial Economy to National Space*, Delhi: Permanent Black.

Griffon, Michel, 2006. *Nourrir la planète*, Paris: Odile Jacob.

Guhan, S., 1995. 'Centre and States in the Reform Process', in R. Cassen, and V. Joshi (eds.), *India: The Future of Economic Reform*, Delhi, Oxford University Press, pp. 71–111.

Gulati, Ashok and Kelley, Tim, 1999. *Trade Liberalization and Indian Agriculture*, Delhi: Oxford University Press.

Gulati, Ashok and Narayanan, Sudha, 2003. *The Subsidy Syndrome in Indian Agriculture*, Delhi: Oxford University Press.

Gulati, Leela, 1977. 'Rationing in a Peri-Urban Community: Case Study of a Squatter Habitat', *EPW*, 12, 12, 19 March, pp. 501–6.

Gumuchian, Hervé, 1991. *Représentations et aménagement du territoire*, Paris: Anthropos-Economica, 1991.

Gupta, Dipankar, 2000, *Culture, Space and the Nation-State: From Sentiment to Structure*, Delhi: Sage.

Harriss, Barbara, 1984. *State and Market: State Intervention in Agricultural Exchange in a Dry Region of Tamil Nadu*, Delhi: Concept.

———, 1995, 'The Intrafamily Distribution of Hunger in South Asia', in Drèze, Sen and Hussain (eds.), *The Political Economy of Hunger*, Delhi: Oxford University Press, pp. 224–97.

Harriss-White, Barbara, 1996. *A Political Economy of Agricultural Markets in South India: Masters of the Countryside*, Delhi: Sage.

———, 2003. *India Working: Essays on Society and Economy*, Cambridge: Cambridge University Press.

Hatekar, Neeraj and Rode, Sanjay, 2003, 'Truth about Hunger and Disease in Mumbai: Malnourishment Among Slum Children', *EPW*, 38, 43, 25 October, pp. 4604–10.

Heinrich, Steven A. and Landy, Frédéric, 1995. 'Le barbier et ses clients : usages diversifiés des codes culturels et permanence de l'Inde', *Etudes rurales*, no. 137, January–March, pp. 7–22.

Heuzé, Gérard, 1993. 'Bombay : la Shiv Sena et le territoire urbain', *Hérodote*, 71, issue on 'L'Inde et la question nationale', pp. 149–68.

———, 2004. 'The price of Progress': A Large Planned Project with Different Players', in. Landy and Chaudhuri (eds.), *Globalization and Local Development in India: Examining the Spatial Demension*, Delhi: Manohar, pp. 139–70.

High Level Committee on Long Term Grain Policy, 2002 : http://fcamin.nic.in/hlc_contents.htm.

Hirway, Indira, 2003, 'Identification of BPL Households for Poverty Alleviation Programmes', *EPW*, 38, 45, 8 November, pp. 4803–8.

Howes, Stephen and Jha, Shikha, 1994. 'Public Distribution of Food in India: A Comment', *Food Policy*, 19, 1, pp. 65–8.

IFPRI, 2002. *Sustainable Food Security for All by 2020. Proceedings of an International Conference Sept. 4-6, 2001*, Bonn, Washington.

Inden, R., 1990. *Imagining India*, Oxford: Basil Blackwell.

Islam, Nurul and Thomas, Saji, 1996. *Foodgrain Price Stabilization in Developing Countries: Issues and Experiences in Asia*, Food Policy Review 3, IFPRI, Washington.

Jaffrelot, Christophe, 1993. 'Nationalisme hindou, territoire et société', *Hérodote*, 71, issue on 'L'Inde et la question nationale', pp. 93–111.

———, 1996. 'La question du territoire en Inde: de l'universalisme aux particularisme ?', in B. Badie and M.C. Smouts (eds.), *L'international sans territoire, Cultures et conflits*, nos. 21-22, L'Harmattan, pp. 75-102.

———, 1998. *La démocratie en Inde: Religion, caste et politique*, Paris: Fayard.

Jenkins, Rob and Goetz, A-M., forthcoming, 'Civil Society, Food Security and

Accountability: Lessons from the Rationing Kruti Samiti's Engagement with the Public Distribution System in Mumbai', in Venkatesh Kumar (ed.), *Civil Society and Governance in Contemporary India*, Delhi : Oxford University Press.

Jha, D., 2001, 'Trade Liberalisation, Agricultural Prices and Social Welfare', in Acharya and Chaudhri (eds.), *Indian Agricultural Policy at the Crossroads*, Delhi: Rawat, pp. 17–126.

Jha, S.N. and Mathur, P.C. (eds.), 1999. *Decentralization and Local Politics*, Readings in Indian Govt and Politics-2, Delhi: Sage.

Jharwal, Sanwhar M., 1998. *Public Distribution System in India Reassessed*, Delhi: Manak.

Jodhka, Surinder S., 2002. 'Nation and Village: Images of Rural India in Gandhi, Nehru and Ambedkar', *EPW*, 37, 32, 10 August, pp. 3343–53.

Kabra, Kamal Nayan, and Ittyerah, Anil Chandy, 1992. *The Public Distribution System in India*, Delhi: Eastern Books.

Kannan, R. et al., 2004. 'Finance Commission Awards and Fiscal Stability in States', *EPW*, 39, 5, 31 January, pp. 477–91.

Kaplan, Steven L., 1988. *Les ventres de Paris. Pouvoir et approvisionnement dans la France d'Ancien Régime*, Paris: Fayard.

Khera, Reetika, 2006. 'Political Economy of State Response to Drought in Rajasthan, 2000-03', *EPW*, 41, 50, 16 December, pp. 5163–72.

Khilnani, Sunil, 1999. *The Idea of India*, New Delhi: Penguin India.

Knight, Sir Henry, 1954. *Food Administration in India 1939-47*, Stanford: Stanford University Press.

Kothari, Rajni, 1988. *State Against Democracy: In Search of Humane Governance*, Delhi: Ajanta Publications.

Krishna, Jai and Jha, S.C., 1969. 'Buffer Stocks: Concepts and Objectives', in *Seminar*, pp. 35–48.

Krishnaji, N., 1990, 'Agricultural Price Policy: A Survey with Reference to Indian Foodgrain Economy', *EPW*, XXV, 26, 30 June, pp. A.54-A.63.

Krishnaji, N. and Krishnan, T.N. (eds.), 2000, *Public Support for Food Security: The Public Distribution System in India*, Delhi: Sage.

Kundu, A., 1992. 'Urban Bias in PDS: Reexamination of NSS Data', *EPW*, 27 June, pp. 1340–1.

———, 1992b. *In the Name of the Poor: Access to Basic Amenities*, Delhi: Sage.

Kurian, N.J., 2000, 'Widening Regional Disparities in India', *EPW*, 12 February, pp. 538–50.

Khusro, A.M., 1969, 'Stocks and Storage of Major Food grains', in *Seminar*, pp. 134–47.

———, 1973. *Buffer Stocks and Storage of Foodgrains in India*, Bombay: Tata McGraw-Hill.

Lall, Marie-Carine, 2001. *India's Missed Opportunity: India's Relationship with the Non Resident Indians*, Aldershot: Ashgate.

Landes, Rip and Gulati, Ashok, 2004. 'Farm Sector Performance and Reform Agenda', *EPW*, 39, 32, 7 August, pp. 3611–19.

Landy, Frédéric, 1994. *Paysans de l'Inde du Sud: Le choix et la contrainte*, Paris: Karthala-IFP.

———, 1999, 'Entre villes et campagnes, la politique alimentaire de l'Inde', in J.L. Chaléard, A. Dubresson (eds.), *Villes et campagnes dans les pays du Sud*, Paris: Karthala, pp. 21–45.

——— (dir), 2001. 'La libéralization économique en Inde: inflexion ou rupture ?', *Revue Tiers-Monde*, 165.

———, 2002. *L'Union Indienne*, Nantes: Editions du Temps.

———, 2004. 'From the Top or from the Bottom? Rural Development and Food Security', in F. Landy and B. Chaudhuri (eds.), *Globalization and Local Development in India: Examining the Spatial Dimension*, Delhi: Manohar, pp. 221–48.

Landy, Frédéric et al., 2007, 'Urban governance through the Lens of the PDS: can we compare Hyderabad and Mumbai?', seminar 'Actors, Policies and Urban Governance', ICC–CSH, Delhi, 23 January.

Landy, Frédéric and Chaudhuri, Basudeb (eds.), 2004. *Globalization and Local Development in India: Examining the Spatial Dimension*, Delhi: Manohar.

Lardinois, Roland, 1982. 'Une conjoncture de crise démographique en Inde du Sud au XIXe siècle: La famine de 1876-1878', *Population*, 2, pp. 371–404.

Lefort, Isabelle, 1992. *La lettre et l'esprit. Géographie scolaire et géographie savante en France*, Paris: Ed. du CNRS.

Lele, Uma J., 1971, *Food Grain Marketing in India: Private Performance and Public Policy*: Ithaca: Cornell University Press.

Levinson, F. James et al., 2003. 'Nutritional Well-Being and Gender Differences: After 30 Years of Rapid Growth in Rural Punjab', *EPW*, 38, 32, 9 August, pp. 3340–1.

Lewis, John P., 1995. *India's Political Economy: Governance and Reform*, Delhi: Oxford University Press.

Lipton, Michael, 1976. *Why Poor People Stay Poor? Urban Bias in World Development*, Londres: Temple Smith.

Mahendra Dev, S., 2003. *Right to Food in India*, CESS, Working Paper 50, Hyderabad.

Mahendra Dev, S., Kannan, K.P. and Ramachandran, Nira (eds.), 2003. *Towards Food Secure India*, Delhi: IHD–CESS–Manohar.

Mahendra Dev, S. et al., 2004, *Economic Liberalisation, Targeted Programmes and Household Food Security: A Case Study of India*, MTID Paper 68, Washington.

Maire, Bernard and Delpeuch, Francis, 2004. 'La transition nutritionnelle, l'alimentation et les villes dans les PVD', Montrouge: *Cahiers agricultures*, 13, 1, pp. 23–30.

Marchand, Bernard, 2001, 'La haine de la ville : Paris et le désert français de J.F. Gravier', *L'information géographique*, 65, September, pp. 239–53.

Markovits, Claude (ed.), 1994. *Histoire de l'Inde moderne 1480-1950*, Paris: Fayard.

Maxwell, Simon, 1996. 'Food Security: A Post-Modern Perspective', *Food Security*, 21, 2, pp. 155–70.

Mazoyer, Marcel and Roudart, Laurence, 2002. *Histoire des agricultures du monde*, Paris: Seuil.

Mishra, Amina, 2005. 'Local Perceptions of Famine: Study of a Village in Orissa', *EPW*, 40, 6, 5 February, pp. 572–8.

Misra, R.P., 1983. 'Growth Poles and Growth Centres in the Context of India's Urban and Regional Problems', in R.P. Misra, *Contributions to Indian Geography*, vol. 1 *Concepts and Approaches*, Delhi: Heritage, pp. 223–46.

Mitra, Arup, 1994. *Urbanization, Slums, Informal Sector Employment and Poverty*, Delhi: B.R. Publishing Corp.

Mooij, Jos, 1999a, *Food Policy and the Indian State : The Public Distribution System in South India*, Delhi: Oxford University Press.

———, 1999b. 'Real Targeting: The Case of Food Distribution in India', *Food Policy*, 24, pp. 49–69.

———, 2002. 'Welfare Studies and Politics: A Study of Three Government Interventions in Andhra Pradesh, India', Working Paper 181, Overseas Development Institute, London.

———, 2003. 'Food and power in Bihar and Jharkhand', in S. Mahendra Dev et al. (eds.), *Towards Food Secure India*, Delhi: IHD–CESS–Manohar, pp. 232–53.

Motiram, Sripad, Vakulabharanam, Vamsi, and Prashad, Vijay, 2004. 'Iowa is not far from Telengana: Some Arguments for Food Security in India', http://www.geocities.com/wgfs2004.

Mukarji, Nirmal, 1999. 'The Third Stratum', in Jha and Mathur (eds.), *Decentralization and Local Politics*, Delhi: Sage, pp. 70–81.

M.S. Swaminathan Foundation, WFP, 2001. *Food Insecurity Atlas of Rural India*, Chennai.

———, 2002. *Food Insecurity Atlas of Urban India*, Chennai.

Nadkarni, M.V., 2002. 'Review Article: Land Reforms in India', *Indian Journal of Agricultural Economics*, 57, 4, October–December, pp. 751–61.

Nair, K.N., 2000. 'Food Security and PDS in Kerala', in Krishnaji and Krishnan (eds.), *Public Support for Food Security: The Public Distribution System in India*, Delhi: Sage, pp. 313–31.

Nawani, N.P., 1995. *Towards Food for All: Ideas for a New PDS*, Delhi: Min. of Information.

Nayyar, Deepak and Sen, Abhijit, 1994. 'International Trade and Agricultural Sector in India', in G.S. Bhalla (ed.), *Economic Liberalisation and Indian Agriculture*, Delhi: ISID, pp. 61–102.

Nehru, Jawaharlal, 1968. *Jawaharlal Nehru's Speeches*, Delhi: Govt. of India, Publications Division, 5 vols. published until 1968.

———, 1985 [1946]. *The Discovery of India*, Delhi: Oxford University Press.

Nora, Pierre (ed.), 1984. *Les lieux de mémoire*, t.1, Paris: Gallimard.

Olsen, Wendy K., 1989. 'Eat Now Pay Later. Impact of Rice Subsidy Scheme', *EPW*, 24, 28, 15 July, pp. 1597–1611.

Padilla, Martine, 1996. *Les politiques alimentaires*, Paris: Cujas.

Pal, S., D.K., Mruthyunjaya, Bahl, 1993. 'Government Interventions in Food grain Markets. The Case of India', *Food Policy*, 18, 5, October, pp. 414–27.

Parikh, K.S., Kumar, A. Ganesh and Darbha, G., 2002, 'Growth and Welfare Consequences of Rise in MSP', *EPW*, 38, 9, 1 March, pp. 891–5.

Pasha, G., and A. Hafiz, et al., n.d. 'Evaluation of Social Safety Nets in Pakistan', www.spdc-pak.com/pub/rr/rr32.pdf.

Patnaik, Utsa, 1991. 'Food Availability and Famine: A Longer View', *Journal of Peasant Studies*, 19, 1, October, pp. 1–25.

———, 1997. 'Political Economy of State Intervention in Food Economy', *EPW*, 32, 20–1, 17 May, pp. 1105–12.

———, 2004a. 'Rural India in Ruins', *Frontline*, 12 March, pp. 16–27.

———, 2004b. 'The Republic of Hunger', *Social Scientist*, 32, 9–10, pp. 9–35, www.networkideas.org/featart/ apr2004/Republic_Hunger.pdf

Petitier, Paule, 2000. 'D'un tableau l'autre', in M.C. Robic (ed.), *Le Tableau de la geographie de la France de Paul Vidal de la Blache: Dans le labyrinthe des formed*, Ed. du CTHS, pp. 127–50.

Pouchepadass, Jacques, 1996. 'Le monde rural', in Christophe Jaffrelot (ed.), *L'Inde contemporaine de 1950 à nos jours*, Paris: Fayard, pp. 316–48.

———, 2003. 'Nation, mémoire, histoire: le cas de l'Inde', presentation at the symposium *Archives et mémoire*, CEIAS, 25 November.

Pruvost Giron, Corinne, 2002. *Palakkad Pass and the Cattle Trail: An Example of a Territory of Reference in South India*, Pondy Papers in Social Sciences, 28, Pondichéry: French Institute.

Racine, Jean-Luc, 1986. 'Autosuffisance alimentaire et transition nutritionnelle' in Sylvie Brunel (ed.), *Asie-Afrique: greniers vides, greniers pleins*, Economica, Paris, pp. 37–50.

Radhakrishna, R., 1996. 'Food Trends, Public Distribution System and Food Security Concerns', Bombay, *Indian Journal of Agricultural Economics*, 51, 1-2, January–June, pp. 168–83.

Radhakrishna, R. et al., 1996. *India's Public Distribution System: A National and International Perspective*, Washington: Poverty and Social Policy Dept., World Bank.

Radhakrishna, R. and Ravi, C., 2004. 'Malnutrition in India: Trends and Determinants', *EPW*, 39, 7, 14 February, pp. 671–6.

Radhakrishna, R., et al., 2004. 'Chronic Poverty and Malnutrition in 1990s', *EPW*, 39, 28, 10 July, pp. 3121–30.

Raffestin, Claude, 1980, *Pour une géographie du pouvoir*, Paris: Litec.

———, 1985. 'Religions, relations de pouvoir et géographie politique', *Cahiers de géographie du Québec*, 76.

Raghavan, M., 2004, 'Politics of Procurement and Price Support', *EPW*, 39, 5, pp. 506–8.

———, 2006. 'Wheat Imports: Food Security or Politics?', *EPW*, 41, 21, 27 May, pp. 2057–9.

Raj, Kapil, 2003, 'Circulation and the Emergence of Modern Mapping: Great Britain and Early Colonial India, 1764–1820', in C. Markovits et al., *Society and Circulation. Mobile People and Itinerant Cultures in South Asia 1750-1950*, Delhi: Permanent Black, pp. 23–54.

Ramaswami, Bharat, 2002. 'Efficiency and Equity of Food Market Interventions', *EPW*, 37, 12, 23 March, pp. 1129–35.

Ramaswami, Bharat and Balakrishnan, P., 2002, 'Food Prices and the Efficiency of Public Intervention: The Case of the Public Distribution System in India', *Food Policy*, 27, pp. 419–36.

Ramaswamy, S., 2006. 'Enshrining the Map of India: Cartography, Nationalism and the Politics of Deity in Varanasi', in M. Gaenszle, and J. Gengnagel (eds.), *Visualizing Space in Banaras*, Wiesbaden: Harrassowitz Verlag, pp. 165–90.

Rangarajan, C. and Srivastava, D.K., 2004. 'Fiscal Transfers in Australia: Review and Relevance to India', *EPW*, 39, 33, 14 August, pp. 3709–22.

Rao, C.H. Hanumantha, 2000. 'Declining Demand for Foodgrain in Rural India: Causes and Implications', *EPW*, 22 January, pp. 201–6.

Rao, V.M. and Deshpande, R.S., 2002. 'Food Security in Drought-Prone Areas: A Study in Karnataka', *EPW*, 37, 35, 31 August, pp. 3677–81.

Ravaillon, Martin, 1987, *Markets and Famines*, Oxford: Clarendon.

Ray S.K., 1970. 'Imbalances, Instability and Government Operations in Foodgrains', *EPW*, V, 39, 26 September, pp. A.115–A.124.

Rath, Nilakantha, 2002. 'D.R. Gadgil on Planning at the District Level', *EPW*, 37, 23, 8 June, pp. 2219–22.

Ravi, C. and S. Indrakant, 2003, 'Food Security and Public Distribution System', in C.H. Hanumantha Rao, and S. Mahendra Dev (eds.), *Andhra Pradesh Development*, Delhi: CESS–Manohar, pp. 498–516.

Robic, Marie-Claire (ed.), 2000. *Le Tableau de la géographie de la France de Paul Vidal de la Blache: Dans le labyrinthe des formes*, Ed. du CTHS, 2000.

Ruby, Donatienne, 2005. *Système de distribution publique alimentaire et gouvernance dans la vieille ville de Hyderabad*, master's dissertation in geography, Université de Paris X.

Rudolph, L.I. and S.H., 1987. *In Pursuit of Lakshmi: The Political Economy of the Indian State*, Delhi: Orient Longman.

Ruet, Joël, 2001. 'Le secteur électrique en Inde: réforme libérale ou persistence d'une forme de développement à l'indienne?', *Revue Tiers-Monde*, 165, January–March, pp. 83–104.

Sagar, Vidya, 2000. 'The Public Distribution System and Food Security in a Region of Large Agricultural Instability: Rajasthan', in Krishnaji, Krishnan (eds.), pp. 227–312.

Saglio-Yatzimirsky, M. Caroline (eds.), 2002. *Inde: Population et développement*, Paris: Ellipses, 2002.

Sahn, D.E. and Alderman, H., 1996. 'The Effect of Food Subsidies on Labour Supply in Sri Lanka', *Economic Develoment and Cultural Change*, 45, 1, pp. 125–45.

Sainath, P., 1996. *Everybody Loves a Good Drought: Stories from India's Poorest Districts*, Delhi: Penguin India.

Sarap, K. and Mahamallik, M., 2003. 'Food Security System and its Operation: A Study of Some Villages in the District of Kalahandi, Orissa', in S. Mahendra Dev et al. (eds.), pp. 364–89.

Sarkar, G.K., 1995. *Agriculture and Rural Transformation in India*, Calcutta: Oxford University Press.

Sathyamurthy, T.V. (ed.), 1995. *Industry and Agriculture in India since Independence*, Delhi: Oxford University Press.

Savarkar, Vinayak Damodar, 1969 [1923]. *Hindutva: Who is a Hindu*, Bombay: Veer Savarkar Prakashan.

Saxena, N.C. and Harsh Mander, 2005. *Sixth Report of the Commissioners.* (www.righttofoodindia.org/comrs/comrs_reports.html).

Seminar on Foodgrains Buffer Stocks in India, 1969, Bombay: Indian Society of Agricultural Economics.

Sen, Amartya K., 1981. *Poverty and Famines: An Essay on Entitlement and Deprivation*, Oxford: Clarendon Press.

Shankar, Kripa, 2004. 'How Efficient is TPDS in Tribal Areas?', *EPW*, 39, 21, 22 May, pp. 2093–6.

Sharma, Jai Prakash, 1987. *Federal Systems of India and Pakistan*, Jaipur: Printwell Publ.

Sharma, Pradeep K., 1997. *Foodgrain Economy of India*, Delhi: Shipra.

Shetty, S.L., 2003. 'Growth of SDP and Structural Changes in State Economies: Interstate Comparisons', *EPW*, 38, 49, 6 December, pp. 5189–5200.

Shiva, Vandana, 2006. 'The Great Grain Robbery by Agribusiness MNC's: A Recipe For More Farmer's Suicides, More Hunger And More Disease', *Znet* (http://www.zmag.org/content/showarticle.cfm?ItemID=1045).

Singh, Jasbir, 1997. *Agricultural Development in South Asia*, Delhi: National Book Organisation.

Singh, S.P., 1973, *Centre-State Relations in Agricultural Development*, Delhi: Vikas.

Sinha, B.K. and Pushpendra (eds.), 2000. *Land Reforms in India: An Unfinished Agenda*, vol. 5, Delhi: Sage.

Social Action, *2004. Special Issue 'Right to Food'*, 54, 3, Delhi.

Sridhar, Kala Seetharam, 2003. 'Firm Location Decisions and Impact on Local Economies', *EPW*, 38, 39, 27 September, pp. 4121–30.

Srinivas, Ch. and S. Abdul Thaha, 2004. *A Study on Alternative Public Distribution System*, Deccan Development Society, Hyderabad. (www.ddsindia.com)

Srinivas, M.N., 1962. *Caste in Modern India and Other Essays*, Bombay: Media Promoters.

Srivastava, H.S., 1968. *History of Indian Famines and Development of Famine Policy 1858-1918*, Agra: Sri Ram Mehra and Co.

Subbarao, K., 1985. 'State Policies and Regional Disparity in Indian Agriculture', *Development and Change*, vol. 16, pp. 523–46.

Suryanarayana, M.H., 1995a. 'PDS Reform and Scope for Commodity-Based Targeting', *EPW*, XXX, 13, 1 April, pp. 687–95.

———, 1995b. 'Some Experiments with Food Stamps', *EPW*, 30, 52, pp. A.151–A.159.

———, 1995c. 'PDS: Beyond Implicit Subsidy and Urban Bias: The Indian Experience', *Food Policy*, 20, 4, pp. 259–78.

Svedberg, Peter, 2002. 'Undernutrition Overestimated', *Economic Development and Cultural Change*, 51, 1, pp. 5–36.

Swaminathan, Madhura, 2000. *Weakening Welfare: The Public Distribution of Food in India*, Delhi: Left Word Books.

Swaminathan, M.S., 1996. *Sustainable Agriculture. Towards an Evergreen Revolution*, Delhi: Konark.

Tauger, Mark B., 2003. 'Entitlement, Shortage and the 1943 Bengal Famine: Another Look', *Journal of Peasant Studies*, 31, 1, pp. 45–72.

Thamarajakshi R., 1997. 'Economic Reforms and State Intervention in Foodgrain Market', *EPW*, XXXII, 30, 26 July, pp. 1894–1900.

Thireau, Isabelle, and HUA, Linshan, 2003. 'Entre le local et le national : migrations et citoyenneté au lendemain des réformes', 1st Asia Network Congress (MSH), 24 September, Paris.

Tilly, Charles, 1986. *La France conteste: De 1600 à nos jours*, Paris: Fayard.

Timmer, C. Peter, 1989. 'Food Price Policy: The Rationale for Government Interventions', *Food Policy*, 14, 1, February, Oxford, pp. 17–27.

Timmer, C. Peter, Falcon, Walter P. and Pearson, Scott R., 1986. *Food Policy Analysis*, Baltimore: Johns Hopkins University Press (http://cesp.stanford.edu/docs/pubs/falcon/foodpolicy/fronttoc.fm.html)

Tinker, Hugh, 1977, *The Banyan Tree. Overseas Emigrants from India, Pakistan and Bangladesh*, Oxford: Oxford University Press.

Tyagi, D.S., 1990. *Managing India's Food Economy: Problems and Alternatives*, Delhi: Sage.

van der Veer, Peter, 1994. *Religious Nationalism: Hindus and Muslims in India*, Berkeley: University of California Press.

Varshney, Ashutosh, 1994. *Democracy, Development and the Countryside: Urban-Rural Struggles in India*, Cambridge: Cambridge University Press.

Varshney, Vibha, and Pandey, Pratap, 2003,'Nutrition', *Down to Earth*, Delhi, 15 July, pp. 27–35.

Varshneya, J.S., 1969. 'Financing of Buffer Stock Operations', in *Seminar*, pp. 128–33.

Venugopal, K.R., 1992. *Deliverance from Hunger: The Public Distribution System in India*, Delhi: Sage

Visaria, Leela and Visaria, Pravin, 1982. 'Population (1757–1947)', in Dharma Kumar (ed.), *The Cambridge Economic History of India*, vol. 2, Cambridge: Orient Longman–Cambridge University Press, pp. 463–532.

Vithal, B.P.R. and Sastry, M.L., 2002, *The Gadgil Formula for Allocation of Central Assistance for State Plans*, Delhi: Manohar–CESS.

Wade, Robert, 1982. 'The System of Administrative and Political Corruption: Canal Irrigation in South India', *Journal of Development Studies*, 18, 3, pp. 287–328.

Whadhwa, D.C., 2000. 'Zoning for Sugar Co-operatives: Note of Dissent', *EPW*, 34, 25, 17 June, pp. 2155–70.

Whitehead, Judy, 2003. 'Space, Place and Primitive Accumulation in Narmada Valley and Beyond', *EPW*, 38, 40, 4 October, pp. 4224–30.

Zhou, Zhang-Yue and Guang-Hua, Wan, 2005. 'The Public Distribution Systems of Foodgrains and their Implications on Food Security: The Indian and Chinese Experience Compared', colloque ICSSR-WIDER, 4-6 March, Jaipur.

INTERNET SITES

Ministry of Food (access to the Department of Public Distribution and FCI site): http://fcamin.nic.in

Agricultural statistics: http://agricoop.nic.in

National Sample Survey Organisation: http://mospi.nic.in

International Food Policy Research Institute (several publications on India, free): www.ifpri.org

Right to Food Campaign: www.righttofood.org.

NEWSPAPERS AND MAGAZINES

The Hindu Business Line (daily): www.blonnet.com

Frontline (bi-weekly): www.flonnet.com

Economic and Political Weekly (weekly): www.epw.org.in

Index